Lecture Notes in Computer Science 11652

More information about this series at http://www.springer.com/series/7407

Majid Zamani · Damien Zufferey (Eds.)

Numerical Software Verification

12th International Workshop, NSV 2019
New York City, NY, USA, July 13–14, 2019
Proceedings

 Springer

Editors
Majid Zamani
University of Colorado Boulder
Boulder, CO, USA

Damien Zufferey
Max Planck Institute
for Software Systems
Kaiserslautern, Germany

ISSN 0302-9743　　　　　　ISSN 1611-3349　(electronic)
Lecture Notes in Computer Science
ISBN 978-3-030-28422-0　　　　ISBN 978-3-030-28423-7　(eBook)
https://doi.org/10.1007/978-3-030-28423-7

LNCS Sublibrary: SL1 – Theoretical Computer Science and General Issues

This Springer imprint is published by the registered company Springer Nature Switzerland AG
The registered company address is: Gewerbestrasse 11, 6330 Cham, Switzerland

Preface

The 12th International Workshop on Numerical Software Verification (NSV 2019) was held during July 13–14, 2019, in New York, USA. NSV 2019 was co-located with CAV 2019, the 31st International Conference on Computer-Aided Verification.

Numerical computations are ubiquitous in digital systems: Supervision, prediction, simulation, and signal processing rely heavily on numerical calculus to achieve desired goals. Design and verification of numerical algorithms has a unique set of challenges, which set it apart from rest of software verification. To achieve the verification and validation of global properties, numerical techniques need to precisely represent local behaviors of each component. The implementation of numerical techniques on modern hardware adds another layer of approximation because of the use of finite representations of infinite precision numbers that usually lack basic arithmetic properties, such as commutativity and associativity. Finally, the development and analysis of cyber-physical systems (CPS), which involve the interacting continuous and discrete components, pose a further challenge. It is hence imperative to develop logical and mathematical techniques for the reasoning about programmability and reliability. The NSV workshop is dedicated to the development of such techniques.

This edition of NSV put more emphasis on the challenges related to the automation of driving tasks. This subject was discussed both by invited speakers (from academia and industry) and in contributed papers.

A highlight of NSV 2019 is the presence of high-profile invited speakers from computer science, control theory, and industry: Calin Belta from Boston University, Karl Henrik Johansson from KTH, Jens Oehlerking from Robert Bosch GmbH, and Martin Rinard from MIT. NSV 2019 also added two tutorials, one given by Susmit Jha from SRI International, and the other one by Ashutosh Trivedi from CU Boulder. Regarding the contributed papers, NSV 2019 had 10 submissions which each received 3 reviews, and 7 of them were accepted.

We would like to thank Denso for sponsoring NSV 2019, the CAV organizers for the local organization and support, and the Steering Committee, in particular Sergiy Bogomolov, for allowing us to organize NSV 2019.

July 2019

Majid Zamani
Damien Zufferey

Preface

Organization

Program Committee

Matthias Althoff	Technical University of Munich, Germany
Olivier Bouissou	Mathworks, France
Samuel Coogan	Georgia Institute of Technology, USA
Rémi Delmas	ONERA, France
Sicun Gao	University of California San Diego, USA
Alberto Griggio	Fondazione Bruno Kessler, Italy
Ashutosh Gupta	IIT Bombay, India
Ichiro Hasuo	National Institute of Informatics, Japan
Susmit Jha	SRI International, USA
James Kapinski	Toyota, USA
Soonho Kong	Toyota Research Institute, USA
Jun Liu	University of Waterloo, Canada
Manuel Mazo Jr.	Delft University of Technology, The Netherland
Tatjana Petrov	University of Konstanz, Germany
Ruzica Piskac	Yale University, USA
Sylvie Putot	LIX, Ecole Polytechnique, France
Akshay Rajhans	MathWorks, USA
Stefan Ratschan	Institute of Computer Science, Czech Academy of Sciences, Czech Republic
Matthias Rungger	ABB Corporate Research, Germany
Sadra Sadraddini	MIT, USA
Krishna Shankaranarayanan	IIT Bombay, India
Sadegh Soudjani	Newcastle University, UK
Laura Titolo	National Institute of Aerospace, USA
Ashutosh Trivedi	University of Colorado Boulder, USA
Jana Tumova	KTH Royal Institute of Technology, Sweden
Caterina Urban	Inria, France
Xiang Yin	Shanghai Jiao Tong University, China
Majid Zamani	University of Colorado Boulder, USA
Damien Zufferey	Max Planck Institute for Software Systems, Germany

Abstracts of Invited Talks

Correctness and Optimality
for Control Systems

Calin Belta

Boston University, Boston, USA

Abstract. In control theory, complicated dynamics such as systems of (non-linear) differential equations are mostly controlled to achieve stability. This fundamental property is often linked with optimality, which requires minimization of a certain cost along the trajectories of a stable system. In formal synthesis, simple systems such as finite state transition graphs modeling computer programs or digital circuits are controlled from specifications such as safety, liveness, or richer requirements expressed as formulas of temporal logics. With the development and integration of cyber physical and safety critical systems, there is an increasing need for computational tools for controlling complex systems from rich, temporal logic specifications. In this talk, I will introduce some recent results on the connection between optimal control and formal synthesis. Specifically, I will focus on the following problem: given a cost and a correctness temporal logic specification for a dynamical system, generate an optimal control strategy that satisfies the specification. I will first talk about automata-based methods, in which the dynamics of the system are mapped to a finite abstraction that is then controlled using an automaton corresponding to the specification. I will then focus on optimization-based methods, which rely on mapping the specification and the dynamics to constraints of an optimization problem. I will illustrate the usefulness of these approaches with examples from robotics and traffic control.

Modeling, Control, and Verification of an Automated Transport System

Karl H. Johansson

KTH Royal Institute of Technology, Sweden

Abstract. Freight transportation is of utmost importance for our society. It accounts for a significant amount of all energy consumption and greenhouse gas emissions. In this talk, we will discuss the potential future of road goods transportation and how it can be made more robust and efficient, from the automation of individual long-haulage trucks to the optimisation of fleet management and logistics. Such an integrated transportation system benefits from having trucks travelling together in vehicle platoons. From the reduced air drag, platooning trucks travelling close together can save more than 10% of their fuel consumption. In addition, by automating the driving, it is possible to change driver regulations and thereby increase the efficiency even more. Control and optimization problems on various level of this transportation system will be presented. It will be argued that a system architecture utilising vehicle-to-vehicle and vehicle-to-infrastructure communication enable robust and safe control of individual trucks as well as optimised vehicle fleet collaborations and new market opportunities. Extensive experiments done on European highways will illustrate system performance and safety requirements. The presentation will mainly be based on joint work over the last ten years with collaborators at KTH and with the truck manufacturers Scania and Volvo.

Formal Methods for Highly Automated Driving Applications

Jens Oehlerking

Robert Bosch GmbH, Stuttgart, Germany

Abstract. In highly automated driving (HAD), the complexity of the environment leads to challenges in perception, planning, and control that go beyond those encountered in classical cyber-physical systems. These include the need to certify systems including artificial neural networks for perception, the need to predict human behavior in complex situations and the need to give safety guarantees without a human driver as a fallback.

Coming from concepts that are heavily used in the design of HAD system, such as criticality metrics, this talk gives perspectives on the applicability of formal methods. Formal methods of interest include hybrid systems, reachability computations, control invariants and the formal analysis of neural networks. Drawing from this discussion, a case is made for new specification languages that are tailored to the domain of autonomous systems.

Contents

Tutorials

Trust, Resilience and Interpretability of AI Models

Susmit Jha$^{(\boxtimes)}$

Computer Science Laboratory, SRI International, Menlo Park, USA
susmit.jha@sri.com

Abstract. In this tutorial, we present our recent work on building trusted, resilient and interpretable AI models by combining symbolic methods developed for automated reasoning with connectionist learning methods that use deep neural networks. The increasing adoption of artificial intelligence and machine learning in systems, including safety-critical systems, has created a pressing need for developing scalable techniques that can be used to establish trust over their safe behavior, resilience to adversarial attacks, and interpretability to enable human audits. This tutorial is comprised of three components: review of techniques for verification of neural networks, methods for using geometric invariants to defend against adversarial attacks, and techniques for extracting logical symbolic rules by reverse engineering machine learning models. These techniques form the core of TRINITY: Trusted, Resilient and Interpretable AI framework being developed at SRI. In this tutorial, we identify the key challenges in building the TRINITY framework, and report recent results on each of these three fronts.

1 Introduction

The rapid integration of intelligent and autonomous agents into our industrial and social infrastructure has created an immediate need for establishing trust between these agents and their human users. Decision-making and planning algorithms central to the operation of these systems currently lack the ability to explain the choices and decisions that they make. This is particularly problematic when the results returned by these algorithms are counter-intuitive. It is important that intelligent agents become capable of responding to inquiries from human users. For example, when riding in an autonomous taxi, we might expect to query the AI driver using questions similar to those we would ask a human driver, such as "why did we not take the Bay Bridge", and receive a response such as "there is too much traffic on the bridge" or "there is an accident on the ramp leading to the bridge or in the middle lane of the bridge." These explanations are essentially formulae in propositional logic formed by combining the atomic propositions corresponding to the user-observable system and the environment states using Boolean connectives.

Even though the decisions of intelligent agents are the consequence of algorithmic processing of perceived system and environment states, the straightforward approach of reviewing this processing is not practical. There are three

© Springer Nature Switzerland AG 2019
M. Zamani and D. Zufferey (Eds.): NSV 2019, LNCS 11652, pp. 3–25, 2019.
https://doi.org/10.1007/978-3-030-28423-7_1

key reasons for this. First, AI algorithms use internal states and intermediate variables to make decisions which may not be observable or interpretable by a typical user. For example, reviewing decisions made by the A* planning algorithm [38] could reveal that a particular state was never considered in the priority queue. But this is not human-interpretable, because a user may not be familiar with the details of how A* works. Second, the efficiency and effectiveness of many AI algorithms relies on their ability to intelligently search for optimal decisions without deducing information not needed to accomplish the task, but some user inquiries may require information that was not inferred during the original execution of the algorithm. For example, a state may never be included in the queue of a heuristic search algorithm like A* because either it is unreachable or it has very high cost. Thus, the ability to explain why this state is not on the computed path will require additional effort. Third, artificial intelligence is often a composition of numerous machine learning and decision-making algorithms, and explicitly modeling each one of these algorithms is not practical. Instead, we need a technique which can treat these algorithms as black-box oracles, and obtain explanations by observing their output on selected inputs. This is the first challenge addressed in the TRINITY framework of improving interpretability of AI models by extracting logical symbolic rules.

Among AI models, deep neural networks (DNNs) have emerged as an ubiquitous choice of representation in machine learning due to the relative ease and computational efficiency of training these models in the presence of large amounts of data. The massive increase in computational power fueled by Moore's law and the emergence of architectures supporting parallel processing at a large scale have made it possible to train these highly nonlinear deep learning networks with thousands of parameters using millions of samples in a reasonable amount of time. This has led to a quantum leap in the prediction accuracy of machine learned models, and encouraged their rapid adoption in different aspects of our social, economic and military infrastructure. Deep neural networks currently provide state-of-the-art results in various applications ranging from computer vision, network security, natural language processing to automatic control.

Unlike other traditional system design approaches, there are few known and scalable methods to verify DNN models. This is the second challenge addressed by the TRINITY framework for building trusted AI systems by developing techniques for verifying DNNs [11,12] that has been implemented in a publicly available open-source tool, Sherlock. Sherlock uses mixed-integer linear programming (MILP) solver but it does not merely compile the verification into an MILP problem. Sherlock first uses sound piecewise linearization of the nonlinear activation function to define an encoding of the neural network semantics into mixed-integer constraints involving real-valued variables and binary variables that arise from the (piecewise) linearized activation functions. Such an encoding into MILP is a standard approach to handling piecewise linear functions. As such, the input constraints $\phi(\mathbf{x})$ are added to the MILP and next, the output variable is separately maximized and minimized to infer the corresponding guarantee that holds on the output. This enables us to infer an assume-guarantee contract on the overall deep neural network. Sherlock augments this simple use of MILP solving with a local search that exploits the local continuity and differentiability properties of the function represented by the network. These properties are not exploited by MILP solvers which typically use a branch-and-cut approach. On the other hand, local search alone may get "stuck" in local minima. Sherlock handles local minima by using the MILP solver to search for a solution that is "better" than the current local minimum or conclude that no such solution exists. Thus, by alternating between inexpensive local search iterations and relatively expensive MILP solver calls, Sherlock can exploit local properties of the neural network function but at the same time avoid the problem of local minima, and thus, solve the verification of deep neural networks more efficiently.

Further, DNN models have been shown to be very brittle and vulnerable to specially crafted adversarial perturbations to examples: given an input x and any target classification t, it is possible to find a new input x' that is similar to x but classified as t. These adversarial examples often appear almost indistinguishable from natural data to human perception and are yet incorrectly classified by the neural network. Recent results have shown that accuracy of neural networks can be reduced from close to 100% to below 5% using adversarial examples. This creates a significant challenge in deploying these deep learning models in security-critical domains where adversarial activity is intrinsic, such as cyber-networks, and surveillance. The use of neural networks in computer vision and speech recognition have brought these models into the center of security-critical systems where authentication depends on these machine learned models. How do we ensure that adversaries in these domains do not exploit the limitations of machine learning models to go undetected or trigger a non-intended outcome? The third challenge addressed in TRINITY framework is to use geometric methods for identifying invariants in training data that can be used for detecting adversarial examples.

2 Interpretability of AI Models

2.1 Motivating Example

We describe a motivating example to illustrate the problem of providing human-interpretable explanations for the results of an AI algorithm. We consider the A* planning algorithm [38], which enjoys widespread use in path and motion planning due to its optimality and efficiency. Given a description of the state space and transitions between states as a weighted graph where weights are used to encode costs such as distance and time, A* starts from a specific node in the graph and constructs a tree of paths starting from that node, expanding paths in a best-first fashion until one of them reaches the predetermined goal node. At each iteration, A* determines which of its partial paths is most promising and should be expanded. This decision is based on the estimate of the cost-to-go to the goal node. Specifically, A* selects an intermediate node n that minimizes $\texttt{totalCost}(n) = \texttt{partialCost}(n) + \texttt{guessCost}(n)$, where $\texttt{totalCost}$ is the estimated total cost of the path that includes node n, obtained as the sum of the cost ($\texttt{partialCost}(n)$) of reaching n from the initial node, and a heuristic estimate of the cost ($\texttt{guessCost}(n)$) of reaching the goal from n. The heuristic function $\texttt{guessCost}$ is problem-specific: e.g., when searching for the shortest path on a Manhattan grid with obstacles, a good $\texttt{guessCost}$ is the straight line distance from the node n to the final destination. Typical implementations of A* use a priority queue to perform the repeated selection of intermediate nodes. This priority queue is known as the open set or fringe. At each step of the algorithm, the node with the lowest $\texttt{totalCost}$ value is removed from the queue, and "expanded", This means that the $\texttt{partialCost}$ values of its neighbors are updated accordingly based on whether going through n improves them, and these neighbors are added to the queue. The algorithm continues until some goal node has the minimum cost value, $\texttt{totalCost}$, in the queue, or until the queue is empty (in which case no plan exists). The $\texttt{totalCost}$ value of the goal node is then the cost of the optimal path. We refer readers to [38] for a detailed description of A*. In rest of this section, we illustrate the need for providing explanations using a simple example map and application of A* on it to find the shortest path.

Figure 1 depicts the result of running A* on a 50×50 grid, where cells that form part of an obstacle are colored red. The input map (Fig. 1(a)) shows the obstacles and free space. A* is run to find a path from lower right corner to upper left corner. The output map is shown in Fig. 1(b).

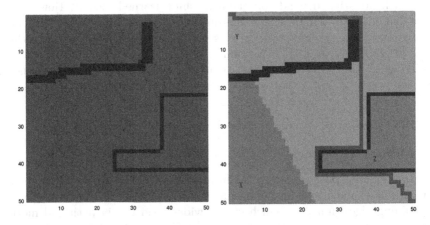

Fig. 1. (a) Input map to A* (b) Output showing final path and internal states of A*. Cells on the computed optimal path are colored dark blue. Cells which entered A*'s priority queue are colored light cyan, and those cells that never entered the queue are colored yellow. (Color figure online)

Consider the three cells X, Y, Z marked in the output of A* in Fig. 1(b) and the following inquiries on the optimal path discovered by A*:

– *Why was the cell Y not selected for the optimal path?* Given the output and logged internal states of the A* algorithm, we know that Y was considered as a candidate cell but discarded due to non-optimal cost.
– *Why was the cell X not selected for the optimal path?* If we logged the internal states of the A* algorithm, we would find that X was not even considered as a candidate and it never entered the priority queue of the A* algorithm. But this is not a useful explanation because a non-expert user cannot be expected to understand the concept of a priority queue, or the details of how A* works.
– *Why was the cell Z not selected for the optimal path?* The cell Z was also never inserted into the priority queue and hence, it was never a candidate to be selected on the optimal path similar to cell X. When responding to a user query about why X and Z were not selected in the optimal path, we cannot differentiate between the two even if all the internal decisions and states of the A* algorithm were logged. So, we cannot provide the intuitively expected explanation that Z is not reachable due to obstacles, while X is reachable but has higher cost than the cells that were considered.

This example scenario illustrates the need for new information to provide explanation in addition to the usual deduction by AI algorithm while solving the original decision making problem.

2.2 Logic Extraction and Formal Synthesis

Our approach relies on learning logical explanations in the form of sparse Boolean formula from examples that are obtained by carefully selected introspective simulations of the decision-making algorithm. The area of active learning Boolean formula from positive and negative examples has been studied in literature [1,33] in both exact and probably approximately correct (PAC) setting. Exact learning Boolean formula [3,34] requires a number of examples exponential in the size of the vocabulary. Under the PAC setting, learning is guaranteed to find an approximately correct concept given enough independent samples [2,43,50]. It is known that k-clause conjunctive normal form Boolean formula are not PAC learnable with polynomial sample-size, even though monomials and disjunctive normal form representations are PAC learnable [13,50]. Changing the representation from CNF to DNF form can lead to exponential blow-up. In contrast, we consider only sparse Boolean formula and our goal is to learn the exact Boolean formula with probabilistic confidence, and not its approximation. Efficient learning techniques exist for particular classes of Boolean formulae such as monotonic and read-one formulae [18,23], but explanations do not always take these restricted forms, and hence, our focus on sparse Boolean formulae is better suited for this context.

Another related research area is the newly emerged field of formal synthesis, which combines induction and deduction for automatic synthesis of systems from logical or black-box oracle specifications [25,29]. Unlike active learning, formal synthesis is also concerned with defining techniques for the generation of interesting examples and not just its inductive generalization, much like our approach. While existing formal synthesis techniques have considered completion of templates by inferring parameters [6,52,55], composition of component Boolean functions or uplifting to bitvector form [10,21,25,63], inferring transducers and finite state-machines [7,8,17], and synthesis of invariants [56,57], our work is the first to consider sparsity as a structural assumption for learning Boolean formulae.

The need for explanations of AI decisions to increase trust of decision-making systems has been noted in the literature [40]. Specific approaches have been introduced to discover explanations in specific domains such as MDPs [14], HTNs [22] and Bayesian networks [64]. Explanation of failure in robotic systems by detecting problems in the temporal logic specification using formal requirement analysis was shown to be practically useful in [51]. Inductive logic programming [15] has also been used to model domain-specific explanation generation rules. In contrast, we propose a domain-independent approach to generate explanations by treating the decision-making AI algorithm as an oracle. Domain-independent approaches have also been proposed in the AI literature for detecting sensitive input components that determine the decision in a classification problem [53,60]. While these approaches work in a quantitative setting, such as measuring sensitivity from the gradient of a neural network classifier's output, our approach is restricted to the discrete, qualitative setting. Further, we not only detect sensitive inputs (support of Boolean formulae) but also generate the explanation.

2.3 Sparse Boolean Formula Learning for Explanations

A decision-making AI algorithm `Alg` can be modelled as a function that computes the values of output variables `out` given input variables `in`, that is,

$$\text{Alg} : \text{in} \rightarrow \text{out}$$

The outputs are the decision variables, while the inputs include the environment and system states as observed by the system through the perception pipeline. While the decision and state variables can be continuous and real valued, the inquiries and explanations are framed using predicates over these variables, such as comparison of a variable to some threshold. These predicates can either be directly provided by the user or the developer of the AI system, or they can be automatically extracted from the implementation of the AI system by including predicates that appear in the control flow of the AI system. These must be predicates over the input and output variables, that is, `in` and `out`, which are understood by the users. Our approach exploits the sparsity of Boolean formula for learning the explanations and so, the vocabulary can include all possible predicates and variables that might be useful for explaining AI decisions. We propose methods to efficiently find relevant variables where these methods only depend logarithmically on the size of the vocabulary. This ensures that the definition of vocabulary can conveniently include all possible variables, and our approach can automatically find the relevant subset and synthesize the corresponding explanation.

We denote the vocabulary of atomic predicates used in the inquiry from the user and the provided explanation from the system by $\mathcal{V}$. We can separate the vocabulary $\mathcal{V}$ into two subsets: $\mathcal{V}_Q$ used to formulate the user inquiry and $\mathcal{V}_R$ used to provide explanations.

$$\mathcal{V}_Q = \{q_1, q_2, \ldots q_m\}, \mathcal{V}_R = \{r_1, r_2, \ldots r_n\} \text{ where } q_i, r_i : \text{in} \cup \text{out} \rightarrow \text{Bool}$$

Intuitively, $\mathcal{V}$ is the shared vocabulary that describes the interface of the AI algorithm and is understood by the human-user. For example, the inquiry vocabulary for a planning agent may include propositions denoting selection of a waypoint in the path, and the explanation vocabulary may include propositions denoting presence of obstacles on a map.

An *inquiry* ϕ_Q from the user is an observation about the output (decision) of the algorithm, and can be formulated as a Boolean combination of predicates in the vocabulary $\mathcal{V}_Q$. Hence, we can denote it as $\phi_Q(\mathcal{V}_Q)$ where the predicates in $\mathcal{V}_Q$ are over the set $\text{in} \cup \text{out}$, and the corresponding grammar is:

$$\phi_Q := \phi_Q \wedge \phi_Q \mid \phi_Q \vee \phi_Q \mid \neg\phi_Q \mid q_i \text{ where } q_i \in \mathcal{V}_Q$$

While conjunction and negation are sufficient to express any Boolean combination, we include disjunction and implication for succinctness of inquiries. Similarly, the *response* $\phi_R(\mathcal{V}_R)$ is a Boolean combination of the predicates in the vocabulary $\mathcal{V}_R$ where the predicates in $\mathcal{V}_R$ are over the set $\text{in} \cup \text{out}$, and the corresponding grammar is:

$$\phi_R := \phi_R \wedge \phi_R \mid \phi_R \vee \phi_R \mid \neg\phi_R \mid r_i \text{ where } r_i \in \mathcal{V}_R$$

Definition 1. *Given an AI algorithm* Alg *and an inquiry* $\phi_Q(\mathcal{V}_Q)$, $\phi_R(\mathcal{V}_R)$ *is a necessary and sufficient explanation when* $\phi_R(\mathcal{V}_R) \iff \phi_Q(\mathcal{V}_Q)$ *where* $\mathcal{V}_R, \mathcal{V}_Q$ *are predicates over* $\text{in} \cup \text{out}$ *as explained earlier, and* $\text{out} = \text{Alg(in)}$. $\phi_R(\mathcal{V}_R)$ *is a sufficient explanation when* $\phi_R(\mathcal{V}_R) \Rightarrow \phi_Q(\mathcal{V}_Q)$.

If the algorithm $\text{out} = \text{Alg(in)}$ could be modeled explicitly in appropriate logic, then the above definition could be used to generate explanations for a given inquiry using techniques such as satisfiability solving. However, such an explicit modeling of these algorithms is currently outside the scope of existing logical deduction frameworks, and is impractical for large and complicated AI systems even from the standpoint of the associated modeling effort. The AI algorithm Alg is available as an executable function; hence, it can be used as an oracle that can provide an outputs for any given input. This motivates oracle-guided learning of the explanation from examples using the notion of confidence associated with it.

Definition 2. *Given an AI algorithm* Alg *and an inquiry* $\phi_Q(\mathcal{V}_Q)$, $\phi_R(\mathcal{V}_R)$ *is a* necessary and sufficient explanation with probabilistic confidence κ *when* $Pr(\phi_R(\mathcal{V}_R) \iff \phi_Q(\mathcal{V}_Q)) \geq \kappa$, *where* $\mathcal{V}_R, \mathcal{V}_Q$ *are predicates over* $\text{in} \cup \text{out}$ *as explained earlier,* $\text{out} = \text{Alg(in)}$ *and* $0 \leq \kappa \leq 1$. *The probability of satisfaction of* $\phi_R(\mathcal{V}_R) \iff \phi_Q(\mathcal{V}_Q)$ *is computed using uniform distribution over the variables in* $\mathcal{V}$. *This uniform distribution is not an assumption over the context in* *which an AI algorithm* Alg *is used. This uniform distribution is only used to estimate the probability of finding the correct explanation. Similarly, $\phi_R(\text{in})$ is a sufficient explanation with confidence κ when $Pr(\phi_R(\mathcal{V}_R) \Rightarrow \phi_Q(\mathcal{V}_Q)) \geq \kappa$.*

The oracle used to learn the explanation uses the AI algorithm. It runs the AI algorithm on a given input in_i to generate the decision output out_i, and then marks the input as a positive example if $\phi_Q(out_i)$ is true, that is, the inquiry property holds on the output. It marks the input as a negative example if $\phi_Q(out_i)$ is not true. We call this an *introspection oracle* which marks each input as either positive or negative.

Definition 3. *An* introspection oracle $\mathcal{O}_{\phi_Q,\text{Alg}}$ *for a given algorithm* Alg *and inquiry ϕ_Q takes an input in_i and maps it to a positive or negative label, that is, $\mathcal{O}_{\phi_Q,\text{Alg}} : \text{in} \to \{\oplus, \ominus\}$.*

$\mathcal{O}_{\phi_Q,\text{Alg}}(in_i) = \oplus$ *if $\phi_Q(\mathcal{V}_Q(out_i))$ and $\mathcal{O}_{\phi_Q,\text{Alg}}(in_i) = \ominus$ if $\neg\phi_Q(\mathcal{V}_Q(out_i))$, where*

$out_i = \text{Alg}(in_i)$, *and $\mathcal{V}_Q(out_i)$ is the evaluation of the predicates in $\mathcal{V}_Q$ on out_i*

We now formally define the problem of learning Boolean formula with specified confidence κ given an oracle that labels the examples.

Definition 4. *The problem of oracle-guided learning of Boolean formula from examples is to identify (with confidence κ) the target Boolean function ϕ over a set of atomic propositions $\mathcal{V}$ by querying an oracle $\mathcal{O}$ that labels each input in_i (which is an assignment to all variables in $\mathcal{V}$) as positive or negative $\{\oplus, \ominus\}$ depending on whether $\phi(in_i)$ holds or not, respectively.*

We make the following observations which relates the problem of finding explanations for decisions made by AI algorithms to the problem of learning Boolean formula.

Observation 1. *The problem of generating explanation ϕ_R for the AI algorithm* Alg *and an inquiry ϕ_Q is equivalent to the problem of oracle-guided learning of Boolean formula ϕ_R using oracle $\mathcal{O}_{\phi_Q,\text{Alg}}$ as described in Definition 4.*

$\phi[r_i]$ denotes the restriction of the Boolean formula ϕ by setting r_i to true in ϕ and $\phi[\overline{r_i}]$ denotes the restriction of ϕ by setting r_i to false. A predicate r_i is in the support of the Boolean formula ϕ, that is, $r_i \in \text{support}(\phi)$ if and only if $\phi[r_i] \neq \phi[\overline{r_i}]$.

Observation 2. *The explanation ϕ_R over a vocabulary of atoms $\mathcal{V}_R$ for the AI algorithm* Alg *and a user inquiry ϕ_Q is a sparse Boolean formula, that is, $|\text{support}(\phi_R)| << |\mathcal{V}_R|$.*

These observations motivate the following problem definition for learning sparse Boolean formula.

Definition 5. *Boolean function ϕ is called k-sparse if $|\text{support}(\phi_R)| \leq k$. The problem of oracle-guided learning of k-sparse Boolean formula from examples is to identify (with confidence κ) the target k-sparse Boolean function ϕ over a set of atomic propositions $\mathcal{V}$ by querying an oracle $\mathcal{O}$ that labels each input in_i (which is an assignment to all variables in $\mathcal{V}$) as positive or negative $\{\oplus, \ominus\}$ depending on whether $\phi(in_i)$ holds or not, respectively.*

The explanation of decisions made by an AI algorithm can be generated by solving the problem of oracle-guided learning of k-sparse Boolean formula. We recently formulated two algorithms to learn sparse Boolean formula where the size of required examples grows logarithmically (in contrast to exponentially in the general case) with the size of the overall vocabulary. The first algorithm is based on a binary search in the Hamming space first described in our earlier work [27]. The second algorithm is based on random walk in the Boolean hypercube reported in our earlier work [28]. We refer the reader to [27,28] for technical details of the formulation, and detailed case studies for empirical evaluation.

3   Verification of DNNs

At an abstract level, a deep neural network computes a function from a set of inputs to some set of outputs. The question that we address here is as follows:

> Given a neural network (NN), and constraints (assumptions) which define a set of inputs to the network, provide a *tight* over-approximation (guarantee) of the output set.

This serves as one of the main primitives in verification of neural networks. Deep neural networks are very common in applications such as image classification and autonomous control. In image classification networks, since each image is a point in the high dimensional pixel space, a polyhedral set may be used to represent all possible bounded perturbations to a given image. If, for such a set, we can guarantee that the output of the classification remains unaltered, then we have proved that the neural network is *robust* to bounded pixel noise. Besides image classification, neural networks are increasingly used in the control of autonomous systems, such as self-driving cars, unmanned aerial vehicles, and other robotic systems. A typical approach to verify these systems involves a *reachability computation* to estimate the forward reachable set as time evolves. Using this, it is possible to prove that, no matter what the initial condition of a system is, it always reaches a target region in finite time. For instance, we wish prove that, an autonomous car whose inputs are provided by a neural network controller's feedback, will remain within a fixed lateral distance from the center of the road (desired trajectory), while remaining under the speed limit.

We address the output range analysis problem for a neural network with a single output. The extension to multiple output neural networks is straightforward. Let $x \in \Re^n$ be an input to a NN, and $y \in \Re$ be the output of the network. A typical neural network consists of layers, where each layer computes some function on the outputs of the previous layer and feeds it's output to the next layer. That is, for a k layer neural network, we get a composition of k functions. Each function is a matrix multiplication, followed by an element wise computation of an activation function. A k layer neural network with N neurons in each hidden layer is described by a set of matrices: $[(W_0, b_0), \ldots, (W_{k-1}, b_{k-1}), (W_k, b_k)]$.

Definition 6 (ReLU Unit). *Each neuron in the network implements a nonlinear function σ linking its input value to the output value. We consider ReLU units that implement the function $\sigma(z) : \max(z, 0)$. We extend the definition of σ to apply component-wise to vectors z as $\sigma(z) : (\sigma(z_1), \sigma(z_2) \ldots \sigma(z_n))$.*

Taking σ to be the ReLU function, we describe the overall function defined by a given network N as follows:

Definition 7 (Function Computed by neural networks). *Given a neural network N as described above, the function $F : \Re^n \to \Re$ computed by the neural network is given by the composition $F := F_k \circ \cdots \circ F_0$ wherein $F_i(z) : \sigma(W_i z + b_i)$ is the function computed by the ith hidden layer with F_0 denoting the function linking the inputs to the first layer and F_k linking the last layer to the output.*

3.1   Range Estimation

Let N be a neural network with n input vector, x, a single output y, and weights $[(W_0, b_0), \ldots, (W_k, b_k)]$. Let F_N be the function defined by such a network. The general problem of verifying neural network and establishing an assume-guarantee contract on its inputs and outputs can be simplified to range estimation problem by suitably transforming the inputs and outputs such that the assumption constraints are described by a polyhedron and the guarantee constraints to be derived over the outputs can be represented as intervals. The universal approximation property of neural networks can be used to approximately encode such transformation as a part of the network itself. Thus, we focus on range estimation problem and rely on reducing other verification problems to it. The *range estimation* problem is defined as follows:

- INPUTS: Neural Network N, input constraints $P : Ax \leq b$ and a tolerance parameter $\delta > 0$.
- OUTPUT: An interval $[\ell, u]$ such that $(\forall\ x \in P)\ F_N(x) \in [\ell, u]$. i.e., $[\ell, u]$ contains the range of F_N over inputs $x \in P$. Furthermore, we require the interval to be *tight*:

$$(\max_{x \in P}\ F_N(x) \geq u - \delta),\ (\min_{x \in P}\ F_N(x) \leq \ell + \delta).$$

We will assume that the input polyhedron P is compact: i.e., it is closed and has a bounded volume. It was shown in [32] that even proving simple properties is NP complete. Simple properties, like proving that there exists an assignment from input set to an output set, which respects the constraints imposed by the neural network. So, one of the fundamental challenges in this problem is to tackle the exponential nature.

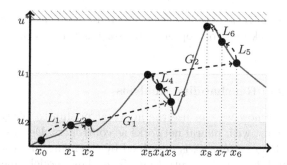

Fig. 2. A schematic figure showing our approach showing alternating series of local search $L_1, \ldots, L_6$ and "global search" G_1, G_2 iterations. The points x_2, x_5, x_8 represent local minima wherein our approach transitions from local search iterations to global search iterations.

3.2   MILP Based Approach

Without loss of generality, we will focus on estimating the upper bound u. The case for the lower bound will be entirely analogous. First, we note that a single Mixed Integer Linear Programming (MILP) problem can be formulated, and then query a solver to directly compute u. Unfortunately, that can be quite expensive in practice. Therefore, our approach will combine a series of MILP feasibility problems alternating with local search steps.

Figure 2 shows a pictorial representation of the overall approach. The approach incrementally finds a series of approximations to the upper bound $u_1 < u_2 < \cdots < u^*$, culminating in the final bound $u = u^*$.

1. The first level u_1 is found by choosing a randomly sampled point $x_0 \in P$.
2. Next, we perform a series of local iteration steps resulting in samples $x_1, \ldots, x_i$ that perform gradient ascent until these steps cannot obtain any further improvement. We take $u_2 = F_N(x_i)$.
3. A "global search" step is now performed to check if there is any point $x \in P$ such that $F_N(x) \geq u_2 + \delta$. This is obtained by solving a MILP feasibility problem.
4. If the global search fails to find a solution, then we declare $u^* = u_2 + \delta$.
5. Otherwise, we obtain a new *witness* point x_{i+1} such that $F_N(x_{i+1}) \geq u_2 + \delta$.
6. We now go back to the local search step.

The ideas discussed here for the output range analysis have been implemented in Sherlock [12]. For neural networks with multiple outputs, we can individually find the bounds for each of the network outputs, and then combine them to form a hyper-rectangle in the output dimensional space. This can be extended to using a template polyhedron to obtain tighter bounds, in the output dimension, described in the next section. In general, we can obtain guarantees on the output from a given class defined by the constraint template used in the minimization/maximization step of the presented approach. Our current implementation in Sherlock built on top of MILP solvers requires the template to be linear.

3.3 Application: Reachability Analysis

We briefly describe how we can use the above algorithm to verify behaviors of autonomous systems, with neural networks as controllers. Details are presented in [11]. A closed loop system, $\mathcal{C}$, is described by the neural networks f_p, for the system model, and f_h, for the control law. The plant model function f_p, gives the state of the system in the next time step, given the states of the system at the current time step. That is, $x(t+1) = f_p(x(t), f_h(x(t)))$, where $x(t) \in \Re^n$, is the state of the system at time t, in an n dimensional space.

Thus, given an initial state X_0 (represented as a polyhedron over the state space), we wish to compute symbolic representations for sets $X_1, X_2, \ldots, X_K$ wherein X_i represents the reachable states of the closed loop system given by the composition of the plant f_p and the feedback law f_h, in i steps. Here K is some fixed time horizon. We will use range computation, as a primitive for checking reachability, invariance and stability properties.

The computation of the reach sets of the closed loop system starts with an effort to compute over-approximation of the post operator:

$$\mathsf{post}(X; f_p, f_h) : \ \{\mathbf{x} \in \mathbb{R}^n \mid (\exists \mathbf{x}_0 \in X) \ \mathbf{x} = f_p(\mathbf{x}_0, f_h(\mathbf{x}_0))\}.$$

For an input set X, the exact set of the output map of the post operator can be prohibitively expensive to compute: in general, it's a union of polyhedrons, the count of which is exponential in the number of neurons in the two given networks f_p and f_h. Instead, we use a single polyhedron $P(X)$ that approximates the post condition.

For that purpose, we use a template polyhedra:

Definition 8 (Template Polyhedra). *A template T is a set of expressions $T : \{\mathbf{e}_1, \ldots, \mathbf{e}_r\}$ wherein each $\mathbf{e}_i$ is an linear expression of the form $\mathbf{c}_i^t \mathbf{x}$ over the state variables. A template polyhedron P over a template T is of the form:*

$$\bigwedge_{j=1}^{r} \ell_j \leq \mathbf{e}_j \leq u_j,$$

for bounds ℓ_j, u_j over each template expression $\mathbf{e}_j$.

For a fixed template T, the reachable sets are represented by template polyhedra over the above templates. The post condition operation $\mathsf{post}(X; f_p, f_h)$, can now be substituted by a template-based post-condition operator $\mathsf{post}_T(X; f_p, f_h)$ that produces bounds ℓ_j, u_j for each $\mathbf{e}_j \in T$ by solving the following optimization problem:

$$\ell_j(u_j) : \ \min(\max) \ \mathbf{e}_j[\mathbf{x}] \ \text{s.t.} \mathbf{x}_0 \in X_0, \ \mathbf{u} = f_h(\mathbf{x}_0), \ \mathbf{x} = f_p(\mathbf{x}_0, \mathbf{u}).$$

The above optimization problem, is defined using neural network functions f_h and f_p. However, the combination of local search and MILP encoding used in our tool SHERLOCK can be modified almost trivially to solve this optimization problem. Furthermore, the guarantees used in SHERLOCK extend. Thus, we guarantee that the reported result is no more than ϵ away from the true value, for the given tolerance parameter ϵ.

The computation of reach sets can be extended beyond single step using Sherlock. It is possible to use the tool for a k step reachability $\mathrm{post}_T^{(k)}(X; f_p, h)$ with the tolerance factor ϵ, in a very straight forward manner. A fundamental goal in computing reachable sets is to prove that the system trajectories converge to a target set, starting from the initial set. It suffices to show that the reach sets computed eventually land inside the target set T, in a finite number of time steps. Thus, the problem of checking reachability of a target set T is performed iteratively as

Table 1. Performance results on networks trained on functions with known maxima and minima. **Legend:** x number of inputs, k number of layers, N: total number of neurons, T: CPU time taken, Nc: number of nodes explored. All the tests were run on a Linux server running Ubuntu 17.04 with 24 cores, and 64 GB RAM (DNC: Did Not Complete)

| | | | | 23 cores | | | | single core | | | | Reluplex |
| | | | | Sherlock | | Monolithic | | Sherlock | | Monolithic | | |
ID	x	k	N	T	Nc	T	Nc	T	Nc	T	Nc	T
N_0	2	1	100	1s	94	2.3s	24	0.4s	44	0.3s	25	9.0
N_1	2	1	200	2.2s	166	3.6s	29	0.9s	71	0.8s	38	1m50s
N_2	2	1	500	7.8s	961	12.6s	236	2s	138	2.9s	257	15m59s
N_3	2	1	500	1.5s	189	0.5s	43	0.6s	95	0.2s	53	12m25s
N_4	2	1	1000	3m52s	32E3	3m52s	3E3	1m20s	4.8E3	35.6s	5.3E3	1h06m
N_5	3	7	425	4s	6	6.1s	2	1.7s	2	0.9s	2	DNC
N_6	3	4	762	3m47s	3.3E3	4m41s	3.6E3	37.8s	685	56.4s	2.2E3	DNC
N_7	4	7	731	3.7s	1	7.7s	2	3.9s	1	3.1s	2	1h35m
N_8	3	8	478	6.5s	3	40.8s	2	3.6s	3	3.3s	2	DNC
N_9	3	8	778	18.3s	114	1m11s	2	12.5s	12	4.3s	73	DNC
N_{10}	3	26	2340	50m18s	4.6E4	1h26m	6E4	17m12s	2.4E4	18m58s	1.9E4	DNC
N_{11}	3	9	1527	5m44s	450	55m12s	6.4E3	56.4s	483	130.7s	560	DNC
N_{12}	3	14	2292	24m17s	1.8E3	3h46m	2.4E4	8m11s	2.3E3	1h01m	1.6E4	DNC
N_{13}	3	19	3057	4h10m	2.2E4	61h08m	6.6E4	1h7m	1.5E4	15h1m	1.5E5	DNC
N_{14}	3	24	3822	72h39m	8.4E4	111h35m	1.1E5	5h57m	3E4	timeout	-	DNC
N_{15}	3	127	6845	2m51s	1	timeout	-	3m27s	1	timeout	-	DNC

We did comparisons with a recent solver for deep neural networks called Reluplex [32], and detailed study is available in [11,12]. Even though Reluplex is an SMT solver, it can be used to perform set propagation using a binary search wrapper. The preliminary comparison shows that Sherlock is much faster than Reluplex used with a binary search wrapper. Another set of comparisons was using Sherlock, against a monolithic mixed integer linear programming (MILP) solver. The results of the comparison has been presented in Table 1.

We used Sherlock for verifying properties of various closed-loop cyberphysical systems that have neural networks as controller. We could prove that in finite number of steps, the sets did converge to the goal region. Details of the technical approach and empirical evaluation are presented in [11,12].

4   Resilience of DNNs

There has been a recent explosion of methods for adversarial attacks on neural network models along with techniques for making neural networks resilient to attacks. No single resilient mechanism has yet been discovered which can be used against any feasible attack method. We take a different approach to resilience by focusing on the identification of suspicious adversarial examples. The overall idea is to ensure that the machine learning models can identify adversarial attacks, and not provide a prediction on them instead of providing a wrong prediction. An approach to detect these adversarial examples will act as a runtime monitor that finds the limits of the machine learning model.

We recently developed an approach to detect adversarial examples by identifying a low dimensional manifold in which the training data lie, and then measuring the distance of a new sample to this manifold. The manifold corresponds to a geometric invariant of the training data. Adversarial examples often rely on lying outside this manifold, and since the model was learned using data samples in the manifold, the model naturally mis-predicts on examples farther away from the manifold. In our experiments, we used the CleverHans system [46] and employed the Projected Gradient Descent (PGD) attack method implemented in it. This is an implementation of a very recent attack method described in Madry et al. [42]. We control the strength of the attack using one of the parameters in this method ϵ that bounds the maximum distortion of adversarial example compared to the original input. Increasing this norm bound generates adversarial examples with higher confidence.

Our empirical study on MNIST [39] and CIFAR10 [36] datasets suggests that adversarial examples not only lie farther away from the data manifold, but this distance from manifold of an adversarial example increases with the confidence of adversarial examples. Consequently, our detection approach can more easily detect adversarial examples generated with higher norm bound and hence, more likely to cause mis-prediction in the machine learned model. Our efforts constitute a first step towards formulating a computational geometric approach to identifying boundaries of a machine learning model, and using it to detect adversarial attacks. The details are described in [26].

4.1 Adversarial Attacks and Defenses

Multiple methods have been proposed in literature to generate adversarial examples as well as defend against adversarial examples. Adversarial example generation methods include both white-box and black-box attacks on neural networks [19,47,48,61], targeting feedforward classification networks [9], generative networks [35], and recurrent neural networks [49]. These methods leverage gradient based optimization for normal examples to discover perturbations that lead to mis-prediction - the techniques differ in defining the neighborhood in which perturbation is permitted and the loss function used to guide the search. For example, one of the earliest attacks [19] used a fast sign gradient method (FGMS) that looks for a similar image x' in the L^∞ neighborhood of x. Given a loss function $Loss(x, l)$ specifying the cost of classifying the point x as label l, the adversarial example x' is calculated as

$$x' = x + \epsilon \cdot sign(\nabla_x Loss(x, l_x))$$

FGMS was improved to iterative gradient sign approach (IGSM) in [37] by using a finer iterative optimization strategy where the attack performs FGMS with a smaller step-width α, and clips the updated result so that the image stays within the ϵ boundary of x. In this approach, the i-th iteration computes the following:

$$x'_{i+1} = clip_{\epsilon,x}(x'_i + \alpha \cdot sign(\nabla_x Loss(x, l_x)))$$

In contrast to FGSM and IGSM, DeepFool [45] attempts to find a perturbed image x' from a normal image x by finding the closest decision boundary and crossing it. In practice, DeepFool relies on local linearized approximation of the decision boundary. Another attack method that has received a lot of attention is Carlini attack that relies on finding a perturbation that minimizes change as well as the hinge loss on the logits (pre-softmax classification result vector). The attack is generated by solving the following optimization problem:

$$min_\delta[||\delta||_2 + c \cdot \max(Z(x')_{l_x} - maxZ(x')_i : i \neq l_x, -\kappa)]$$

where Z denotes the logits, l_x is the ground truth label, κ is the confidence (raising which will force searcher for larger perturbations), and c is a hyperparameter that balances the perturbation and the hinge loss. Another attack method is projected gradient method (PGM) proposed in [42]. PGD attempts to solve this constrained optimization problem:

$$\max_{||x^{adv}-x||_\infty \leq \epsilon} Loss(x^{adv}, l_x)$$

where S is the constraint on the allowed perturbation usually given as bound ϵ on the norm, and l_x is the ground truth label of x. Projected gradient descent is used to solve this constrained optimization problem by restarting PGD from several points in the l_∞ balls around the data points x. This gradient descent increases the loss function $Loss$ in a fairly consistent way before reaching a plateau with a fairly well-concentrated distribution and the achieved maximum value is considerably higher than that of a random point in the data set. We focus on this PGD attack because it is shown to be a universal first order adversary [42], that is, developing detection capability or resilience against PGD also implies defense against many other first order attacks.

Defense of neural networks against adversarial examples is more difficult compared to generating attacks. Madry et al. [42] propose a generic saddle point formulation where $\mathcal{D}$ is the underlying training data distribution, $Loss(\theta, x, l_x)$ is a loss function at data point x with ground truth label l_x for a model with parameter θ:

$$\min_{\theta} E_{(x,y)\sim\mathcal{D}} \Big[\max_{||x^{adv}-x||_\infty \leq \epsilon} Loss(\theta, x^{adv}, l_x) \Big]$$

This formulation uses robust optimization over the expected loss for worst-case adversarial perturbation for training data. The internal maximization corresponds to finding adversarial examples, and can be approximated using IGSM [37]. This approach falls into a category of defenses that use *adversarial training* [59]. Instead of training with only adversarial examples, using a mixture of normal and adversarial examples in the training set has been found to be more effective [45,61]. Another alternative is to augment the learning objective with a regularizer term corresponding to the adversarial inputs [19]. More recently, logit pairing has been shown to be an effective approximation of adversarial regularization [31].

Another category of defense against adversarial attacks on neural networks are defensive distillation methods [48]. These methods modify the training process of neural networks to make it difficult to launch gradient based attacks directly on the network. The key idea is to use distillation training technique [24] and hide the gradient between the pre-softmax layer and the softmax outputs. Carlini and Wagner [9] found methods to break this defense by changing the loss function, calculating gradient directly from pre-softmax layer and transferring attack from easy-to-attack network to distilled network. More recently, Athalye et al. [4] showed that it is possible to bypass several defenses proposed for the whitebox setting.

Our approach falls into the category of techniques that focus on only detecting adversarial examples. Techniques based on manually identified statistical features [20] or a dedicated learning model [44] trained separately to identify adversarial examples have been previously proposed in literature. These explicit classification methods do not generalize well across different adversarial example generation techniques.

In contrast to these defensive methods, our approach does not require any augmentation of training data, modification of the training process or change in the learned model. The design and training of the neural network is independent to the manifold based filtering approach. Thus, our approach to detection is orthogonal to learning robust machine learning models and can benefit from these methods. Further, we do not require access to the adversarial example generation method, and thus this defense is likely to generalize well across different attack methods. Our approach relies on just identifying the manifold of typical data which need not be even labeled and hence, this method is more practical in contexts where labeled training data is very difficult to obtain.

4.2 Manifold Learning

Learning manifold in which data points lie has been itself an active area of research [41,54,58,62]. ISOMAP, t-SNE and spectral embedding have been proposed to learn the data manifold. The spectral embedding method performs dimensionality reduction in a way that preserves dot products between data points as closely as possible by minimizing $\sum_i (x_i^T x_j - y_i^T y_j)^2$ where y_i is embedding of x_i. ISOMAP [62] embeds the data points in a low dimensional space while preserving the geodesic distances between data points. The geodesic distances are measured in terms of shortest paths between the points in a graph formed by computing k-nearest neighbors and introducing an edge between the neighbors. After computing the geodesic distances, spectral methods can be used to compute the embeddings that preserve this geodesic distance instead of Euclidean distance. t-distributed Stochastic Nearest Embedding (t-SNE) [41] is another method for computing manifold. It constructs a probability distribution over pairs of high-dimensional data points in such a way that similar objects have a high probability of being picked. This is followed by defining a similar distribution in the low dimension and minimized the KL divergence between the two distributions.

LLE [54] is another graph-based dimensionality reduction method that tries to preserve the local linear structure. LLE linearly approximates each data point in the training set manifold with its closest neighbors where the approximation is learned using linear regression. LLE requires computations of the k-nearest neighbors followed by computing the weight matrix W that represents each point as a linear combination of its neighbors. W is computes such that the overall reconstruction error $\sum_i ||x_i - \sum_j W_{ij} x_j||^2$ is minimized subject to constraints that $W_{ij} = 0$ when x_i and x_j are not neighbors, and $\sum_j W_{ij} = 1$ for all i. The low dimensional embedding is computed in LLE by minimizing the following objective: $\sum_i ||y_i - \sum_j W_{ij} y_j||^2$, where y_i denotes the low dimensional embedding of x_i, and we can normalize the representation by requiring $\sum_i y_i = 0$ and $Y^T Y = I$. W is constructed locally for each point, but the low dimensional embeddings y_i are computed globally in a single optimization step. This enables LLE to uncover global structure. Further, the embedding discovered by LLE is scale and rotation independent due to constraints on y_i. Our experiments found LLE to be most effective because of LLE's better discovery of nonlinearity, and sharper embedding in lower dimension.

Our approach relies on computing the distance of the new sample point from the manifold of training data. The kernel density estimation can be used to measure the distance $d(x)$ of x from the data manifold of training set. Specifically, $d(x) = \frac{1}{|X|} \sum_{x_i \in X} k(x_i, x)$, where X is the full data set and $k(\cdot, \cdot)$ is a kernel function such as Gaussian or a simple L_∞ or L_2 norm. In case of using Gaussian kernel, the bandwidth σ needs to be carefully selected to avoid 'spiky' density estimate or an overly smooth density estimate. A typical good choice for bandwidth is a value that maximizes the log-likelihood of the training data [30]. Further, we can restrict the set of training points to be considered from the full set X to a set of immediate neighbors of x. The neighborhood can be defined using the maximum distance or bound on the number of neighbors. In our experiments, we use L_∞ norm with bound on the number of neighbors which yielded good result.

It has been hypothesized in literature [5, 16] that the deeper layers of a deep neural network provide more linear and unwrapped manifolds in comparison to the input space. Thus, the task of identifying the manifold becomes easier as we progress from the input space to the more abstract feature spaces all the way to the logit space. But the adversarial perturbations are harder to detect at higher levels and might get hidden by the lower layers of the neural network. In our experiments, we learned manifolds in input space as well as the logit space.

4.3 Empirical Evaluation

We evaluated our approach on MNIST dataset [39] and CIFAR10 dataset [36]. We report the key findings in this section.

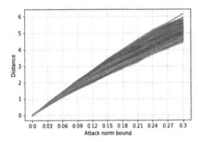 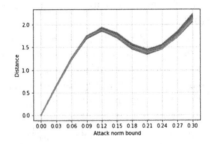

Fig. 3. Increase in adversarial distance from manifold for MNIST in input space (Left) and logit space (Right). Each line of different color shows the increase in distance with attack norm for one sample of a 1000 images. The distance monotonically increased in each of the 100 experiments in the input space. The logit space shows increase in distance with norm up to a threshold after which the distance decreases before again increasing. This is because of high norm bound allowing occasional discovery of 'clever' adversarial examples that are closer to the logit manifold though farther from the input manifold. (Color figure online)

As the norm bound in the PGD method for generating adversarial examples is increased, the distance of adversarial examples from the manifold increases. While the success of attack on the neural network increases with high norm bound, it also becomes easier to detect these adversarial examples. We observed this behavior to be common across MNIST and CIFAR10 data set as illustrated in Fig. 4. The distance from manifold monotonically increases in the input space but in the logit space, higher norm bound beyond a threshold allows the attack

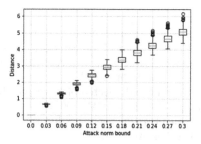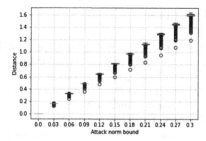

Fig. 4. Increase in adversarial example's distance from input manifold with increase in attack norm: Left: MNIST, Right: CIFAR. The boxes in the box plot denote the first and third quartile of the distance at a given attack norm.

method to find examples that decrease the distance from logit manifold even though they are farther from the input manifold. The consistent rise and fall of distance in logit space for all the 100 samples is likely a property of the used PGD method. This result is illustrated in Fig. 3. The detection rate of adversarial examples for MNIST as well as CIFAR10 improves with increase in norm bound and increased distance from the manifold as illustrated in Fig. 5.

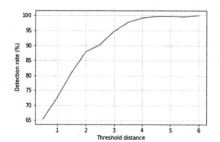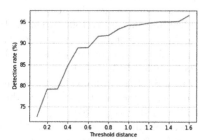

Fig. 5. (Left) Detection rate for MNIST data set (Right) Detection rate for CIFAR

5   Conclusion

We summarized recent work on building trusted, resilient and interpretable AI models. We identify the key challenges for each of these three fronts, and describe recently proposed techniques that make progress on these challenges. These techniques comprise the key elements of TRINITY framework for high-assurance artificial intelligence being developed at SRI.

Acknowledgement. The author acknowledges support from the US ARL Cooperative Agreement W911NF-17-2-0196 on Internet of Battlefield Things (IoBT) and National Science Foundation (NSF) #1750009 and #1740079.

References

1. Abouzied, A., Angluin, D., Papadimitriou, C., Hellerstein, J.M., Silberschatz, A.: Learning and verifying quantified boolean queries by example. In: ACM Symposium on Principles of Database Systems, pp. 49–60. ACM (2013)
2. Angluin, D.: Computational learning theory: survey and selected bibliography. In: ACM Symposium on Theory of Computing, pp. 351–369. ACM (1992)
3. Angluin, D., Kharitonov, M.: When won't membership queries help? In: ACM Symposium on Theory of Computing, pp. 444–454. ACM (1991)
4. Athalye, A., Carlini, N., Wagner, D.: Obfuscated gradients give a false sense of security: circumventing defenses to adversarial examples. arXiv preprint arXiv:1802.00420 (2018)
5. Bengio, Y., Mesnil, G., Dauphin, Y., Rifai, S.: Better mixing via deep representations. In: International Conference on Machine Learning, pp. 552–560 (2013)
6. Bittner, B., Bozzano, M., Cimatti, A., Gario, M., Griggio, A.: Towards pareto-optimal parameter synthesis for monotonie cost functions. In: FMCAD, pp. 23–30, October 2014
7. Boigelot, B., Godefroid, P.: Automatic synthesis of specifications from the dynamic observation of reactive programs. In: Brinksma, E. (ed.) TACAS 1997. LNCS, vol. 1217, pp. 321–333. Springer, Heidelberg (1997). https://doi.org/10.1007/BFb0035397
8. Botinčan, M., Babić, D.: Sigma*: symbolic learning of input-output specifications. In: POPL, pp. 443–456 (2013). https://doi.org/10.1145/2429069.2429123
9. Carlini, N., Wagner, D.: Towards evaluating the robustness of neural networks. arXiv preprint arXiv:1608.04644 (2016)
10. Cook, B., Kroening, D., Rümmer, P., Wintersteiger, C.M.: Ranking function synthesis for bit-vector relations. FMSD **43**(1), 93–120 (2013). https://doi.org/10.1007/s10703-013-0186-4
11. Dutta, S., Jha, S., Sankaranarayanan, S., Tiwari, A.: Learning and verification of feedback control systems using feedforward neural networks. IFAC-PapersOnLine **51**(16), 151–156 (2018)
12. Dutta, S., Jha, S., Sankaranarayanan, S., Tiwari, A.: Output range analysis for deep feedforward neural networks. In: Dutle, A., Muñoz, C., Narkawicz, A. (eds.) NFM 2018. LNCS, vol. 10811, pp. 121–138. Springer, Cham (2018). https://doi.org/10.1007/978-3-319-77935-5_9
13. Ehrenfeucht, A., Haussler, D., Kearns, M., Valiant, L.: A general lower bound on the number of examples needed for learning. Inf. Comput. **82**(3), 247–261 (1989). https://doi.org/10.1016/0890-5401(89)90002-3
14. Elizalde, F., Sucar, E., Noguez, J., Reyes, A.: Generating explanations based on Markov decision processes. In: Aguirre, A.H., Borja, R.M., Garciá, C.A.R. (eds.) MICAI 2009. LNCS, vol. 5845, pp. 51–62. Springer, Heidelberg (2009). https://doi.org/10.1007/978-3-642-05258-3_5
15. Feng, C., Muggleton, S.: Towards inductive generalisation in higher order logic. In: 9th International Workshop on Machine Learning, pp. 154–162 (2014)
16. Gardner, J.R., et al.: Deep manifold traversal: changing labels with convolutional features. arXiv preprint arXiv:1511.06421 (2015)
17. Godefroid, P., Taly, A.: Automated synthesis of symbolic instruction encodings from I/O samples. SIGPLAN Not. **47**(6), 441–452 (2012). https://doi.org/10.1145/2345156.2254116

18. Goldsmith, J., Sloan, R.H., Szörényi, B., Turán, G.: Theory revision with queries: horn, read-once, and parity formulas. Artif. Intell. **156**(2), 139–176 (2004)
19. Goodfellow, I.J., Shlens, J., Szegedy, C.: Explaining and harnessing adversarial examples. arXiv preprint arXiv:1412.6572 (2014)
20. Grosse, K., Manoharan, P., Papernot, N., Backes, M., McDaniel, P.: On the (statistical) detection of adversarial examples. arXiv preprint arXiv:1702.06280 (2017)
21. Gurfinkel, A., Belov, A., Marques-Silva, J.: Synthesizing safe bit-precise invariants. In: Ábrahám, E., Havelund, K. (eds.) TACAS 2014. LNCS, vol. 8413, pp. 93–108. Springer, Heidelberg (2014). https://doi.org/10.1007/978-3-642-54862-8_7
22. Harbers, M., Meyer, J.J., van den Bosch, K.: Explaining simulations through self explaining agents. J. Artif. Soc. Soc. Simul. (2010). http://EconPapers.repec.org/RePEc:jas:jasssj:2009-25-1
23. Hellerstein, L., Servedio, R.A.: On PAC learning algorithms for rich boolean function classes. Theoret. Comput. Sci. **384**(1), 66–76 (2007)
24. Hinton, G., Vinyals, O., Dean, J.: Distilling the knowledge in a neural network. arXiv preprint arXiv:1503.02531 (2015)
25. Jha, S., Gulwani, S., Seshia, S.A., Tiwari, A.: Oracle-guided component-based program synthesis. In: ICSE, pp. 215–224. IEEE (2010)
26. Jha, S., Jang, U., Jha, S., Jalaian, B.: Detecting adversarial examples using data manifolds. In: 2018 IEEE Military Communications Conference (MILCOM), MILCOM 2018, pp. 547–552. IEEE (2018)
27. Jha, S., Raman, V., Pinto, A., Sahai, T., Francis, M.: On learning sparse boolean formulae for explaining AI decisions. In: Barrett, C., Davies, M., Kahsai, T. (eds.) NFM 2017. LNCS, vol. 10227, pp. 99–114. Springer, Cham (2017). https://doi.org/10.1007/978-3-319-57288-8_7
28. Jha, S., Sahai, T., Raman, V., Pinto, A., Francis, M.: Explaining AI decisions using efficient methods for learning sparse boolean formulae. J. Autom. Reason. 1–21 (2018)
29. Jha, S., Seshia, S.A.: A theory of formal synthesis via inductive learning. Acta Informatica **54**, 693–726 (2016). Special Issue on Synthesis
30. Jones, M.C., Marron, J.S., Sheather, S.J.: A brief survey of bandwidth selection for density estimation. J. Am. Stat. Assoc. **91**(433), 401–407 (1996)
31. Kannan, H., Kurakin, A., Goodfellow, I.: Adversarial logit pairing. arXiv preprint arXiv:1803.06373 (2018)
32. Katz, G., Barrett, C., Dill, D.L., Julian, K., Kochenderfer, M.J.: Reluplex: an efficient SMT solver for verifying deep neural networks. In: Majumdar, R., Kunčak, V. (eds.) CAV 2017. LNCS, vol. 10426, pp. 97–117. Springer, Cham (2017). https://doi.org/10.1007/978-3-319-63387-9_5
33. Kearns, M., Li, M., Valiant, L.: Learning boolean formulas. J. ACM **41**(6), 1298–1328 (1994)
34. Kearns, M., Valiant, L.: Cryptographic limitations on learning boolean formulae and finite automata. J. ACM (JACM) **41**(1), 67–95 (1994)
35. Kos, J., Fischer, I., Song, D.: Adversarial examples for generative models. arXiv preprint arXiv:1702.06832 (2017)
36. Krizhevsky, A., Nair, V., Hinton, G.: The CIFAR-10 dataset (2014). http://www.cs.toronto.edu/kriz/cifar.html
37. Kurakin, A., Goodfellow, I., Bengio, S.: Adversarial examples in the physical world. arXiv preprint arXiv:1607.02533 (2016)
38. LaValle, S.M.: Planning Algorithms. Cambridge University Press, Cambridge (2006)

39. LeCun, Y.: The MNIST database of handwritten digits (1998). http://yann.lecun.com/exdb/mnist/

40. Lee, J., Moray, N.: Trust, control strategies and allocation of function in human-machine systems. Ergonomics **35**(10), 1243–1270 (1992)

41. van der Maaten, L., Hinton, G.: Visualizing data using t-SNE. J. Mach. Learn. Res. **9**(Nov), 2579–2605 (2008)

42. Madry, A., Makelov, A., Schmidt, L., Tsipras, D., Vladu, A.: Towards deep learning models resistant to adversarial attacks. arXiv preprint arXiv:1706.06083 (2017)

43. Mansour, Y.: Learning boolean functions via the Fourier transform. In: Roychowdhury, V., Siu, K.Y., Orlitsky, A. (eds.) Theoretical Advances in Neural Computation and Learning, pp. 391–424. Springer, Boston (1994). https://doi.org/10.1007/978-1-4615-2696-4_11

44. Metzen, J.H., Genewein, T., Fischer, V., Bischoff, B.: On detecting adversarial perturbations. arXiv preprint arXiv:1702.04267 (2017)

45. Moosavi-Dezfooli, S.M., Fawzi, A., Frossard, P.: DeepFool: a simple and accurate method to fool deep neural networks. In: Proceedings of the IEEE Conference on Computer Vision and Pattern Recognition, pp. 2574–2582 (2016)

46. Papernot, N., et al.: CleverHans v2.0.0: an adversarial machine learning library. arXiv preprint arXiv:1610.00768 (2016)

47. Papernot, N., McDaniel, P., Goodfellow, I., Jha, S., Celik, Z.B., Swami, A.: Practical black-box attacks against machine learning. In: Proceedings of the 2017 ACM on Asia Conference on Computer and Communications Security, pp. 506–519. ACM (2017)

48. Papernot, N., McDaniel, P., Jha, S., Fredrikson, M., Celik, Z.B., Swami, A.: The limitations of deep learning in adversarial settings. In: 2016 IEEE European Symposium on Security and Privacy (EuroS&P), pp. 372–387. IEEE (2016)

49. Papernot, N., McDaniel, P., Swami, A., Harang, R.: Crafting adversarial input sequences for recurrent neural networks. In: 2016 IEEE Military Communications Conference, MILCOM 2016, pp. 49–54. IEEE (2016)

50. Pitt, L., Valiant, L.G.: Computational limitations on learning from examples. J. ACM (JACM) **35**(4), 965–984 (1988)

51. Raman, V., Lignos, C., Finucane, C., Lee, K.C.T., Marcus, M.P., Kress-Gazit, H.: Sorry Dave, I'm afraid I can't do that: explaining unachievable robot tasks using natural language. In: Robotics: Science and Systems (2013)

52. Reynolds, A., Deters, M., Kuncak, V., Tinelli, C., Barrett, C.: Counterexample-guided quantifier instantiation for synthesis in SMT. In: Kroening, D., Păsăreanu, C.S. (eds.) CAV 2015. LNCS, vol. 9207, pp. 198–216. Springer, Cham (2015). https://doi.org/10.1007/978-3-319-21668-3_12

53. Ribeiro, M.T., Singh, S., Guestrin, C.: "Why Should I Trust You?": explaining the predictions of any classifier. In: KDD, pp. 1135–1144 (2016). https://doi.org/10.1145/2939672.2939778

54. Roweis, S.T., Saul, L.K.: Nonlinear dimensionality reduction by locally linear embedding. Science **290**(5500), 2323–2326 (2000)

55. Sankaranarayanan, S., Miller, C., Raghunathan, R., Ravanbakhsh, H., Fainekos, G.: A model-based approach to synthesizing insulin infusion pump usage parameters for diabetic patients. In: Annual Allerton Conference on Communication, Control, and Computing, pp. 1610–1617, October 2012. https://doi.org/10.1109/Allerton.2012.6483413

56. Sankaranarayanan, S.: Automatic invariant generation for hybrid systems using ideal fixed points. In: HSCC, pp. 221–230 (2010). https://doi.org/10.1145/1755952.1755984

57. Sankaranarayanan, S., Sipma, H.B., Manna, Z.: Constructing invariants for hybrid systems. FMSD **32**(1), 25–55 (2008). https://doi.org/10.1007/s10703-007-0046-1
58. Saul, L.K., Roweis, S.T.: Think globally, fit locally: unsupervised learning of low dimensional manifolds. J. Mach. Learn. Res. **4**(Jun), 119–155 (2003)
59. Shaham, U., Yamada, Y., Negahban, S.: Understanding adversarial training: increasing local stability of neural nets through robust optimization. arXiv preprint arXiv:1511.05432 (2015)
60. Štrumbelj, E., Kononenko, I.: Explaining prediction models and individual predictions with feature contributions. KIS **41**(3), 647–665 (2014). https://doi.org/10.1007/s10115-013-0679-x
61. Szegedy, C., et al.: Intriguing properties of neural networks. arXiv preprint arXiv:1312.6199 (2013)
62. Tenenbaum, J.B., De Silva, V., Langford, J.C.: A global geometric framework for nonlinear dimensionality reduction. Science **290**(5500), 2319–2323 (2000)
63. Urban, C., Gurfinkel, A., Kahsai, T.: Synthesizing ranking functions from bits and pieces. In: Chechik, M., Raskin, J.-F. (eds.) TACAS 2016. LNCS, vol. 9636, pp. 54–70. Springer, Heidelberg (2016). https://doi.org/10.1007/978-3-662-49674-9_4
64. Yuan, C., Lim, H., Lu, T.C.: Most relevant explanation in Bayesian networks. J. Artif. Intell. Res. (JAIR) **42**, 309–352 (2011)

Reinforcement Learning and Formal Requirements

Fabio Somenzi[1] and Ashutosh Trivedi[2(✉)]

[1] Department of Electrical, Computer, and Energy Engineering,
University of Colorado Boulder, Boulder, CO 80309, USA
`fabio@colorado.edu`
[2] Department of Computer Science, University of Colorado Boulder,
Boulder, CO 80309, USA
`ashutosh.trivedi@colorado.edu`

Abstract. Reinforcement learning is an approach to controller synthesis where agents rely on reward signals to choose actions in order to satisfy the requirements implicit in reward signals. Oftentimes non-experts have to come up with the requirements and their translation to rewards under significant time pressure, even though manual translation is time consuming and error prone. For safety-critical applications of reinforcement learning a rigorous design methodology is needed and, in particular, a principled approach to requirement specification and to the translation of objectives into the form required by reinforcement learning algorithms.

Formal logic provides a foundation for the rigorous and unambiguous requirement specification of learning objectives. However, reinforcement learning algorithms require requirements to be expressed as scalar reward signals. We discuss a recent technique, called limit-reachability, that bridges this gap by faithfully translating logic-based requirements into the scalar reward form needed in model-free reinforcement learning. This technique enables the synthesis of controllers that maximize the probability to satisfy given logical requirements using off-the-shelf, model-free reinforcement learning algorithms.

1 Introduction

Reinforcement Learning (RL) is an approach to sequential decision making where agents rely on reward signals to choose actions so as to achieve given objectives [40]. Model-free RL [39] refers to a class of techniques that are asymptotically space-efficient because they do not construct a full model of the environment. These techniques include classic algorithms like Q-learning as well as their extensions to deep neural networks [35]. Progress in deep neural networks have highlighted the potential benefits of widespread adoption of model-free reinforcement learning in autonomous agents [26,28]. At the same time, accidents involving learning-enabled systems [29,42,47] have received intense publicity and have raised concerns that current design techniques may provide insufficient guarantees that the system requirements are met.

© Springer Nature Switzerland AG 2019
M. Zamani and D. Zufferey (Eds.): NSV 2019, LNCS 11652, pp. 26–41, 2019.
https://doi.org/10.1007/978-3-030-28423-7_2

For safety-critical applications of RL a rigorous design methodology is needed and, in particular, a principled approach to requirement specification and to the translation of objectives into the form required by RL algorithms. Four decades of formal methods [9,32,34] have shown that logic is a powerful and effective tool in specifying and verifying properties of reactive systems. Therefore to develop safety-critical RL applications at scale, we must develop logic-based approaches to formally specify the requirements for RL-enabled systems, with emphasis on *model-free* RL. The emphasis on model-free algorithms is motivated by their success in the aforementioned large RL problems and by the inherent difficulty in scaling verification of stochastic systems using model-based algorithms [2,4]. Model-free RL algorithms are a natural fit for nonlinear function approximators (deep neural networks) [31,35,41].

Reinforcement learning relies on scalar rewards. Reachability objectives, like running a maze, are naturally expressed in terms of scalar rewards; in other cases the translation is less obvious. For example, ω-regular objectives like repeated reachability and eventual stability (e.g., the LTL formula [4,10] G F goal $\wedge$ F G stable) are about the long-term behavior of a system; the frequency of reward collected is not what matters. A policy that guarantees no negative reward and some positive reward every ten steps, is better than a policy that promises a positive reward at each step, but with probability 0.5 results in no reward.

Therefore, bridging the gap between logic specifications and model-free RL requires a translation from specification to scalar reward such that a model-free RL algorithm maximizing scalar rewards produces a policy that maximizes the probability of satisfaction of the specification. In this tutorial, we present *Limit Reachability* (LR) as a foundation for such translations and present its applications to synthesis of RL-enabled systems.

Related Work. The problem of ω-regular rewards in the context of model-free RL was first tackled in [36] by translating the objective into a deterministic Rabin automaton and deriving positive and negative rewards directly from the acceptance condition of the automaton. Hahn et al. [18] showed that their algorithm, and the extension of [21] may fail to find optimal strategies, and may underestimate the probability of satisfaction of the objective. In [19,20] the use of limit-deterministic Büchi automata avoids the problems connected with the use of a Rabin acceptance condition. However, as shown by Hahn et al., that approach may still produce incorrect results.

Related problems include model-based RL [15], RL for finite-horizon objectives [27], and learning for efficient verification [7]. The closest relation to the limit reachability approach are algorithms that use a model based and model dependent translation to reachability by first identifying winning end-components of a learned MDP with a suitable automaton, and then essentially trying to maximize the chance of reaching them [7,19]. As opposed to that, limit reachability construction is a model independent reduction to a reachability problem. A series of papers [1,24,25,44] studied the problem of learning controllers satisfying bounded signal temporal logic [12] based requirements using

RL where reward is characterized by robustness [12–14] of the trace against STL specification.

Organization. We begin the technical exposition by introducing key definitions and ideas in reinforcement learning in the next section. In Sect. 3 we provide the necessary background for ω-regular requirements and linear temporal logic. Section 4 presents the limit reachability technique and its applications in model-free RL of ω-regular requirements.

The presentation in this invited tutorial paper is primarily based on the work of Hahn et al. [18] and does not contain any original technical contribution.

2 Reinforcement Learning

2.1 Markov Decision Processes

Let $\mathcal{D}(S)$ be the set of distributions over S. A *Markov decision process* $\mathcal{M}$ is a tuple (S, A, T, AP, L) where S is a finite set of states, A is a finite set of *actions*, $T: S \times A \rightharpoonup \mathcal{D}(S)$ is the probabilistic transition (partial) function, AP is the set of *atomic propositions*, and $L: S \to 2^{AP}$ is the *proposition labeling function*.

Example 1. Figure 4 shows an MDP with four states $S = \{0, (1, b), (2, g), (3, g)\}$ and five actions $A = \{a, b, c, d, e, f\}$. Probabilistic distributions are shown by branching the transition arrow into successor states with corresponding probabilities labeling these branches. We use colors to show the proposition labeling of a state—here green (g) and blue (b)—and when convenient, we also write the label of a state next to it (see Fig. 1).

For any state $s \in S$, we let $A(s)$ denote the set of actions that can be selected in state s. For states $s, s' \in S$ and $a \in A(s)$, $T(s, a)(s')$ equals $p(s'|s, a)$. A *run* of $\mathcal{M}$ is an ω-word $\langle s_0, a_1, s_1, \ldots \rangle \in S \times (A \times S)^\omega$ such that $p(s_{i+1}|s_i, a_{i+1}) > 0$ for all $i \geq 0$. A finite run is a finite such sequence. For a *run* $r = \langle s_0, a_1, s_1, \ldots \rangle$ we define the corresponding labeled run as $L(r) = \langle L(s_0), L(s_1), \ldots \rangle \in (2^{AP})^\omega$. We write $Runs^{\mathcal{M}}(FRuns^{\mathcal{M}})$ for the set of runs (finite runs) of the MDP $\mathcal{M}$ and $Runs^{\mathcal{M}}(s)(FRuns^{\mathcal{M}}(s))$ for the set of runs (finite runs) of the MDP $\mathcal{M}$ starting from state s. We write $last(r)$ for the last state of a finite run r.

A strategy in $\mathcal{M}$ is a function $\sigma: FRuns \to \mathcal{D}(A)$ such that $supp(\sigma(r)) \subseteq A(last(r))$, where $supp(d)$ denotes the support of the distribution d. Let $Runs_\sigma^{\mathcal{M}}(s)$ denote the subset of runs $Runs^{\mathcal{M}}(s)$ that correspond to strategy σ with initial state s. Let $\Sigma_{\mathcal{M}}$ be the set of all strategies. A strategy σ is *pure* if $\sigma(r)$ is a point distribution for all runs $r \in FRuns^{\mathcal{M}}$ and we say that σ is *stationary* if $last(r) = last(r')$ implies $\sigma(r) = \sigma(r')$ for all runs $r, r' \in FRuns^{\mathcal{M}}$. A strategy that is not pure is *mixed*. A strategy is *positional* if it is both pure and stationary.

The behavior of an MDP $\mathcal{M}$ under a strategy σ is defined on a probability space $(Runs_\sigma^{\mathcal{M}}(s), \mathcal{F}_{Runs_\sigma^{\mathcal{M}}(s)}, \Pr_\sigma^{\mathcal{M}}(s))$ over the set of infinite runs of σ with starting state s. Given a real-valued random variable over the set of infinite runs

$f\colon Runs^{\mathcal{M}} \to \mathbb{R}$, we denote by $\mathbb{E}_\sigma^{\mathcal{M}}(s)\{f\}$ the expectation of f over the runs of $\mathcal{M}$ originating at s that follow strategy σ.

A *rewardful* MDP is a pair $(\mathcal{M}, \rho)$, where $\mathcal{M}$ is an MDP and $\rho\colon S \times A \to \mathbb{R}$ is a reward function assigning utility to state-action pairs. A rewardful MDP $(\mathcal{M}, \rho)$ under a strategy σ determines a sequence of random rewards $\rho(X_{i-1}, Y_i)_{i \geq 1}$, where X_i and Y_i are the random variables denoting the i-th state and action, respectively. Depending upon the problem of interest, different performance objectives are proposed in literature:

1. The *Reachability Probability* $Reach(T)_\sigma^{\mathcal{M}}(s)$ (with $T \subseteq S$) is defined as

$$\mathrm{Pr}_\sigma^{\mathcal{M}}(s)\left\{\langle s, a_1, s_1, \ldots\rangle \in Runs_\sigma^{\mathcal{M}}(s)\colon \exists i \,.\, s_i \in T\right\}$$

2. *Discounted Reward* (with discount factor $\lambda \in [0, 1)$):

$$Disct(\lambda)_\sigma^{\mathcal{M}}(s) = \lim_{N \to \infty} \mathbb{E}_\sigma^{\mathcal{M}}(s)\left\{\sum_{1 \leq i \leq N} \lambda^{i-1} \rho(X_{i-1}, Y_i)\right\}$$

3. *Average Reward*

$$Avg_\sigma^{\mathcal{M}}(s) = \limsup_{N \to \infty} \frac{1}{N} \mathbb{E}_\sigma^{\mathcal{M}}(s)\left\{\sum_{1 \leq i \leq N} \rho(X_{i-1}, Y_i)\right\}.$$

For an objective $Cost^{\mathcal{M}} \in \{Reach(T)^{\mathcal{M}}, Disct(\lambda)^{\mathcal{M}}, Avg^{\mathcal{M}}\}$ and an initial state s, we define the optimal reward $Cost_*^{\mathcal{M}}(s)$ as $\sup_{\sigma \in \Sigma_{\mathcal{M}}} Cost_\sigma^{\mathcal{M}}(s)$. A strategy $\sigma \in \Sigma_{\mathcal{M}}$ is optimal for $Cost^{\mathcal{M}}$ if $Cost_\sigma^{\mathcal{M}}(s) = Cost_*^{\mathcal{M}}(s)$ for all $s \in S$.

The problem of computing an optimal strategy for the reachability probability objective can be reduced to the problem of computing an optimal strategy for the average reward objective by equipping the target states with self-loops with unit rewards. Due to the following Blackwell-optimality theorem, the average-optimal strategies are discounted-optimal for some large discount factor.

Theorem 1 (Blackwell-Optimality [22]). *For every rewardful MDP $(\mathcal{M}, \rho)$ there exists a discount factor $\lambda_0 \in (0, 1)$ such that, for all $\lambda \in [\lambda_0, 1)$, every optimal strategy for the discounted reward objective is also an optimal strategy for the average reward objective.*

For these reasons, we can restrict our attention to algorithms for computing optimal strategies for the discounted performance objective.

2.2   Computation of Discounted Reward Optimal Strategies

The optimal discounted value $Disct(\lambda)_*^{\mathcal{M}} = V : S \to \mathbb{R}$ can be characterized [33] using the following *Bellman optimality equations*:

$$V(s) = \max_{a \in A(s)} \left\{\rho(s, a) + \lambda \sum_{s' \in S} p(s' \mid s, a) \cdot V(s')\right\}. \tag{1}$$

Being a *contraction*, the unique fixed point of the following *value improvement operator* $\Phi : \mathbb{R}^{|S|} \to \mathbb{R}^{|S|}$, defined as

$$\Phi : F \mapsto \max_{a \in A(s)} \left\{ \rho(s,a) + \lambda \sum_{s' \in S} p(s' \mid s,a) \cdot F(s') \right\},$$

gives the solution for the discounted optimality Eq. (1). From the Banach fixed point theorem [5], the following sequence of iterates converges to the optimal value $Disct(\lambda)_*^{\mathcal{M}}$:

$$V_{t+1}(s) = \max_{a \in A(s)} \left\{ \rho(s,a) + \lambda \sum_{s' \in S} p(s' \mid s,a) \cdot V_t(s') \right\}$$

starting from an arbitrary value function $V_0 \in [S \to \mathbb{R}]$. This sequence of iterates are often represented in the following equivalent form by using $Q_t(s,a)$ as the estimate for the value of a state-action pair at step t of the iteration:

$$Q_{t+1}(s,a) = \rho(s,a) + \lambda \sum_{s' \in S} p(s' \mid s,a) \cdot V_t(s') \ \text{ and } \ V_{t+1}(s) = \max_{a \in A(s)} Q_{t+1}(s,a).$$

Let $Q_*(s,a) = \lim_{t \to \infty} Q_t(s,a)$ for all $s,a \in S \times A$. We refer to such value associated with the state-action pair as the Q-value or the "quality" of the pair.

2.3 Q-Learning Algorithm and Its Convergence

When the MDP transition and reward structures are unknown, the aforementioned value iteration algorithm is not applicable. In such situations, *reinforcement learning* [40] provides a framework to approximate optimal values and Q-values from repeated interactions with the environment. The Q-learning algorithm of Watkins [46] is one such classical reinforcement learning algorithm.

The Q-learning algorithm assumes that instead of knowing the MDP beforehand, we are given data samples of the form $(s_t, a_t, r_{t+1}, s_{t+1}) \in S \times A \times \mathbb{R} \times S$ for $t = 0,1,2,\ldots$ such that $p(s_{t+1} \mid s_t, a) > 0$ and $\rho(s_t, a_t) = r_{t+1}$. The Q-learning algorithm iteratively applies the following update to the state-action value function:

$$Q_{t+1}(s,a) = \begin{cases} (1-\alpha_t)Q_t(s,a) + \alpha_t(r_{t+1}+\lambda \cdot \max_{a' \in A(s)} Q_t(s_{t+1}, a')), & \text{if } (s,a) = (s_t, a_t) \\ Q_t(s,a), & \text{otherwise,} \end{cases}$$

where $0 \le \alpha_t < 1$ is the learning-rate at the step $t \ge 0$. Watkins and Dayan [45] showed the following convergence result for the Q-learning algorithm.

Theorem 2. *For bounded rewards $|r_t| \le B$ and learning rates $0 \le \alpha_t < 1$ satisfying:*

$$\sum_{t=0}^{\infty} \alpha_t = \infty \ \text{ and } \ \sum_{t=0}^{\infty} \alpha_t^2 < \infty,$$

we have that $Q_t(x,a) \to Q_*(s,a)$ as $t \to \infty$ for all $s,a \in S \times A$ almost surely.

Borkar and Meyn [6] give a simple derivation of the asymptotic convergence by exploiting the O.D.E. method for the convergence of stochastic approximation.

3 Formal Requirements

3.1 ω-Regular Objectives

A *nondeterministic Büchi automaton* (NBW) is a tuple $\mathcal{A} = (\Sigma, Q, q_0, \delta, F)$, where Σ is a finite *alphabet*, Q is a finite set of *states*, $q_0 \in Q$ is the *initial state*, $\delta \colon Q \times \Sigma \to 2^Q$ is the *transition function*, and $F \subseteq Q \times \Sigma \times Q$ is the set of *accepting transitions*.

A *run* r of $\mathcal{A}$ on $w \in \Sigma^\omega$ is an ω-word $r_0, w_0, r_1, w_1, \ldots$ in $(Q \cup \Sigma)^\omega$ such that $r_0 = q_0$ and, for $i > 0$, $r_i \in \delta(r_{i-1}, w_{i-1})$. Each triple (r_{i-1}, w_{i-1}, r_i) is a *transition* of $\mathcal{A}$. We write $\inf(r)$ for the set of transitions that appear infinitely often in the run r. A run r of $\mathcal{A}$ is *accepting* if $\inf(r) \cap F \neq \emptyset$. The *language* of $\mathcal{A}$ (or, *accepted* by $\mathcal{A}$) is the subset of words in Σ^ω that have accepting runs in $\mathcal{A}$. A language is *ω-regular* if it is accepted by a nondeterministic Büchi automaton.

A Büchi automaton $\mathcal{A} = (\Sigma, Q, q_0, \delta, F)$ is *deterministic* if $|\delta(q, \sigma)| \leq 1$ for all $q \in Q$ and all $\sigma \in \Sigma$. $\mathcal{A}$ is *complete* if $|\delta(q, \sigma)| \geq 1$. A word in Σ^ω has exactly one run in a deterministic, complete automaton. Note that deterministic Büchi automata (DBWs) are strictly less expressive than NBWs as there are ω-regular languages—such as $(0 + 1)^* 0^\omega$—that are not accepted by any DBW.

Example 2. An NBW accepting the language of words containing infinitely many g's or infinitely many b's is shown in Fig. 1, while a DBW for the same language is shown in Fig. 2. In our figures, we depict the final transitions using a green dotted transition.

Given an MDP $\mathcal{M}$ and an ω-regular objective φ given as a Büchi automaton $\mathcal{A}_\varphi = (\Sigma, Q, q_0, \delta, F)$, we are interested in computing an optimal strategy satisfying the objective. We define the satisfaction probability of a strategy σ from initial state s as:

$$\mathrm{Pr}_\sigma^{\mathcal{M}}(s \models \varphi) = \mathrm{Pr}_\sigma^{\mathcal{M}}(s) \left\{ r \in \mathit{Runs}_\sigma^{\mathcal{M}}(s) \colon \inf(r) \cap F \neq \emptyset \right\}.$$

The optimal satisfaction probability $\mathrm{Pr}_*^{\mathcal{M}}(s \models \varphi)$ for MDP $\mathcal{M}$ and objective φ is defined as $\sup_{\sigma \in \Sigma_{\mathcal{M}}} \mathrm{Pr}_\sigma^{\mathcal{M}}(s \models \varphi)$ and we say that $\sigma \in \Sigma_{\mathcal{M}}$ is an optimal strategy for φ if $\mathrm{Pr}_*^{\mathcal{M}}(s \models \varphi) = \mathrm{Pr}_\sigma^{\mathcal{M}}(s \models \varphi)$.

3.2 Product MDP

Given a Markov decision process $\mathcal{M} = (S, A, T, AP, L)$ with a designated initial state $s_0 \in S$, and a deterministic Büchi automaton $\mathcal{A} = (2^{AP}, Q, q_0, \delta, F)$, the *product* MDP $\mathcal{M} \times \mathcal{A}$ is the tuple $(S \times Q, (s_0, q_0), A, T^\times, F^\times)$. The probabilistic transition function $T^\times \colon (S \times Q) \times A \to \mathcal{D}(S \times Q)$ is such that

$$T^\times((s, q), a)((\hat{s}, \hat{q})) = \begin{cases} T(s, a)(\hat{s}) & \text{if } \hat{q} = \delta(q, L(s)) \\ 0 & \text{otherwise.} \end{cases}$$

The set of final transitions $F^\times$ is defined by $F \subseteq Q \times 2^{AP} \times Q$; then $F^\times \subseteq (S \times Q) \times A \times (S \times Q)$ defines $\mathsf{Acc}^\times$ as follows: $((s, q), a, (s', q')) \in F^\times$ if and

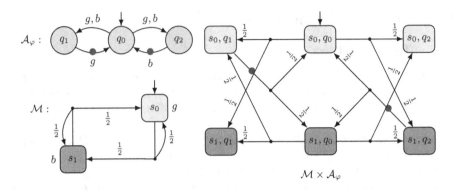

Fig. 1. Product does not preserve probability. An NBW $\mathcal{A}_\varphi$ (above left) accepting the language of infinitely many g's or infinitely many b's (accepts all ω-words) and a Markov decision process $\mathcal{M}$ whose set of actions is a singleton (a Markov chain). Notice that the MDP $\mathcal{M}$ satisfies the property with probability 1. Their product is shown on the right side, where there is no accepting BSCC. Hence, the probability of reaching the BSCC (under any strategy) is 0. (Color figure online)

only if $(q, L(s), q') \in F$ and $T(s, a)(s') \neq 0$. If $\mathcal{A}$ is an NBW, the actions in the product must be enriched to identify both the actions of the original MDP and the choice of the successor state of the NBW.

Given a product MDP $\mathcal{M} \times \mathcal{A} = (S \times Q, (s_0, q_0), A, T^\times, F^\times)$, we define its directed underlying graph $\mathcal{G}_{\mathcal{M} \times \mathcal{A}} = (V, E)$ where $V = S \times Q$ and $E \subseteq V \times V$ is such that $((s, q), (s', q')) \in E$ if $T^\times((s, q), a, ((\hat{s}, \hat{q})) > 0$ for some $a \in A(s)$. A sub-MDP of the product $\mathcal{M} \times \mathcal{A}$ is an MDP $\mathcal{M}'$ whose states and actions are sub-sets of that of $\mathcal{M} \times \mathcal{A}$ and probabilistic transitions are analogous to $\mathcal{M} \times \mathcal{A}$ when restricted to the states and actions of $\mathcal{M}'$. An *end-component* [2] of $\mathcal{M} \times \mathcal{A}$ is a sub-MDP $\mathcal{M}'$ such that $\mathcal{G}_{\mathcal{M}'}$ is strongly connected.

Theorem 3 (End-Component Properties [2]**).** *Once an end-component C of an MDP is entered, there is a strategy that visits every state-action combination in C with probability 1 and stays in C forever. Moreover, for every strategy the union of the end-components is visited with probability 1.*

A Markov chain is an MDP whose set of actions is a singleton. A *bottom strongly connected component* (BSCC) of a Markov chain is any of its end-components. A BSCC is accepting if it contains an accepting transition (see below) and otherwise it is rejecting. For any MDP $\mathcal{M}$ and positional strategy σ, let $\mathcal{M}_\sigma$ be the Markov chain resulting from resolving the nondeterminism in $\mathcal{M}$ using σ. End-components and runs are defined for products just like for MDPs. A run of $\mathcal{M} \times \mathcal{A}$ is accepting if it satisfies the product's acceptance condition. An *accepting end-component* of $\mathcal{M} \times \mathcal{A}$ is an end-component such that every run of the product MDP that eventually dwells in it is accepting.

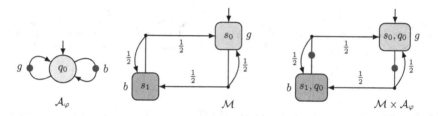

Fig. 2. Product preserves probability. A DBW $\mathcal{A}_\varphi$ (left) accepting the language of infinitely many g's or infinitely many b's (accepts all ω-words) and a Markov decision process $\mathcal{M}$ (center) whose set of actions is singleton (a Markov chain). Notice that the MDP $\mathcal{M}$ satisfies the property with probability 1. Their product is shown on the right side where the whole MDP is one accepting BSCC. Hence, the probability of reaching the BSCC (under any strategy) is 1. (Color figure online)

Example 3. Figure 1 shown an NBW $\mathcal{A}_\varphi$, a Markov chain $\mathcal{M}$, and their product Markov chain $\mathcal{M} \times \mathcal{A}_\varphi$. There are two BSCCs in $\mathcal{M} \times \mathcal{A}_\varphi$:–one with the state s_1, q_1 and other with the state s_0, q_2. Note that none of the BSCCs are accepting.

In view of Theorem 3, satisfaction of an ω-regular objective φ by an MDP $\mathcal{M}$ can be formulated in terms of the accepting end-components of the product $\mathcal{M} \times \mathcal{A}_\varphi$, where $\mathcal{A}_\varphi$ is a DBW accepting φ. For deterministic Büchi automata $\mathcal{A}_\varphi$, the maximum probability of satisfaction of φ by $\mathcal{M}$ is the maximum probability, over all strategies, that a run of the product $\mathcal{M} \times \mathcal{A}_\varphi$ eventually dwells in one of its accepting end-components. Unfortunately, DBWs cannot express all ω-regular objectives. On the other hand, NBWs can not be used in the product construction since the product does not preserve the optimal probability of satisfaction as shown in the following example.

Example 4. Figure 2 shows that for DBW, the optimal probability of reaching an accepting BSCC is equal to the optimal probability of satisfying the objective. On the other hand, consider the Markov chain $\mathcal{M}$ and the NBW $\mathcal{A}_\varphi$ shown in Fig. 1. It is clear that the Markov chain satisfies the property with probability 1 as both g's and b's are seen infinitely often. On the other hand, there are no accepting BSCCs in the product MDP $\mathcal{M} \times \mathcal{A}_\varphi$ and hence the probability of reaching an accepting BSCC is 0.

3.3 Limit-Deterministic Büchi Automata

In spite of the expressiveness gap between NBWs and DBWs, even a very restricted form of nondeterminism is sufficient to make DBWs as expressive as NBWs. A limit-deterministic Büchi automaton (LDBW) behaves deterministically once it has seen an accepting transition. Formally, a *limit-deterministic Büchi automaton* (LDBW) is an NBW $\mathcal{A} = (\Sigma, Q_i \cup Q_f, q_0, \delta, F)$ such that $Q_i \cap Q_f = \emptyset$, $F \subseteq Q_f \times \Sigma \times Q_f$; $|\delta(q, \sigma) \cap Q_i| \leq 1$ for all $q \in Q_i$ and $\sigma \in \Sigma$; $|\delta(q, \sigma)| \leq 1$ for all $q \in Q_f$ and $\sigma \in \Sigma$; $\delta(q, \sigma) \subseteq Q_f$ for all $q \in Q_f$ and $\sigma \in \Sigma$.

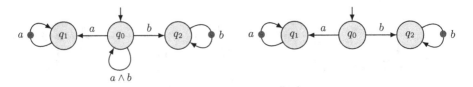

Fig. 3. Suitable (left) and unsuitable (right) LDBWs for the LTL formula $(G\,a) \vee (G\,b)$.

LDBWs are as expressive as general NBWs. Moreover, NBWs can be translated into LDBWs that can be used for the qualitative and quantitative analysis of MDPs [11,17,37,43]. We use the translation from [17], which uses LDBWs that consist of two parts: an initial deterministic automaton (without accepting transitions) obtained by a subset construction; and a final part produced by a breakpoint construction. They are connected by a single "guess", where the automaton guesses a singleton subset of the reachable states to start the breakpoint construction. Like in other constructions (e.g. [37]), one can compose the resulting automata with an MDP, such that the optimal control of the product defines a control on the MDP that maximizes the probability of obtaining a word from the language of the automaton. We refer to such an LDBW as a *suitable limit-deterministic automata* (SLDBWs).

Definition 1 (Suitable LDBW). *An SLDBW $\mathcal{A}$ for property φ is an LDBW that recognizes φ and such that, for every finite MDP $\mathcal{M}$, there exists a positional strategy $\sigma \in \Sigma_{\mathcal{M} \times \mathcal{A}}$ such that the probability of satisfying the Büchi condition in the Markov chain $(\mathcal{M} \times \mathcal{A})_\sigma$ is $\mathrm{Pr}_*^{\mathcal{M}}(s \models \varphi)$.*

Although the construction of a suitable LDBW reaches back to the 80s [43], not all LDBWs are suitable. Broadly speaking, the nondeterministic decisions taken in the initial part may not depend on the future—though it may depend on the state of an MDP. The example LDBW from Fig. 3 (left) satisfies the property: it can try to delay to progress to one of the accepting states to when an end-component in an MDP is reached that always produces a's or b's, respectively. In contrast, the LDBW from Fig. 3 (right)—which recognizes the same language—will have to make the decision of seeing only a's or only b's immediately, without the option to wait for reaching an end-component. This makes it unsuitable for the use in MDPs.

Theorem 4 ([11,17,37,43]). *Suitable limit-deterministic Büchi automata exist for all ω-regular languages.*

SLDBWs—and their properties described in Definition 1—are used in the qualitative and quantitative model checking algorithms in [11,17,37,43]. The accepting end-components of the product MDPs are all using only states from the final part of the SLDBW. Büchi acceptance then allows for using memoryless almost sure winning strategies in the accepting end-components, while outside of accepting end-components a memoryless strategy that maximizes the chance

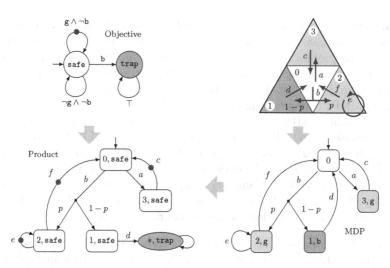

Fig. 4. A grid-world example (top right). The labeled arrows represent actions. When action b is performed, Cell 2 is reached with probability p and Cell 1 is reached with probability $1-p$, for $0 < p < 1$. Atomic propositions b and g hold in Cell 1 and Cells 2–3, respectively. MDP for the grid (bottom right). An automaton for $\varphi = (\mathsf{G}\,\neg\mathsf{b}) \wedge (\mathsf{G}\,\mathsf{F}\,\mathsf{g})$ (top left). The transition marked with a dot is the only accepting transition. Product MDP (bottom left). (Color figure online)

of reaching such an end-component can be used. The distinguishing property is the guarantee that they provide the correct probability, while using a product with a general NBW would only provide a value that cannot exceed it.

3.4   Linear Time Logic Objectives

LTL (Linear Time Logic) is a temporal logic whose formulae describe a subset of the ω-regular languages, which is often used to specify objectives in human-readable form. Translations exist from LTL to various forms of automata, including NBW and SLDBW. Given a set of atomic propositions AP, a is an LTL formula for each $a \in AP$. Moreover, if φ and ψ are LTL formulae, so are

$$\neg\varphi, \varphi \vee \psi, \mathsf{X}\,\varphi, \psi\,\mathsf{U}\,\varphi.$$

Additional operators are defined as abbreviations: $\top \overset{\text{def}}{=} a \vee \neg a$; $\bot \overset{\text{def}}{=} \neg\top$; $\varphi \wedge \psi \overset{\text{def}}{=} \neg(\neg\varphi \vee \neg\psi)$; $\varphi \to \psi \overset{\text{def}}{=} \neg\varphi \vee \psi$; $\mathsf{F}\,\varphi \overset{\text{def}}{=} \top\,\mathsf{U}\,\varphi$; and $\mathsf{G}\,\varphi \overset{\text{def}}{=} \neg\mathsf{F}\,\neg\varphi$. We write $w \models \varphi$ if ω-word w over 2^{AP} satisfies LTL formula φ. The satisfaction relation is defined inductively [4,30].

3.5   Probabilistic Model Checking

Formal verification of stochastic against temporal logic requirements has received considerable attention [3,4,8,23]. For system modeled as MDPs and requirements expressed using ω-regular specification (given as either LTL specification or Büchi automata), the key verification problem "probabilistic model-checking" is to compute optimal satisfaction probabilities and strategies. The probabilistic model checking problem against SLDBW requirements can be solved [2,8,16,38] using graph-theoretic techniques (by computing accepting end-component and then maximizing the probability to reach states in such components) over the product of MDPs and ω-automata.

For a given finite MDP $\mathcal{M}$, and an LTL requirement φ, the probability model checking consists of the following steps: (1) translate the LTL objective φ into a suitable LDBA $\mathcal{A}_\varphi$; (2) compute the product MDP $\mathcal{M} \times \mathcal{A}_\varphi$ for the MDP $\mathcal{M}$ and SLDBW $\mathcal{A}_\varphi$; (3) use graph-theoretic approaches [2] to compute the accepting end-component of $\mathcal{M} \times \mathcal{A}_\varphi$; and (4) compute a strategy that maximizes the probability of reaching states in accepting end-components of $\mathcal{M} \times \mathcal{A}_\varphi$ by using value iteration, policy iteration, or linear programming [33].

Example 5. Consider the grid-world example shown in Fig. 4 and corresponding MDP representation. Suppose we want to find a strategy that maximizes the probability of satisfaction of the the LTL requirement $\varphi = (\mathsf{G}\,\neg\mathsf{b}) \wedge (\mathsf{G}\,\mathsf{F}\,\mathsf{g})$, i.e. we want to always avoid the "bad" region (grid 1), while infinitely often visiting one of the "good" regions (grid 2 or 3). It is clear that starting from the initial state (grid 0), choosing sequence of actions $(a, c)^\omega$ satisfies this property with probability 1. To apply the above probabilistic model checking algorithm, we compile the LTL objective in to the DBW shown in Fig. 4 and then compute its product with the MDP. There are two accepting end-components in the product: the first one consists of the states $(0, \mathtt{safe})$ and $(3, \mathtt{safe})$, while the second one consists of the state $(2, \mathtt{safe})$. It is clear that any strategy that maximizes the probability of reaching these end-components give a strategy on the original MDP to maximize the probability of satisfaction of the LTL requirement.

4   Limit Reachability

The limit reachability technique reduces the model checking problem for given MDP and SLDBW to a reachability problem by slightly changing the structure of the product: We add a target state t that can be reached with a given probability $1 - \zeta$ whenever visiting an accepting transition of the original product MDP.

This reduction avoids the identification of winning end-components and thus allows a natural integration to a wide range of model-free RL approaches. Thus, while the proofs do lean on standard model checking properties that are based on identifying winning end-components, they serve as a justification not to consider them when running the learning algorithm. In the rest of this section, we fix an MDP $\mathcal{M}$ and an SLDBW $\mathcal{A}$ for the ω-regular property φ.

Definition 2 (Augmented Product). *For any $\zeta \in (0, 1)$, the augmented MDP $\mathcal{M}^\zeta$ is an MDP obtained from $\mathcal{M} \times \mathcal{A}$ by adding a "sink" state t with a self-loop to the set of states of $\mathcal{M} \times \mathcal{A}$, and by making t a destination of each accepting transition τ of $\mathcal{M} \times \mathcal{A}$ with probability $1 - \zeta$. The original probabilities of all other destinations of an accepting transition τ are multiplied by ζ.*

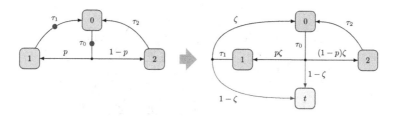

Fig. 5. Adding transitions to the target in the augmented product MDP.

An example of an augmented MDP is shown in Fig. 5. With a slight abuse of notation, if σ is a strategy on the augmented MDP $\mathcal{M}^\varsigma$, we denote by σ also the strategy on $\mathcal{M} \times \mathcal{A}$ obtained by removing t from the domain of σ. The following theorem by Hahn et al. [18] shows the correctness of this the augmented product construction with respect to ω-regular property satisfaction.

Theorem 5 (Limit Reachability Theorem [18]). *There exists a threshold $\varsigma' \in (0,1)$ such that, for all $\varsigma > \varsigma'$ and every state s, any strategy σ that maximizes the probability of reaching the sink in $\mathcal{M}^\varsigma$ is (1) an optimal strategy in $\mathcal{M} \times \mathcal{A}$ from s and (2) induces an optimal strategy for the original MDP $\mathcal{M}$ from s with objective φ. Moreover, $\mathcal{M}$ satisfies φ almost surely if and only if the sink is almost surely reachable in $\mathcal{M}^\varsigma$ for all $0 < \varsigma < 1$.*

Proof (Sketch). Let us fix a strategy σ in both the MDP $\mathcal{M} \times \mathcal{A}$ and the augmented MDP $\mathcal{M}^\varsigma$. Notice that for every state in an accepting end-component of $(\mathcal{M} \times \mathcal{A})_\sigma$, the probability of reaching the sink in $\mathcal{M}^\varsigma$ is 1. Similarly, for every state in a rejecting end-component, the probability of reaching the sink in $\mathcal{M}^\varsigma$ is 0. The only difference between the probability of reaching accepting end-component in $(\mathcal{M} \times \mathcal{A})_\sigma$ and the probability of reaching the sink in $(\mathcal{M}^\varsigma)_\sigma$ occurs due to accepting transient transitions in such a way that the probability of reaching sink in $(\mathcal{M}^\varsigma)_\sigma$ overapproximates the probability of satisfaction in $(\mathcal{M} \times \mathcal{A})_\sigma$. This approximation error tends to 0 as ς tends to 1. Moreover, the the probability of reaching the sink in $(\mathcal{M}^\varsigma)_\sigma$ is 1 only when the probability of satisfaction in $(\mathcal{M} \times \mathcal{A})_\sigma$ is 1. □

Limit Reachability in Model-Free RL. Theorem 5 leads to a very simple model-free RL algorithm, which is illustrated in Fig. 6. The augmented product is not built by the RL algorithm, which does not know the transition structure of the environment MDP. Instead, the observations are used to drive the objective automaton. When the automaton reports an accepting transition, the interpreter tosses a biased coin to give the learner a reward with probability $1 - \varsigma$. The interpreter also extracts the set of actions for the learner to choose from. If the automaton is not deterministic and it has not taken the one nondeterministic transition it needs to take yet, the set of actions the interpreter provides to the learner includes the choice of special "jump" actions that instruct the automaton to move to a chosen accepting component.

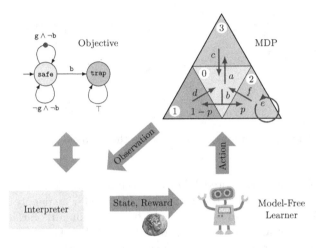

Fig. 6. Model-free reinforcement learning for ω-regular objectives.

When the automaton reports an accepting transition, the interpreter gives the learner a positive reward with probability $1 - \zeta$. When the learner actually receives a reward, the training episode terminates. Any RL algorithm that maximizes this probabilistic reward is guaranteed to converge to a policy that maximizes the probability of satisfaction of the ω-regular objective.

5   Conclusion

While limit reachability provides an alternative model-checking algorithm for ω-regular requirements of Markov Decision Processes, its main virtue is to enable model-free reinforcement learning: the translation from logical specification to scalar reward guarantees that a strategy that maximizes the expected reward also maximized the probability of satisfaction of the objective. While not all objectives are conveniently expressed as ω-regular languages, limit reachability provides a foundation on which the translation of more expressive specification languages may be built.

References

1. Aksaray, D., Jones, A., Kong, Z., Schwager, M., Belta, C.: Q-learning for robust satisfaction of signal temporal logic specifications. In: 2016 IEEE 55th Conference on Decision and Control (CDC), pp. 6565–6570 (2016)
2. de Alfaro, L.: Formal verification of probabilistic systems. Ph.D. thesis, Stanford University (1998)
3. Baier, C., Größer, M.: Recognizing ω-regular languages with probabilistic automata. In: Logic in Computer Science (LICS 2005), pp. 137–146, June 2005
4. Baier, C., Katoen, J.P.: Principles of Model Checking. MIT Press, Cambridge (2008)

5. Banach, S.: Sur les opérations dans les ensembles abstraits et leur application aux équations intégrales. Fundam. Math. **3**(1), 133–181 (1922). http://eudml.org/doc/213289
6. Borkar, V.S., Meyn, S.P.: The ode method for convergence of stochastic approximation and reinforcement learning. SIAM J. Control Optim. **38**(2), 447–469 (2000)
7. Brázdil, T., et al.: Verification of Markov decision processes using learning algorithms. In: Cassez, F., Raskin, J.-F. (eds.) ATVA 2014. LNCS, vol. 8837, pp. 98–114. Springer, Cham (2014). https://doi.org/10.1007/978-3-319-11936-6_8
8. Chatterjee, K., Henzinger, M.: Faster and dynamic algorithms for maximal end-component decomposition and related graph problems in probabilistic verification. In: Symposium on Discrete Algorithms (SODA), pp. 1318–1336, January 2011
9. Clarke, E.M., Emerson, E.A.: Design and synthesis of synchronization skeletons using branching time temporal logic. In: Kozen, D. (ed.) Logic of Programs 1981. LNCS, vol. 131, pp. 52–71. Springer, Heidelberg (1982). https://doi.org/10.1007/BFb0025774
10. Clarke, E.M., Grumberg, O., Peled, D.A.: Model Checking. MIT Press, Cambridge (1999)
11. Courcoubetis, C., Yannakakis, M.: The complexity of probabilistic verification. J. ACM **42**(4), 857–907 (1995)
12. Donzé, A., Maler, O.: Robust satisfaction of temporal logic over real-valued signals. In: Chatterjee, K., Henzinger, T.A. (eds.) FORMATS 2010. LNCS, vol. 6246, pp. 92–106. Springer, Heidelberg (2010). https://doi.org/10.1007/978-3-642-15297-9_9
13. Fainekos, G., Pappas, G.J.: Robustness of temporal logic specifications for continuous-time signals. Theor. Comput. Sci. **410**, 4262–4291 (2009)
14. Fainekos, G.E.: Robustness of temporal logic specifications. Ph.D. thesis, Department of Computer and Information Science, University of Pennsylvania (2008)
15. Fu, J., Topcu, U.: Probably approximately correct MDP learning and control with temporal logic constraints. In: Robotics: Science and Systems, July 2014
16. Hahn, E.M., Li, G., Schewe, S., Turrini, A., Zhang, L.: Lazy probabilistic model checking without determinisation. CoRR abs/1311.2928 (2013). http://arxiv.org/abs/1311.2928
17. Hahn, E.M., Li, G., Schewe, S., Turrini, A., Zhang, L.: Lazy probabilistic model checking without determinisation. In: Concurrency Theory, (CONCUR), pp. 354–367 (2015)
18. Hahn, E.M., Perez, M., Schewe, S., Somenzi, F., Trivedi, A., Wojtczak, D.: Omega-regular objectives in model-free reinforcement learning. In: Vojnar, T., Zhang, L. (eds.) TACAS 2019. LNCS, vol. 11427, pp. 395–412. Springer, Cham (2019). https://doi.org/10.1007/978-3-030-17462-0_27
19. Hasanbeig, M., Abate, A., Kroening, D.: Logically-correct reinforcement learning. CoRR abs/1801.08099 (2018). http://arxiv.org/abs/1801.08099
20. Hasanbeig, M., Abate, A., Kroening, D.: Certified reinforcement learning with logic guidance. arXiv e-prints arXiv:1902.00778, February 2019
21. Hiromoto, M., Ushio, T.: Learning an optimal control policy for a Markov decision process under linear temporal logic specifications. In: Symposium Series on Computational Intelligence, pp. 548–555, December 2015
22. Hordijk, A., Yushkevich, A.A.: Blackwell optimality. In: Feinberg, E.A., Shwartz, A. (eds.) Handbook of Markov Decision Processes: Methods and Applications, pp. 231–267. Springer, Boston (2002). https://doi.org/10.1007/978-1-4615-0805-2_8

23. Kwiatkowska, M., Norman, G., Parker, D.: PRISM 4.0: verification of probabilistic real-time systems. In: Gopalakrishnan, G., Qadeer, S. (eds.) CAV 2011. LNCS, vol. 6806, pp. 585–591. Springer, Heidelberg (2011). https://doi.org/10.1007/978-3-642-22110-1_47

24. Lahijanian, M., Andersson, S.B., Belta, C.: Temporal logic motion planning and control with probabilistic satisfaction guarantees. IEEE Trans. Robot. **28**(2), 396–409 (2012)

25. Lahijanian, M., Maly, M.R., Fried, D., Kavraki, L.E., Kress-Gazit, H., Vardi, M.Y.: Iterative temporal planning in uncertain environments with partial satisfaction guarantees. IEEE Trans. Robot. **32**(3), 538–599 (2016)

26. Levine, S., Finn, C., Darrell, T., Abbeel, P.: End-to-end training of deep visuomotor policies. J. Mach. Learn. Res. **17**(1), 1334–1373 (2016). http://dl.acm.org/citation.cfm?id=2946645.2946684

27. Li, X., Vasile, C.I., Belta, C.: Reinforcement learning with temporal logic rewards. In: International Conference on Intelligent Robots and Systems (IROS), pp. 3834–3839 (2017)

28. Lillicrap, T.P., et al.: Continuous control with deep reinforcement learning. CoRR abs/1509.02971 (2015). http://arxiv.org/abs/1509.02971

29. Liu, R., et al.: An intriguing failing of convolutional neural networks and the Coord-Conv solution. ArXiv e-prints 1807.03247, July 2018

30. Manna, Z., Pnueli, A.: The Temporal Logic of Reactive and Concurrent Systems *Specification*. Springer, New York (1992). https://doi.org/10.1007/978-1-4612-0931-7

31. Mnih, V., et al.: Human-level control through reinforcement learning. Nature **518**, 529–533 (2015)

32. Pnueli, A.: The temporal logic of programs. In: IEEE Symposium on Foundations of Computer Science, pp. 46–57 (1977)

33. Puterman, M.L.: Markov Decision Processes: Discrete Stochastic Dynamic Programming. Wiley, New York (1994)

34. Queille, J.P., Sifakis, J.: Specification and verification of concurrent systems in CESAR. In: Dezani-Ciancaglini, M., Montanari, U. (eds.) Programming 1982. LNCS, vol. 137, pp. 337–351. Springer, Heidelberg (1982). https://doi.org/10.1007/3-540-11494-7_22

35. Riedmiller, M.: Neural fitted Q iteration – first experiences with a data efficient neural reinforcement learning method. In: Gama, J., Camacho, R., Brazdil, P.B., Jorge, A.M., Torgo, L. (eds.) ECML 2005. LNCS (LNAI), vol. 3720, pp. 317–328. Springer, Heidelberg (2005). https://doi.org/10.1007/11564096_32

36. Sadigh, D., Kim, E., Coogan, S., Sastry, S.S., Seshia, S.A.: A learning based approach to control synthesis of Markov decision processes for linear temporal logic specifications. In: IEEE Conference on Decision and Control (CDC), pp. 1091–1096, December 2014

37. Sickert, S., Esparza, J., Jaax, S., Křetínský, J.: Limit-deterministic Büchi automata for linear temporal logic. In: Chaudhuri, S., Farzan, A. (eds.) CAV 2016. LNCS, vol. 9780, pp. 312–332. Springer, Cham (2016). https://doi.org/10.1007/978-3-319-41540-6_17

38. Sickert, S., Křetínský, J.: MoChiBA: probabilistic LTL model checking using limit-deterministic Büchi automata. In: Artho, C., Legay, A., Peled, D. (eds.) ATVA 2016. LNCS, vol. 9938, pp. 130–137. Springer, Cham (2016). https://doi.org/10.1007/978-3-319-46520-3_9

39. Strehl, A.L., Li, L., Wiewiora, E., Langford, J., Littman, M.L.: PAC model-free reinforcement learning. In: International Conference on Machine Learning, ICML, pp. 881–888 (2006)
40. Sutton, R.S., Barto, A.G.: Reinforcement Learnging: An Introduction, 2nd edn. MIT Press, Cambridge (2018)
41. Tsitsiklis, J.N., Roy, B.V.: An analysis of temporal-difference learning with function approximation. IEEE Trans. Autom. Control **42**(5), 674–690 (1997)
42. (2018). http://fortune.com/2018/05/08/uber-autopilot-death-reason. Accessed 11 May 2018
43. Vardi, M.Y.: Automatic verification of probabilistic concurrent finite state programs. In: FOCS, pp. 327–338 (1985)
44. Wang, J., Ding, X.C., Lahijanian, M., Paschalidis, I.C., Belta, C.: Temporal logic motion control using actor-critic methods. Int. J. Robot. Res. **34**(10), 1329–1344 (2015)
45. Watkins, C.J.C.H., Dayan, P.: Q-learning. Mach. Learn. **8**(3–4), 279–292 (1992)
46. Watkins, C.J.C.H.: Learning from delayed rewards. Ph.D. thesis, King's College, Cambridge, UK, May 1989
47. (2018). https://en.wikipedia.org/wiki/Waymo#Limitations. Accessed 11 May 2018

Contributed Papers

An Evaluation of Monte-Carlo Tree Search for Property Falsification on Hybrid Flight Control Laws

Rémi Delmas[1(✉)], Thomas Loquen[1], Josep Boada-Bauxell[2], and Mathieu Carton[2]

[1] ONERA/DTIS, Université de Toulouse, Toulouse, France
{remi.delmas,thomas.loquen}@onera.fr
[2] Airbus Operations S.A.S., Toulouse, France
{josep.boada-bauxell,mathieu.carton}@airbus.com

Abstract. The formal verification and validation of real-world, industrial critical hybrid flight controllers remains a very challenging task. An increasingly popular and quite successful alternative to formal verification is the use of optimization and reinforcement learning techniques to maximize some real-valued reward function encoding the robustness margin to the falsification of a property. In this paper we present an evaluation of a simple Monte-Carlo Tree Search property falsification algorithm, applied to select properties of a longitudinal hybrid flight control law: a threshold overshoot property, two frequential properties, and a discrete event-based property.

Keywords: Hybrid flight control laws · Property falsification · Reward function · Monte-Carlo Tree Search · Planning

1 Introduction

The formal verification of advanced hybrid controllers remains a very challenging task, largely due to the fundamental undecidability of hybrid theories and to the difficulty of inferring sufficiently accurate and effectively provable candidate invariants. Another impediment to formal verification is the representation gap between hybrid dataflow formalisms used by control engineers (e.g. Simulink), and hybrid automata formalisms underlying most formal verification techniques. Translation algorithms were proposed [12], however they mainly consist in flattening control-flow configurations to obtain a switched ODE system, and can lead to a combinatorial explosion during translation. So, despite the tremendous progress achieved on techniques such as reachability analysis [4,7,9], set-based simulation [3], etc. high-dimensional hybrid models remain elusive formal verification targets.

An increasingly studied approach is to forego the soundness and completeness guarantees of the above-mentioned techniques and to re-frame the verification

© Springer Nature Switzerland AG 2019
M. Zamani and D. Zufferey (Eds.): NSV 2019, LNCS 11652, pp. 45–59, 2019.
https://doi.org/10.1007/978-3-030-28423-7_3

problem as a real-valued reward optimization problem, in which the reward signal represents a robustness margin for the falsification of the candidate property. Scalable black-box optimization techniques [2,6], Reinforcement Learning (RL) techniques [1] or a combination of both [16] are then used to search for reward-maximizing input sequences, starting from given initial states. Despite being only able to produce falsification witnesses, the scalability of these techniques and the usefulness of the results obtained on high-dimensional hybrid models makes them a very worthwhile alternative when formal verification is not applicable.

The work presented in this paper was conducted as part of the WP10.3 of the IKKY-SEFA project, a 4 year effort in partnership between ONERA, LAAS-CNRS, AIRBUS and DASSAULT, under the french General Delegation of Civilian Aviation (DGAC) funding. The goal was to assess a collection of state-of-the-art analysis techniques for hybrid systems to determine how they could contribute to the efficiency of the design, verification and validation processes of advanced flight controllers. Of particular interest for the industrial partners were techniques that can be applied early in the design process and automatically detect unusual input sequences leading to altered closed-loop performance. This paper reports on experiments conducted with a property falsification algorithm based on Monte-Carlo Tree Search (MCTS), applied to a collection of industrial-sized hybrid controller benchmarks.

The paper is organised as follows: Sect. 2 presents the goals of the study together with the flight controller benchmarks used as input by the algorithms. Section 3 describes the Monte-Carlo tree search algorithm we implemented and used for property falsification. Section 4 presents several examples of property formalisation and falsification results. Section 5 discusses related works. Last, Sect. 6 concludes the paper with a general discussion of the results and some perspectives.

2   Industrial Use Case and Approach

For this study, Airbus provided a closed-loop flight dynamics model and simplified control law, depicted Fig. 1 and including:

- an aircraft model representing the longitudinal flight mechanics, with 10 state variables, 5 inputs and 12 outputs;
- sensor and output filter models representing the dynamics of measuring devices (transient responses, saturations and delays) and associated signal processing (transient filtering, bandwidths, delays and estimators) for the computation of speeds, accelerations, angles, and angular speeds;
- actuator models representing the transient responses, saturations and rate saturations of control surfaces and command allocation functions;
- a wind model translating vertical and horizontal steps or gusts into forces applied to the flight dynamics model;
- a simplified longitudinal hybrid control law including several operational modes (manual control, altitude transition, capture and regulation) and flight control laws (guidance, estimation, control, angle and speed protections).

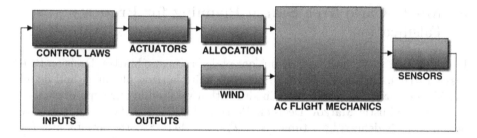

Fig. 1. Airbus benchmark: closed-loop Matlab/Simulink scheme

The controller consists of a feedback law in load factor n_z together with dynamic protections of the flight envelope in angle of attack and pitch angle (converted into vertical speed protections) and supports auto-pilot and manual operation modes. The controllable inputs in closed-loop operation are:

- **bapeng:** a Boolean-valued *auto-pilot engagement* switch allowing to switch between manual and auto-pilot modes,
- **selalt:** a real-valued *selected altitude target* input for the auto-pilot mode,
- **nzcmanche:** a real-valued *pilot stick order* input for the direct mode,
- **wx, wz:** real-valued wind speeds inputs along vertical and horizontal axes, allowing gusts or sustained perturbations.

The complexity of this model is mainly due to the 112 continuous state variables, 27 discrete switches, 4 RS latches, 28 2D lookup tables and 34 saturations. Moreover, as proposed by Airbus for this study, the hybrid simulation framework uses three sample times: continuous-time for continuous dynamics (flight dynamics, sensors, actuators, ...), discrete T_1 for command allocation, target, operational modes and guidance (altitude transition, capture and regulation) and a faster discrete $T_2 \simeq 1.5T_1$ for angle of attack and speed protections, active protection selection and voting and pitch inner loop. On this reference model all classical requirements are satisfied, i.e. for all authorized values of inputs in terms of amplitude and variation rate, protections always play their roles and relevant signals like angle of attack or load factor evolve smoothly and stay controlled within the required envelope.

Several modified versions of the control law were produced, each containing data-flow and/or control-flow alterations introducing undesirable closed-loop behaviours, such as reduced flight quality, threshold overshoots, spurious autopilot disconnections or spurious protection envelope alterations. These behaviours are triggered under very specific, yet unspecified conditions. Each modified control-law was accompanied with a reference scenario demonstrating these undesirable closed-loop effects. The goal of the study was to identify which of these scenarios were amenable to formalization and to efficient analysis with Monte-Carlo Tree Search falsification algorithms.

3   Monte-Carlo Tree Search Planning for Property Falsification

In this section we review basic definitions of deterministic Markov Decision Processes (MDP), cumulative reward functions, finite horizon planning, and detail the Monte-Carlo tree search planning algorithm we used in our experiments.

A deterministic Markov Decision Process (MDP) with finite and discrete action space is defined by a tuple $\langle S, A, T, r, \gamma \rangle$, where S is the set of states (or *state space*), A is the finite discrete action set (or *action space*), $T : S \times A \to S$ is the deterministic transition relation, $r : S \times A \to \mathbb{R}$ is the immediate reward function, $\gamma \in [0, 1]$ is the discount factor. From a state s_t an execution trace for actions $a_0, a_1, a_2, \ldots$ is the sequence of states and immediate rewards $(s_t, a_0) \xrightarrow{r_t} (s_{t+1}, a_1) \xrightarrow{r_{t+1}} (s_{t+2}, a_2) \xrightarrow{r_{t+2}} \ldots$ such that $s_{t+i+1} = T(s_{t+i}, a_i)$ and $r_{t+i+1} = r(s_{t+i}, a_i)$ for all i. The *cumulative reward* over N transitions from instant t, and the cumulative reward for trace suffixes starting at step K are given by $R_t = \sum_{i=0}^{N-1} \gamma^i r_{t+i}$ and $R_{t+K} = \sum_{i=K}^{N-1} \gamma^i r_{t+i}$ respectively[1]. Solving a *finite-horizon sequential planning problem* consists in generating a sequence of actions $a_1, \ldots a_N$ from some initial state such that cumulative rewards $R_t, R_{t+1}, \ldots, R_{t+N-1}$ are maximized at each step starting from the initial state.

Monte-Carlo Tree Search (MCTS) planning algorithms, first introduced by Coulom [5] and Kocsis et al. [8] have produced outstanding results for many hard planning applications, with its most recent extensions reaching superhuman level at the game of Go [13]. In its most basic form, MCTS iteratively builds a search tree over possible action sequences, using stochastic sampling aka *rollout* to estimate the cumulative reward function and guide the search. Nodes in the search tree correspond to reachable set of states, edges of the tree are labelled by actions of A connecting these states through T. Each node i stores an integer *visit counter* n_i and a real-valued $\bar{R}_{t_i}$ the current *empirical mean of cumulative reward* at the instant of occurrence of the node t_i. A *leaf node* is a node missing some outgoing edges, a *terminal node* is a node without outgoing edges.

The planning algorithm is shown in Fig. 2 and embeds an MCTS loop within an eager sequential planning loop as follows. Starting from a fresh root node and an empty plan for each step of the plan *mcts_iterations* MCTS iterations are run. An MCTS iteration consists of four steps: *Selection* traverses the search tree from the root to a leaf, selecting at each step, from node i, the child node j with the best Upper Confidence Bound (UCB) value $UCB1_j = \bar{R}_{t_j} + c \times \sqrt{\frac{\ln(n_i)}{n_j}}$. This tree-search policy strikes an optimal exploration/exploitation balance [8]. *Expansion* randomly selects one of not-yet-explored actions of the leaf node and adds a new terminal node. *Rollout* extends the action sequence of the current branch up to the finite planning horizon by sampling uniformly from A. A black-box simulation is run with the complete action sequence, yielding the cumulative

---

[1] By lack of space and since we are only considering planning problems in the deterministic and finite-horizon case, the definitions of *policy, state-value function S, action value function Q* and *optimal policy synthesis* are deliberately omitted.

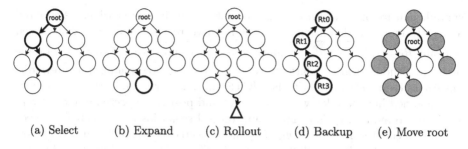

(a) Select   (b) Expand   (c) Rollout   (d) Backup   (e) Move root

Fig. 2. Phases of the Monte-Carlo Tree Search based planning algorithm.

reward signal. The *Backup* step updates the reward and visit statistics of each node of the current branch, using the cumulative reward at the node's own occurrence date. When the MCTS iterations are complete the *Move Root* step re-roots the search process to the best child of the current root according to the current UCB1 score and commits the corresponding action to the plan. Future MCTS iterations ignore the greyed-out nodes and expand the new subtree. Finally, the complete plan is returned.

4 Evaluation Results and Discussion

This section presents how the concrete application benchmark maps to the framework of Sect. 3 together with analysis results for three types of properties[2].

4.1 Connexion with the MDP Framework and Experimental Methodology

Informally, the closed-loop control model described in Sect. 2 maps to the MDP planning framework of Sect. 3 as follows: the state space S is of the form $\mathbb{R}^{nReal} \times \mathbb{Z}^{nInt} \times \mathbb{B}^{nBool}$, where $nReal$, $nInt$ an $nBool$ are respectively the number of real, integer and Boolean state variables of the model. The action space A is a user-definable discrete subset of the cartesian product of controllable inputs domains $\mathbb{B} \times \mathbb{R}^4$, augmented with a scalar dimension representing the *action duration*, i.e. the duration for which constant inputs are maintained. The planning algorithm hence searches in the set of piecewise constant functions over a finite time horizon. The transition relation T is given by the operational semantics of the Simulink engine for selected action duration and ODE solver parameters. The immediate reward function r is modelled as a synchronous observer composed to the Simulink model. Reward functions are designed to capture and generalize the unwanted closed-loop behaviours exemplified in reference scenarios provided with each modified benchmark. Furthermore, to better handle the

---

[2] Disclaimer: some quantitative aspects of the results presented in this section have been omitted for industrial confidentiality reasons.

sporadic nature of reward functions encountered in this application, we adopted a slightly modified definition of the cumulative reward, akin to a generalized p-mean: $R_t = \sqrt[p]{r_t^p + \gamma R_{t+1}^p}$. Values $p > 1$ give more importance to sporadic high amplitude rewards relatively to more frequent lower amplitude rewards. For each modified benchmark, the MCTS analysis is run on both the reference and modified benchmarks, with a negative and positive expected outcome, repsectively. Human analysis of maximum reward scenarios is conducted to check if they indeed result from triggering the expected control-flow and data-flow modifications of each candidate benchmark. The MCTS planning algorithm was implemented in pure matlab to allow efficient communication with the simulink engine used for reward sampling.

4.2 Threshold Property

In this benchmark, incorrect closed-loop behaviour is specified as any situation where a given flight parameter of the aircraft model α exceeds its target value by some given *margin*, expressed as $\alpha \geq \alpha_{target} + margin$. The corresponding reward function, represented in Fig. 3, is expressed as $r = \max(\alpha - (\alpha_{target} + margin), \epsilon)$.

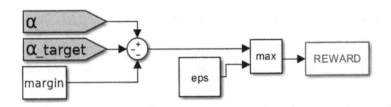

Fig. 3. Matlab/Simulink scheme for threshold property

For this analysis the action space is defined as $bapeng \in \{T, F\}$, $selalt = 10000fts$, $nzcmanche \in \{neutral, half\_up, full\_up\}$, $wx = wz = 0.0$ and an action duration of 5 s. Cumulative reward parameters are set to $\gamma = 0.9999$ and $p = 5$, plan size to 30 with 30 MCTS iterations per plan step. The total duration of analysis was 780 s. Snapshots of the MCTS progress are shown in Fig. 4.

The maximum-reward scenario generated by the analysis, shown in Fig. 5, falsifies the requirement by activating the expected conditions. Under these conditions, the internal saturation value α_{lim} (in black) is erroneously scaled, allowing α (in blue) to exceed the required α_{target} threshold (in red) when the appropriate stick order is maintained for a sufficient duration.

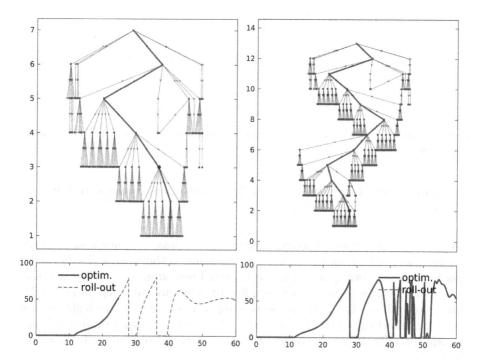

Fig. 4. Search tree and best reward – threshold property. Upper half: snapshots of MCTS tree during search, best branch highlighted in green. Lower half: corresponding immediate reward trace for current best branch, in solid red up to current planning depth, and dashed for best rollout suffix. Remark: the flight dynamics model escapes its domain of validity after $t = 28\,$s, the subsequent reward signal is irrelevant. (Color figure online)

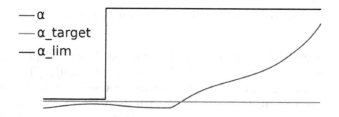

Fig. 5. Falsification of $\alpha \geq \alpha_{target} + margin$.

4.3   Frequential Properties

In this paragraph, we consider properties categorized by flight control engineers as frequency requirements. Two classes of undesirable behaviours are considered:

- long-duration, high-frequency oscillations of n_z around the commanded n_{zc} as shown in Fig. 6–left.

Fig. 6. Blue: n_{zc}, black: n_z (reference benchmark), red: n_z (modified benchmark) (Color figure online)

- short-duration, large amplitude oscillations of n_z uncorrelated to the commanded n_{zc} as shown in Fig. 6–right,

Property 1. The reward function measures the average amplitude of n_z oscillations in a specific frequency band corresponding to the undesired behaviours. Low frequencies, corresponding to the expected response to low frequency pilot orders, and high frequencies corresponding to noise, are cut using an 11th order Butterworth filter. The edge frequencies are defined according to flight control engineers knowledge. The absolute value of the filtered signal is then fed into an exponentially decaying moving average operator to obtain the final reward signal Fig. 7.

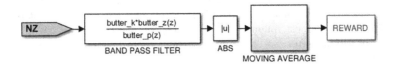

Fig. 7. Reward function for frequential property 1

For this analysis the action space is defined as *bapeng* $\in \{T, F\}$, *selalt* $\in$ $\{25000\mathit{fts}, 28000\mathit{fts}\}$, *nzcmanche* $\in \{\mathit{half\_down}, \mathit{neutral}, \mathit{half\_up}\}$, $wx = wz = 0.0$ and an action duration of $5\,\mathrm{s}$. Cumulative reward parameters are set to $\gamma = 0.9999$ and $p = 10$, plan size to 25 with 2880 MCTS iterations per plan step – needed to handle the complex sequential dependencies of the triggering scenario and the sporadic nature of the reward peaks. The total duration of analysis was $69700\,\mathrm{s}$. Snapshots of the MCTS progress are shown in Fig. 8.

As shown on Fig. 9, MCTS planning manages to generate results that are noticeably different from the reference scenario. The input sequence leads to two oscillating phenomena (with similar amplitude) while only one is present in the reference trace.

The unwanted behaviour corresponds to a spurious disconnection of autopilot on a mode switch of the control law. The n_z load factor perturbation corresponds to an incorrect reset of the internal state of an actuator control loop, introducing a delay effect during a few seconds.

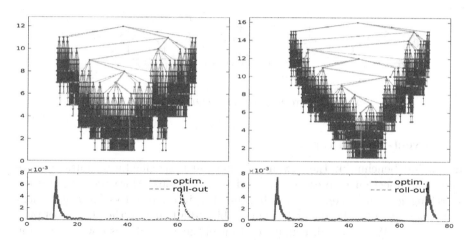

Fig. 8. Search tree and best reward – frequential property 1. For legend see Fig. 4

Property 2. In this case, the unwanted behaviour consists of n_z oscillations around the commanded n_{zc}. Such oscillations are tolerated when they are low frequency, but can become problematic when they are high frequency and sustained over time, regardless of amplitude. The reward function simply counts the number of sign inversions of $n_z - n_{zc}$ in a sliding window of a few seconds, see Fig. 10.

For this analysis the action space is defined as *bapeng* $\in \{T, F\}$, *selalt* $\in \{25000fts, 28000fts\}$, *nzcmanche* $\in \{half\_down, neutral, half\_up\}$, *wx* = *wz* = 0.0 and an action duration of 5 s. Cumulative reward parameters are set to $\gamma = 0.9999$ and $p = 5$, plan size to 25 with 120 MCTS iterations per plan step. The total duration of analysis was 8140 s. Snapshots of the MCTS progress are shown in Fig. 11.

As presented Fig. 12, MCTS manages to generate an input sequence triggering the undesirable behaviour over extended time periods, which results from an incorrect reinitialisation of the inner control loop gains after a mode switch. For a few seconds the control law's extra stiffness leads to oscillations of the load factor n_z around the commanded n_{zc}.

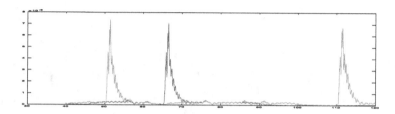

Fig. 9. Reward signal of the reference trace (blue) and MCTS trace (red) (Color figure online)

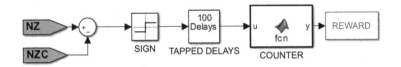

Fig. 10. Reward function for frequential property 2

4.4 Event-Based Property

In this last benchmark, the unwanted behaviour is specified as a spurious auto-pilot disconnection in presence of wind perturbations. More precisely, we are searching for wind scenarios which cause the internal auto-pilot engagement signal *bapeng_int* to become false on a stabilized altitude in the absence of pilot intervention. We use the disconnection time of the auto-pilot as reward function, as shown in Fig. 13.

We defined two different wind profiles, *weak wind* and *strong wind*, with the following MCTS parameters:

- **Weak wind**: *bapeng* = T, *selalt* = 25000*fts*, *nzcmanche* = *neutral*, $(wx, wz) \in \{zero, low\}^2$, an action duration of 5 s, reward parameters $\gamma = 0.9999$, $p = 5$, a plan size of 15 with 20 MCTS iterations per plan step, for a total duration of analysis of 810 s.
- **Strong wind**: *bapeng* = T, *selalt* = 25000*fts*, *nzcmanche* = *neutral*, $(wx, wz) \in \{zero, low, medium, high, very\_high\}^2$, an action duration of 5 s, reward parameters $\gamma = 0.9999$, $p = 5$, a plan size of 15 with 25 MCTS iterations per plan step, for a total duration of analysis of 1056 s.

Snapshots of MCTS progress are shown for the *low wind* and *high wind* cases in Figs. 14 and 15. In each case, MCTS manages to generate the wind

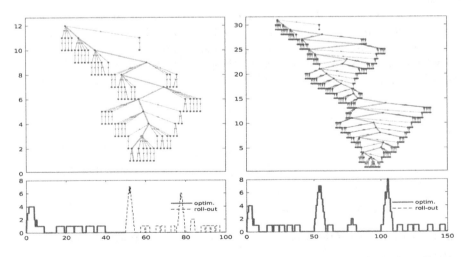

Fig. 11. Search tree and best reward – frequential property 2. For legend see Fig. 4

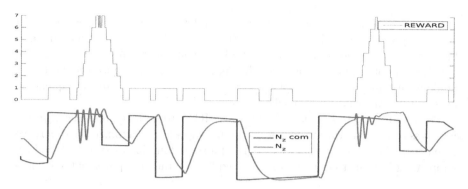

Fig. 12. Frequential property 2: best reward and trace (blue: commanded n_z, red: measured n_z) (Color figure online)

profiles necessary to trigger the spurious auto-pilot disconnection. On the weak wind case, we obtain multiple short disconnections. On the strong wind case, we obtain a single long disconnection, which brings the aircraft dynamics model out of its validity domain.

5 Related Works

Property falsification for cyber-physical systems is a very active research field, in particular for MCTS-based techniques, Q-learning techniques and their various combinations. Our work is heavily inspired by the works of Zhang et al. [16], in which the falsification of STL formulas on Matlab/Simulink models is addressed using a *time-staging* approach (an *eager sequential planning* in our own formulation), and are able to handle continuous action spaces by combining MCTS and stochastic hill-climbing optimizer. In comparison, our approach is simpler since it is restricted to discrete action spaces, a deliberate choice made to reduce the computation cost. Indeed, the closed-loop models we are dealing with have high simulation costs, in the order of seconds on a desktop workstation. Allowing continuous actions spaces using stochastic hill-climbing techniques can only increase dramatically the computation budget.

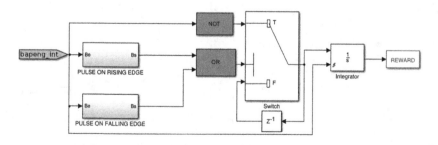

Fig. 13. Reward function for auto-pilot disconnection detection

Worth mentioning is the fact that most related works use some flavour of linear temporal logic with robust semantics (e.g. PSL) as reward functions and that we do not. Indeed the properties of interest identified by the industrial partners did not require the use of such expressive logics, being for the most part simple invariants of the form $\Box p(X)$ with no disjunctions or complex sequencing aspects, yet somewhat numerically complex.

The recent work of Lee et al. in [11] uses MCTS to perform *adaptive differential stress testing*, in order to synthesize input traces that maximize the difference in behaviour between alternative designs of a same function or system. The idea is appealing in that it circumvents the need for a detailed requirement specifica-

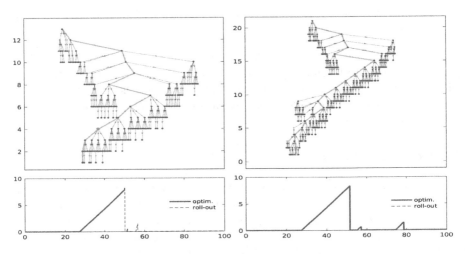

Fig. 14. Search tree and best reward – weak wind profile. For legend see Fig. 4

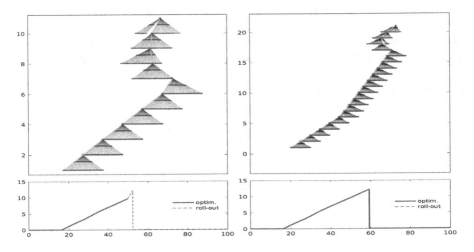

Fig. 15. Search tree and best reward – strong wind profile. For legend see Fig. 4

tion, since the reward function can be essentially reduced to a component-wise distance measure over system outputs. The suitability of this approach for flaw detection for control systems is however not clear: the main reason for making an evolution is to either correct previous bad behaviours (maintenance) or add new behaviours (evolutions), and then by definition the previous version of the model cannot be used as a reference of correct behaviour. Regression testing typically needs a more detailed specification delimiting the impact of evolutions.

6   Conclusion

As a conclusion, we make the following observations. The MCTS-based falsification algorithm we implemented provided surprisingly good results considering its simplicity and the relatively low development effort invested. For each use-case, the MCTS analysis was able to generate maximum-reward traces that pinpointed the control-flow and data-flow modifications that were made to the reference control law. Due to the complexity of Matlab/Simulink models dealt with in this study, the computational budget requirements remained relatively high. The controller part of the models could not be simplified since they are the object of the validation, and the plant part of the models could be simplified only in a few cases. In most cases, a simpler plant model will either loose the unwanted behaviours we are trying to identify or on the contrary introduce new unwanted behaviours and steer the search away from the defect of interest. This motivated the informed choice of small and discrete action spaces and adapted planning parameters to keep the computation budget small. Our experiments have shown that even with such restrictions, the approach can produce valuable results on the most interesting classes of properties of the closed-loop system. The most challenging aspect was, not surprisingly, reward formalisation. For frequential properties in particular the boundary between acceptable and non-acceptable behaviours requires expert knowledge.

Perspectives to this work are the following. Recent work on *memory-augmented Monte-Carlo tree search* [15] uses state memorization and kernel regression to more efficiently share information across branches and perform reward prediction, reducing the rollout budget and improving performance. Adapting the idea to our setting seems natural since the state vector is well defined for closed-loop control models. The selection of appropriate discrete action space for a given requirement still requires expert knowledge on the system. To address this limitation we will study the extension to continuous action spaces, most likely by embedding some form of kernel regression [10] or Gaussian process regression [14] within the eager planning loop, rather than stochastic hill-climbing. The use of biased rollouts is also an interesting point to study in the future, in particular using importance sampling techniques to steer the search towards very rare combinations of inputs with respect to typical aircraft operation scenarios, where the controller's behaviour is most likely to be less robust.

References

1. Akazaki, T., Liu, S., Yamagata, Y., Duan, Y., Hao, J.: Falsification of cyber-physical systems using deep reinforcement learning. In: Havelund, K., Peleska, J., Roscoe, B., de Vink, E. (eds.) FM 2018. LNCS, vol. 10951, pp. 456–465. Springer, Cham (2018). https://doi.org/10.1007/978-3-319-95582-7_27
2. Annpureddy, Y., Liu, C., Fainekos, G., Sankaranarayanan, S.: S-TaLiRo: a tool for temporal logic falsification for hybrid systems. In: Abdulla, P.A., Leino, K.R.M. (eds.) TACAS 2011. LNCS, vol. 6605, pp. 254–257. Springer, Heidelberg (2011). https://doi.org/10.1007/978-3-642-19835-9_21
3. Bouissou, O., Mimram, S., Chapoutot, A.: Hyson: set-based simulation of hybrid systems. In: Proceedings of the 23rd IEEE International Symposium on Rapid System Prototyping, RSP 2012, Tampere, Finland, 11–12 October, pp. 79–85 (2012). https://doi.org/10.1109/RSP.2012.6380694
4. Chen, X., Sankaranarayanan, S., Abraham, E.: Flow* 1.2 - more effective to play with hybrid systems. In: 2nd International Workshop on Applied Verification for Continuous and Hybrid Systems, ARCH@CPSWeek 2015, Seattle, WA, USA, 13 April, pp. 152–159 (2015). https://doi.org/10.29007/1w4t
5. Coulom, R.: Efficient selectivity and backup operators in Monte-Carlo tree search. In: van den Herik, H.J., Ciancarini, P., Donkers, H.H.L.M.J. (eds.) CG 2006. LNCS, vol. 4630, pp. 72–83. Springer, Heidelberg (2007). https://doi.org/10.1007/978-3-540-75538-8_7
6. Donzé, A.: Breach, a toolbox for verification and parameter synthesis of hybrid systems. In: Touili, T., Cook, B., Jackson, P. (eds.) CAV 2010. LNCS, vol. 6174, pp. 167–170. Springer, Heidelberg (2010). https://doi.org/10.1007/978-3-642-14295-6_17
7. Frehse, G., et al.: SpaceEx: scalable verification of hybrid systems. In: Gopalakrishnan, G., Qadeer, S. (eds.) CAV 2011. LNCS, vol. 6806, pp. 379–395. Springer, Heidelberg (2011). https://doi.org/10.1007/978-3-642-22110-1_30
8. Kocsis, L., Szepesvári, C.: Bandit based Monte-Carlo planning. In: Fürnkranz, J., Scheffer, T., Spiliopoulou, M. (eds.) ECML 2006. LNCS (LNAI), vol. 4212, pp. 282–293. Springer, Heidelberg (2006). https://doi.org/10.1007/11871842_29
9. Kong, S., Gao, S., Chen, W., Clarke, E.: dReach: δ-reachability analysis for hybrid systems. In: Baier, C., Tinelli, C. (eds.) TACAS 2015. LNCS, vol. 9035, pp. 200–205. Springer, Heidelberg (2015). https://doi.org/10.1007/978-3-662-46681-0_15
10. Lee, K., Kim, S.A., Choi, J., Lee, S.W.: Deep reinforcement learning in continuous action spaces: a case study in the game of simulated curling. In: Proceedings of the 35th International Conference on Machine Learning, ICML 2018, Stockholmsmässan, Stockholm, Sweden, 10–15 July, pp. 2943–2952 (2018). http://proceedings.mlr.press/v80/lee18b.html
11. Lee, R., et al.: Adaptive stress testing: finding failure events with reinforcement learning. CoRR abs/1811.02188 (2018). http://arxiv.org/abs/1811.02188
12. Schrammel, P., Jeannet, B.: From hybrid data-flow languages to hybrid automata: a complete translation. In: Hybrid Systems: Computation and Control, HSCC 2012, Beijing, China, 17–19 April, pp. 167–176 (2012). https://doi.org/10.1145/2185632.2185658
13. Silver, D., et al.: Mastering the game of go with deep neural networks and tree search. Nature 529(7587), 484–489 (2016). https://doi.org/10.1038/nature16961

14. Silvetti, S., Policriti, A., Bortolussi, L.: An active learning approach to the falsification of black box cyber-physical systems. In: Polikarpova, N., Schneider, S. (eds.) IFM 2017. LNCS, vol. 10510, pp. 3–17. Springer, Cham (2017). https://doi.org/10.1007/978-3-319-66845-1_1
15. Xiao, C., Mei, J., Müller, M.: Memory-augmented Monte Carlo tree search. In: Proceedings of the Thirty-Second AAAI Conference on Artificial Intelligence, New Orleans, Louisiana, USA, 2–7 February, pp. 1455–1462 (2018). https://www.aaai.org/ocs/index.php/AAAI/AAAI18/paper/view/17139
16. Zhang, Z., Ernst, G., Sedwards, S., Arcaini, P., Hasuo, I.: Two-layered falsification of hybrid systems guided by Monte Carlo tree search. IEEE Trans. CAD Integr. Circ. Syst. 37(11), 2894–2905 (2018). https://doi.org/10.1109/TCAD.2018.2858463

Rigorous Continuous Evolution
of Uncertain Systems

Luca Geretti[1], Sanja Živanović Gonzalez[2]([✉]), Pieter Collins[3],
Davide Bresolin[4], and Tiziano Villa[1]

[1] University of Verona, Verona, Italy
{luca.geretti,tiziano.villa}@univr.it
[2] Barry University, Miami Shores, FL 33161, USA
SZivanovic@barry.edu
[3] Maastricht University, Maastricht, The Netherlands
pieter.collins@maastrichtuniversity.nl
[4] University of Padova, Padova, Italy
davide.bresolin@unipd.it

Abstract. Uncertainty is unavoidable in modeling dynamical systems
and it may be represented mathematically by differential inclusions. In
the past, we proposed an algorithm to compute validated solutions of
differential inclusions; here we provide several theoretical improvements
to the algorithm, including its extension to piecewise constant and sinusoidal approximations of uncertain inputs, updates on the affine approximation bounds and a generalized formula for the analytical error. In
addition, we implemented the methodology in Ariadne, a library for the
verification of continuous and hybrid systems. Then we evaluated ten
systems with varying degrees of nonlinearity, number of variables and
uncertain inputs. The results are hereby compared with two state-of-
the-art approaches to time-varying uncertainties in nonlinear systems.

1 Introduction

In this paper we discuss the solution of differential inclusions (DIs) to analyse
uncertain nonlinear dynamical systems. Uncertainty arises due to environmental
disturbances and modeling discrepancies. The former include input and output
disturbances, and noise on sensors and actuators; the latter account for the
unavoidable approximation of a model with respect to the real system due to
unmodeled phenomena, order reduction and parameter variations over changes
of the environment and variations over time of the modeled system. Such uncertainty and imprecision may be modeled by DIs, which issues the challenge to
provide practical algorithms to approximate the reachable set of a nonlinear
inclusion.

DIs are dynamic systems of the form $\dot{x} \in F(x)$, and generalise differential
equations by having multivalued right-hand sides; see [4,20]. They model systems
with (bounded, non-stochastic) uncertainties. DIs can be viewed as systems with
input (control or noise) in the form $\dot{x} = f(x,v)$; $v \in V \subset \mathbb{R}^m$, where $v(\cdot)$ is a

© Springer Nature Switzerland AG 2019
M. Zamani and D. Zufferey (Eds.): NSV 2019, LNCS 11652, pp. 60–75, 2019.
https://doi.org/10.1007/978-3-030-28423-7_4

measurable function [13]. If the set V of inputs is compact and separable, and $f(x, V)$ is continuous in x and convex for all x, the solution sets of the two systems are equivalent [4].

DIs arise in applications in robotics, engineering, physical and biological sciences in a variety of ways. They are used to model differential equations with discontinuities, by taking the closed convex hull of the right-hand side [10]. They can also be used to model systems with uncertain time-varying parameters, by replacing these with the whole set to which they could belong, as in [6,18]. However, the most important use cases arise from the analysis of complex or large-scale systems. One approach to analyse such systems is to apply model-reduction techniques to replace a high-order system of differential equations $\dot{x} = f(x)$ by a low-order system of the form $\dot{z} = h(z) + e$, where $|e| \leq \epsilon$ represents the error introduced in simplifying the model (see [11]). Another way to analyse complex systems is to analyse separately their components. When the components depend on one another, we can decouple them by replacing an input from another component by noise varying over the range of possible values, again resulting in smaller but uncertain systems (see [7]). Note that stochastic models are not appropriate in these cases since the inputs are not random.

To reliably analyse the behaviour and properties of a system, notably safety, uncertainties in the system must be taken into account when modeling, and rigorous numerical methods are necessary in order to provide guaranteed correct solutions. Designing numerical algorithms for computing solutions of DIs rigorously, efficiently and to high precision, remains a point of current research. Different techniques and various types of numerical methods have been proposed in the literature. Some of the recent algorithms include ellipsoidal methods in [15], an interval Taylor-model approach in [16] and [6], Lohner-type algorithms in [18], optimal control in [5], set-based approximations to the Peano-Baker series in [2], hybrid bounding methods in [17], and a set-oriented method in [9]. However, none of these algorithms give both validated enclosures and guaranteed convergence with high-order precision for nonlinear DIs and thus are not of direct interest for comparison. More closely related algorithms implemented on publicly available tools are: [7] implemented within the tool FLOW*, [19] implemented on top of CORA 2015, CORA 2018 (see [1]) and [14] implemented on top of CVODE.

Our algorithm, whose initial version was presented in [23], is implemented and extensively tested in ARIADNE, a tool for verification of hybrid systems, see [3]. The main focus of this paper is showcasing capability and efficiency of our algorithm by analysing ten systems, whose results are then compared with FLOW* and CORA 2018 (from now on, referred to as CORA). These two competitors were chosen as being the most recent and well-known tools able to deal rigorously with nonlinear uncertain systems. In addition, we provide certain theoretical extensions to our algorithm for solving DIs and we compare and test efficiency and accuracy of the algorithm for different orders of error.

The paper is organized as follows: Sects. 2 and 3 discuss the theory, followed by Sect. 4 which is concerned with implementation aspects. Numerical experiments are presented in Sect. 5, with conclusions and future work in Sect. 6.

2   Background

A solution of the DI $\dot{x} \in F(x)$ is an absolutely continuous function $x : [0, T] \rightarrow \mathbb{R}^n$ such that for almost every $t \in [0, T]$, $x(\cdot)$ is differentiable at t and $\dot{x} \in F(x)$. Here $F : \mathbb{R}^n \Rightarrow \mathbb{R}^n$ is considered a multivalued function. The solution set $S(x_0, [0, T]) \subset C([0, T], \mathbb{R}^n)$ (space of continuous functions mapping $[0, T]$ into $\mathbb{R}^n$) is defined as

$$S(x_0, [0, T]) = \{x(\cdot) \in C([0, T], \mathbb{R}^n) \mid x(\cdot) \text{ is a solution}$$
$$\text{of } \dot{x} \in F(x) \text{ with } x(0) = x_0\}.$$

The <u>reachable set at time t</u>, $S(x_0, t) \subset \mathbb{R}^n$, is defined as

$$S(x_0, t) = \{x = x(t) \in \mathbb{R}^n \mid x(\cdot) \in S(x_0)\}.$$

If $F(x) = f(x, V) = \bigcup_{v \in V} f(x, v)$, where the set V is compact and separable, f is continuous, and $f(x, V)$ is convex for all x, then there exists a bounded measurable function $v(t) \in V$, such that $x(t) \in S(x_0, [0, T])$ is the solution of the time-varying system $\dot{x}(t) = f(x(t), v(t))$, $\forall v(t) \in V$, see Chap. 1.14 in [4].

We use the supremum norm for the vector norm in $\mathbb{R}^n$, i.e. for $x \in \mathbb{R}^n$, $\|x\|_\infty = \max\{|x_1|, ..., |x_n|\}$. The corresponding norm for functions $f : D \subset \mathbb{R}^n \rightarrow \mathbb{R}$ is $\|f\|_\infty = \sup_{x \in D} \|f(x)\|_\infty$, and the corresponding matrix norm is

$$\|Q\|_\infty = \max_{i=1,...,n} \left\{ \sum_{j=1}^n |q_{ij}| \right\}$$

Given a square matrix Q and a matrix norm $\|\cdot\|$, the <u>logarithmic norm</u> is defined by $\lambda(Q) = \lim_{h \rightarrow 0^+} \frac{1}{h}(\|I + hQ\| - 1)$, which for the matrix norm above yields

$$\lambda_\infty(Q) = \max_i \left\{ q_{ii} + \sum_{j \neq i} |q_{ij}| \right\}.$$

The logarithmic norm of Q determines how fast trajectories diverge from each other; for the linear system $\dot{x} = Qx$, two solutions $x(\cdot)$ and $y(\cdot)$ satisfy $\frac{d}{dt}\|x(t) - y(t)\| \leq \lambda(Q)\|x(t) - y(t)\|$.

2.1   Brief Summary of Groundwork

In [23], we presented an algorithm for computation of an over-approximation of the solution set of a DI in the form of an input-affine system

$$\dot{x}(t) = f(x(t)) + \sum_{i=1}^m g_i(x(t)) v_i(t); \quad v_i \in [-V_i, V_i] \tag{1}$$

where $v_i(\cdot) \in L^\infty([0, T]; \mathbb{R})$ are measurable functions and V_i are positive real numbers. Our approach relies on reducing the infinite-dimensional space of

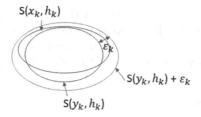

Fig. 1. One time step: exact reachable set $S(x_k, h_k)$ (blue) is over-approximated by computing solution of auxiliary system (2) (red) plus uniform error, i.e. $S(y_k, h_k) + \varepsilon_k$ (green). (Color figure online)

admissible inputs v_i by creating an auxiliary system that approximates the original one

$$\dot{y}(t) = f(y(t)) + \sum_{i=1}^{m} g_i(y(t)) \, w_i(t) \tag{2}$$

and looking at the difference between solutions of the two systems, see Fig. 1. We consider $w_i(\cdot)$ to be functions of finitely many parameters to be defined.

The main focus of [23] was (a) derivation of the difference between solutions, i.e. $x(t_{k+1}) - y(t_{k+1})$, over single time step (k-th time-step is $[t_k, t_{k+1}]$) and (b) presentation of error formulas, namely computation of error ε_k such that

$$\varepsilon_k \geq \sup\{\|x(t_{k+1}) - y(t_{k+1})\| \mid x(\cdot) \text{ solves (1)}$$

$$\text{and } y(\cdot) \text{ solves (2) with } x(t_k) = y(t_k)\}. \tag{3}$$

To provide an error of desired order, the main unknown components are the functions $w_i(\cdot)$. Consequently, we want to choose classes of functions $w_i(\cdot)$ and parameter sets $A_i \subset \mathbb{R}^p$ for which the errors ε_k are small, while keeping the auxiliary system (2) computationally feasible and the number of parameters p small. There are many classes of parameterised functions for which we can obtain high-order approximations. In this paper we provided formulas for the error if $w_i(t)$ is 0 (0-parameter), constant (1-parameter), and linear (2-parameters). The related single step error ε_k was at least of $O(h^2)$, where a time step $h = \max_k h_k = \max_k(t_{k+1} - t_k)$, with $\varepsilon_k \sim O(h^3)$ in two special cases, namely the single input case ($i = 1$) and additive noise case, i.e. $g_i(x(t)) = 1$ for all $i = 1, ..., m$. The numerical capabilities of the algorithm were only illustrated with a simple example.

As the achievable order of error is restricted by the smoothness of the functions f and g_i, to obtain local errors of $O(h^3)$, it suffices to assume that f and the g_i are C^2 functions.

3   Relevant Theory and Extensions

We next present a summary of the different classes of functions $w_i(\cdot)$ that we consider, and the corresponding local error bounds on the difference of the two solutions. Again, the actual derivations of the error formulae were presented in [23] and are not detailed here. However, only linear $w_i(\cdot)$ were considered previously, and here we give two additional choices for two-parameters $w_i(\cdot)$ and an error formula that generalizes to all three cases of two-parameters $w_i(\cdot)$.

3.1   Error Formulas

For the remainder of this section, we fix k to consider the solution of (1) over the interval $[t_k, t_{k+1}]$, with center $t_{k+1/2} = \frac{1}{2}(t_k + t_{k+1})$ and size $h = h_k$. Let B be a bound on the solutions of (1) and (2) over $[t_k, t_{k+1}]$ (see [8] for details), and assume that

$$\|f(z)\| \leq K, \ \|Df(z)\| \leq L, \ \|D^2 f(z)\| \leq H,$$
$$\|g_i(z)\| \leq K_i, \ \|Dg_i(z)\| \leq L_i, \ \|D^2 g_i(z)\| \leq H_i, \tag{4}$$
$$\lambda(Df(z)) \leq \Lambda,$$

for each $i = 1, ..., m$ and for all $z \in B$. Here, $Dp(\cdot)$ is the Jacobian matrix and $D^2 p(\cdot)$ is a third order tensor for some vector function $p(\cdot)$. We also set

$$K' = \sum_{i=1}^{m} V_i K_i, \ L' = \sum_{i=1}^{m} V_i L_i, \ H' = \sum_{i=1}^{m} V_i H_i. \tag{5}$$

As explained in [23], to satisfy desired order of error, we need to obtain appropriate sets of input functions w_i which match the moments of v_i as

$$\mu_{i,0} = \frac{1}{h} \int_{t_k}^{t_{k+1}} v_i(t) \, dt;$$
$$\mu_{i,1} = \frac{4}{h^2} \int_{t_k}^{t_{k+1}} (t - t_{k+1/2}) v_i(t) \, dt.$$

These satisfy $|\mu_{i,0}| \leq V_i$ and $|\mu_{i,1}| \leq (1 - \mu_{i,0}^2/V_i^2)V_i$, so can be parameterised

$$\mu_{i,0} = c_{i,0}, \ \mu_{i,1} = (1 - c_{i,0}^2/V_i^2)c_{i,1} \text{ for } |c_{i,0}|, |c_{i,1}| \leq V_i.$$

Since $|w_i|$ for all $i = 1, ..., m$ affect the size of local error ε, it is desired to choose these functions in such a way that the size of the input set V is not enlarged by a significant amount while they are matching the above moments. After theoretically testing library of standard functions, the following choices of input functions w_i became of interest:

(1) Zero: $w_i(t) = 0$,
(2) Constant: $w_i(t) = a_i$,
(3a) Affine: $w_i(t) = a_i + b_i(t - t_{k+1/2})/h$,
(3b) Sinusoidal: $w_i(t) = a_i + b_i \sin\left(\gamma(t - t_{k+1/2})/h\right)$,
(3c) Piecewise constant: $w_i(t) = \begin{cases} a_i & \text{if } t \in [t_k, t_{k+1/2}) \\ b_i & \text{if } t \in [t_{k+1/2}, t_{k+1}), \end{cases}$

where a_i, b_i are some real parameters to be found. In (1), w_i are zero, we get a local error $O(h)$, and the error bound (3) is

$$\varepsilon = h\,K'\,\varphi(\Lambda h) \tag{6}$$

where $\varphi(x) = (e^x - 1)/x$. Alternatively, we can use

$$\varepsilon = h\,(2K + K'). \tag{7}$$

In (2), the $w_i = a_i$ are constant, with

$$a_i = \frac{1}{h}\int_{t_k}^{t_{k+1}} v_i(t)dt = \mu_{i,0} \tag{8}$$

which means $|w_i| \le V_i$. Then a local error of order $O(h^2)$ is obtained, with

$$\varepsilon \le h^2 \left((K + K')\,L'/3 + 2\,K'\,(L + L')\,\varphi(\Lambda h)\right). \tag{9}$$

If w_i are affine functions as given in (3a), we find $a_i = \mu_{i,0}$ as in (8), and

$$b_i = \tfrac{12}{h^2}\int_{t_k}^{t_{k+1}}(t - t_{k+1/2})\,v_i(t)\,dt = 3\,\mu_{i,1}.$$

Parameterising by $c_{i,0}$ and $c_{i,1}$, we find

$$w_i(t) = c_{i,0} + 3\,(1 - c_{i,0}^2/V_i^2)\,c_{i,1}\,(t - t_{k+1/2})/h;$$
$$|c_{i,0}|, |c_{i,1}| \le V_i; \quad |w_i| \le 5V_i/3 = 1.\overline{6}\,V_i. \tag{10}$$

If w_i are sinusoidal functions in the form (3b), then we find $b_i = p(\gamma)\,\mu_{i,1}$ where $p(2\gamma) = \tfrac{1}{2}\gamma/(\sin(\gamma)/\gamma - \cos(\gamma))$, and that the maximum value of $|w_i|$ is $(p(\gamma) + 1/4p(\gamma))\,V_i$. Minimising this yields $\gamma \approx 4.163152$ with $p(\gamma) \approx 1.146311$, $p(\gamma) + 1/4p(\gamma) \approx 1.364402$. Hence

$$w_i(t) = c_{i,0} + (1 - c_{i,0}^2/V_i^2)\,c_{i,1}\,\sin(4.1632(t - t_{k+1/2})/h);$$
$$|c_{i,0}|, |c_{i,1}| \le V_i; \quad |w_i| \le 1.3645\,V_i.$$

If w_i are step functions as in (3c), then $a_i = \mu_{i,0} - \mu_{i,1}$ and $b_i = \mu_{i,0} + \mu_{i,1}$. Hence,

$$w_i(t) = \begin{cases} c_{i,0} - (1 - c_{i,0}^2)c_{i,1} & \text{if } t \in [t_k, t_{k+1/2}) \\ c_{i,0} - (1 - c_{i,1}^2)c_{i,1} & \text{if } t \in [t_{k+1/2}, t_{k+1}); \end{cases} \tag{11}$$
$$|c_{i,0}|, |c_{i,1}| \le V_i; \quad |w_i| \le 5\,V_i/4 = 1.25\,V_i.$$

In all cases (3a–c) we see that $|w_i| \le r\,V_i$, where r is a constant obtained depending on the choice of functions w_i. The error bound is then given by the following formula:

$$\varepsilon\,(1 - L(h/2) - h\,r\,L') \le (h^2/4)(1 + r^2)\,L'\,K'$$
$$+ (h^3/4)\,(1 + r)\,\varphi(\Lambda h)\,K'$$
$$\quad\left((2rH' + H)\,(K + rK') + L^2 + (3rL + 2r^2L')L'\right) \tag{12}$$
$$+ (h^3/24)(1 + r)(K + K')$$
$$\quad\left(3(H\,K' + L\,L') + 4(H'K + L\,L')\right).$$

When w_i has two parameters, then we achieve an error of $O(h^2) + O(h^3)$ and pure $O(h^3)$ in the case when inputs are additive or there is only one input in the system. In particular, in the case of additive noise, $L' = 0$ so the $O(h^2)$ term vanishes.

For the cases (1) and (2), the respective bounds (6) and (9) for the final error (3) can also be used as the intermediate error bounds. However, for the second-order estimates (3a–c), the intermediate error may be larger than the final error, since the estimates crucially rely on the fact that the moments of the approximating functions w_i agree with those of v_i over the entire interval $[t_t, t_{k+1}]$, while the restrictions $w_i|_{[t_k, t]}$ for $t < t_{k+1}$ need not do so. In these cases, we <u>can</u> use the error bound (9) from case (2) since constant inputs are contained in the possible w_i. Since our formula for error accounts for a single step and we resume evolution from the resulting over-approximated set, an over-approximation of the accumulated error over multiple steps (and hence for the whole evolution time) is the sum of all the errors on each step, i.e., the over-approximation error of the solution set $S(x_0, [0, T])$ is simply $\sum_{k=1}^{N} \varepsilon_k$.

In this following, we will focus on the efficiency and accuracy of the different types of approximations that we obtained via the auxiliary system.

4　Implementation Aspects

While a fully detailed description of the implementation of this approach in ARIADNE is out of the scope of this paper, there are some aspects that are worth mentioning in order to understand the most critical parts of the implementation.

It is important to specify that ARIADNE uses a <u>Taylor function model</u> calculus and differential equation solver, whose theoretical framework has been presented in [8]. A Taylor function model is a representation of a function $f : D \to \mathbb{R}$ by an expression $f(x) = p \circ s^{-1}(x) \pm e$. Here, $D = \prod_{i=1}^{n} [a_i, b_i]$ is a coordinate-aligned box, $s : [-1, +1]^n \to D$ is a scaling function, p is a polynomial with floating-point coefficients, and e is a floating-point bound on the uniform error. A <u>vector</u> Taylor function model is a vector of such functions over a common parameter space D, able to over-approximate a generic function or set. In the following we will use "Taylor model", or just "model", to refer to the vector extension for simplicity. By using rounded arithmetic, inclusion-preserving operations on Taylor models can be implemented, including function composition and antidifferentiation.

4.1　Numerical Accuracy and Representation Complexity

According to the theoretical framework, the approximation error is reduced by decreasing the step size h. However, when an actual implementation is concerned, other numerical aspects contribute to the quality of representation of the sets and the resulting over-approximations.

In order to prevent eventual blow-up of the number of polynomial terms used in the Taylor model, small and/or high-order terms must be "swept" into the uniform error bound e. For this purpose, ARIADNE introduces a <u>sweep threshold</u> σ_{thr} constant that represents the minimum coefficient that a term needs in order to avoid being swept into e. As already discussed, an additional contribution to e is the error originating from the inputs approximation, which is added to the model for each variable. Therefore, over time, e becomes relatively large, ultimately causing the bounds of the represented set to diverge; to address this issue, we need to extract periodically a new parameter for each variable, thus originating n new independent parameters. In particular, our experience with the implementation showed that significantly more accurate results are obtained by parameter extraction at each evolution step, introducing n new parameters at each step. At the same time, each step of the proposed algorithm introduces ℓm additional parameters into the description of the flow, where ℓ is the number of parameters required for each $w_{i,k}$: $\ell = 0$ for the zero case, $\ell = 1$ for the constant case, and $\ell = 2$ for the affine, sinusoidal and piecewise constant cases. Summarizing, after k steps we end up introducing $k(n + \ell m)$ new parameters.

Therefore it is apparent that a critical requirement for the feasibility of the algorithm is to simplify periodically the representation of the reached sets. For the purposes of this paper, we rely on the following basic simplification policy: after a number of steps N_{rst} we keep a number of parameters equal to a multiple β_{rst} of the parameters introduced between two simplifications. To decide which parameters to keep after the simplification, we sum the coefficients of the terms where a parameter is present: the parameters with the lowest sum have the least impact on the set representation and their terms should be simplified into e. Increasing β_{rst} increases the <u>average</u> number of parameters during evolution, while increasing N_{rst} increases the <u>variance</u> of such number.

5   Numerical Results

In this Section we present the experimental results of our approach. First, we briefly present the benchmark suite, composed of ten systems with varying degree of nonlinearity. Then we provide insight on the impact of each approximation in our methodology as implemented in ARIADNE. Finally, comparisons are made against the tool FLOW* as well as CORA. It is important to underline that a strict comparison with ARIADNE would be fair only for FLOW*, due to its use of rigorous rounding in algebraic and geometric operations. Conversely, CORA features a numeric kernel implemented using native MATLAB primitives and as a result it is unable to control the rounding mode of operations.

The results have been collected on a macOS 10.14 laptop with an Intel Core i7-6920HQ processor, using AppleClang 10.0 as a compiler (optimization -O3) in the case of ARIADNE and FLOW* libraries and executables, or running on MATLAB 2018a in the case of CORA.

5.1   Description of the Experimental Setup

We now present ten different systems taken from the literature. In particular, two of them have been used when presenting time-varying uncertainties in FLOW*.

Table 1. List of systems tested, and summary information on the experimental setup.

Name	Alias	Ref	n	m	$\bar{O}$	+	h	T_e
Higgins-Sel'kov	HS	[7]	2	3	3	N	1/50	10
Chemical Reactor	CR	[14]	4	3	2	N	1/16	10
Lotka-Volterra	LV	[14]	2	2	2	N	1/50	10
Jet Engine	JE	[6]	2	2	2	Y	1/50	5
PI Controller	PI	[6]	2	1	2	Y	1/32	5
Jerk Eq. 21	J21	[21]	3	1	5/3	N	1/16	10
Lorenz Attractor	LA	[22]	3	1	5/3	N	1/256	1
Rössler Attractor	RA	[22]	3	1	5/3	Y	1/128	12
Jerk Eq. 16	J16	[21]	3	1	4/3	Y	1/16	10
DC-DC Converter	DC	[19]	2	2	1	N	1/10	5

Table 1 summarises the properties of these systems and part of the experimental setup used. Along with the reference to the literature, we tabulate the number of variables n and inputs m, specify whether the inputs are additive ($+ \in \{Y, N\}$), the step size h used and the evolution time T_e in seconds. Finally we supply the average polynomial order $\bar{O}$ of the system as a measure of the nonlinearity, where $\bar{O} = 1$ implies a linear behavior. Therefore the systems are presented in descending order of nonlinearity. Unfortunately for lack of space we cannot provide full details, but apart from the systems in [21] and [22], the necessary information is available in the provided references. The only deviation is in the case of CR, where we used 1/100 the noise level in [14] since none of the three tools was able to complete evolution otherwise.

In order to guarantee the fairest comparison possible, we collaborated with the authors of FLOW* and CORA to choose appropriate parameters for each system in the test suite.

As for the common configuration settings, we used the following:

- ARIADNE: $\sigma_{thr} = 10^{-8}$, $N_{rst} = 12$, $\beta_{rst} = 6$;
- FLOW*: `fixedOrder=6`, `precision=53`, `cutoff=1e-10`, `remainderEstimation=1e-1`;
- CORA: `reductionTechnique='girard'`, `taylorTerms=5` and for each example a `maxError` high enough to avoid splitting, if possible at all; even a minimum amount of splitting turned out to be detrimental to the score; a high `zonotopeOrder` (≥ 100) was chosen in most cases, which provided better set quality with little impact on the execution speed when plotting wasn't considered.

In terms of metrics for evaluating the systems, we introduce the volume score (from here on simply score) Σ_V as

$$\Sigma_V = \frac{1}{\sqrt[n]{\Pi_{i=1}^n |B_i|}} \tag{13}$$

Table 2. Score Σ_V and execution times t_x in seconds for each system and each approximation. The highest score for a given system is emphasised in bold.

	Z		C		A		S		P	
	Σ_V	t_x	Σ_V	t_x	Σ_V	t_x	Σ_V	t_x	Σ_V	t_x
HS	30.80	84	46.56	35	**48.40**	38	41.76	131	44.17	47
CR	101.2	21	214.3	14	**502.3**	21	219.6	146	428.9	23
LV	5.265	219	10.89	89	**14.53**	60	12.83	169	13.53	76
JE	**15.47**	25	13.72	26	14.43	26	14.37	54	14.56	28
PI	2.604	11	4.469	7.3	**5.399**	8.1	5.391	15	5.398	12
J21	15.08	31	19.37	17	23.10	13	22.90	20	**23.23**	15
LA	3.983	41	6.187	23	8.979	14	8.992	19	**9.045**	18
RA	71.70	46	107.2	28	114.2	25	109.8	34	**120.0**	36
J16	12.00	14	19.49	6.5	23.78	5.3	**23.784**	6.2	23.27	7.7
DC	0.907	2.7	1.888	5.4	**1.906**	5.9	1.902	13	1.906	11

where B is the bounding box of a set. The formula over-approximates a set into a box for simplicity, evaluates its volume and normalises on the number of variables. In particular, halving the set on each dimension yields twice the score. Without extra notation, we evaluate Σ_V on the final set of evolution to measure the quality of the whole trace. It must be noted that since a bounding box returns an over-approximation, this measure is not entirely reliable: for two different sets with equal exact bounds, it may return a slightly larger box for the set with the more complex representation. Still, it is an intuitive and affordable measure that can be used across tools with different internal representations.

Given the large number of systems in the suite, and due to the limited space, we chose to present the results in tabular form only instead of providing any graphical comparison. Finally, all the score and execution time values in the following are rounded to the nearest least significant digit.

5.2 Evaluation of Input Approximations Using Ariadne

As a first step, we are interested in the impact of using each approximation. In the following, we will use the letters Z, C, A, S and P to refer to the zero, costant, affine, sinusoidal and piecewise constant approximations.

Table 2 shows the results for each system and each approximation, where the best approximation (i.e., the one with the highest Σ_V) is emphasised in bold. We see that 2-parameter approximations are not always better than C or Z: this is due to the impact of the more complex set representations required by using a higher-order approximation. In particular S in some cases suffers from representing sinusoidal functions accurately. In addition, our experiments showed that the accuracy parameters have a major impact on the best static approximation.

Table 3. Score Σ_V and execution time t_x in seconds for each system and different setups: (1) pick the best from Table 2; (2) dynamically evaluate each approximation at each step and select the best one; (3) dynamically evaluate each approximation with a frequency proportional to its quality. a% represents the % of approximations chosen dynamically. The highest score for a given system is emphasised in bold.

	Best static		Tight dynamic			Loose dynamic		
	Σ_V	t_x	Σ_V	t_x	a%	Σ_V	t_x	a%
HS	48.40	38	**49.49**	243	A88P12	48.91	39	A94P6
CR	502.3	21	**504.5**	191	A91P9	502.4	26	A91P9
LV	14.53	60	**14.54**	381	A93P7	14.54	62	A94P6
JE	**15.47**	25	14.38	160	Z79P21	**15.47**	27	Z100
PI	**5.399**	8.1	5.391	47	A2S82P16	5.391	17	S78P21
J21	23.23	15	**23.73**	64	C1A86P13	23.10	14	A100
LA	9.045	18	**9.080**	72	A58S6P36	9.070	18	A46S4P50
RA	**120.0**	36	117.7	138	A96P4	113.8	27	A99P1
J16	**23.78**	6.2	23.77	29	A96P4	23.77	6.1	A96P4
DC	1.906	5.9	**1.906**	35	A71P29	1.906	7.7	A88P12

Given these considerations, we are interested in dynamically identifying the best approximation on a given time step, i.e., the approximation that yields the highest Σ_V (equivalently, the lowest volume of the bounding box of the evolved set) after a single time step. The first approach would be to check each approximation at each step, which we call here <u>tight dynamic</u> evaluation of the approximations. Table 3 compares this approach with the best <u>static</u> score extracted from Table 2. Here a% represents the percentage of specific approximations chosen along evolution, e.g., A88P12 means that 88% of the time steps A yielded the smallest volume, while P was the best approximation 12% of the time steps. We see that a dynamic choice is able to give a small edge over a static one, with the cost of a significantly higher computation time (though still below the sum of the times required for each approximation). Please note that, since Σ_V is an inexact measure, dynamically choosing the approximation may return an a% inconsistent with the best static result. This is quite apparent in the case of J16, for which Table 2 suggests that the sinusoidal approximation should be chosen, while a dynamic choice yields the affine approximation instead: here an initial choice of the affine approximation influences the evolved set and makes the affine approximation preferable for the remaining steps in respect with the sinusoidal one. Finally, we can improve on the performance by using a <u>loose dynamic</u> evaluation of the approximations, in which each approximation is evaluated periodically after N_{ev} steps; N_{ev} is reset to 1 if the approximation is identified as the best one, and doubled otherwise. Table 3 shows how the impact on Σ_V is minimal with respect to a tight dynamic evaluation, while the execution time is drastically reduced. Compared to the best static choice, we obtain similar results with the added advantage of abstracting the selection of the approximation. For this reason, the comparison of the next Subsection will be based on a loose dynamic evaluation of the approximations.

5.3 Comparison with Other Tools

In this Subsection we compare our results with those from CORA and FLOW*. However, since CORA performs approximate rounding, its numerical results can't be rigorous even if using interval arithmetics. For this reason, in the following Tables the actual comparison is between ARIADNEand FLOW*, while CORA is used as a reference.

Table 4. Comparison with CORA and FLOW* for different noise levels. For each approach and each system, the score Σ_V is shown. Since the execution time t_x is the same for FLOW* regardless of the noise level, it is shown only for the nominal noise. The highest score between ARIADNE and FLOW* for each system and each noise level is emphasised in bold. When CORA produces the best result, it is underlined for reference.

Setup			System									
Noise	Tool		HS	CR	LV	JE	PI	J21	LA	RA	J16	DC
×¼	ARIADNE	Σ_V	**109.1**	**1573**	**69.31**	**29.21**	**12.82**	**36.31**	**33.48**	**385.6**	**58.56**	4.877
		t_x	22	13	12	13	7.1	6.8	9.5	18	3.6	3.9
	CORA	Σ_V	16.92	<u>2539</u>	14.39	18.40	11.53	7.459	11.08	264.0	51.47	<u>7.605</u>
		t_x	4.0	1.0	2.5	3.8	2.5	3.3	4.0	2.7	3.7	0.26
	FLOW*	Σ_V	71.78	762.1	2.242	23.18	11.10	15.75	17.14	263.5	52.96	**7.559**
×½	ARIADNE	Σ_V	**76.77**	**943.3**	**32.70**	**21.85**	**8.849**	**30.47**	**17.64**	**221.5**	**39.67**	**3.816**
		t_x	27	19	26	19	7.5	9.2	11	20	4.3	5.4
	CORA	Σ_V	13.62	<u>1632</u>	5.970	15.55	8.420	6.803	8.983	177.3	38.30	<u>3.827</u>
		t_x	3.9	1.0	2.6	3.8	2.3	6.5	4.1	4.0	3.5	0.26
	FLOW*	Σ_V	56.97	384.5	N/A	19.01	7.994	14.28	12.33	174.6	39.11	3.804
×1	ARIADNE	Σ_V	**48.91**	**502.4**	**14.54**	**15.47**	**5.492**	**23.10**	**9.070**	**113.8**	23.77	**1.906**
		t_x	39	26	62	28	8.8	14	18	27	6.1	7.7
	CORA	Σ_V	8.162	<u>930.2</u>	1.680	11.81	5.472	5.710	6.543	110.4	25.20	<u>1.915</u>
		t_x	3.9	1.0	3.5	3.7	2.5	6.2	4.1	4.0	3.3	0.26
	FLOW*	Σ_V	37.78	169.9	N/A	13.87	5.107	11.99	8.113	107.5	**25.49**	1.902
		t_x	29	19	13	7.4	3.7	19	12	81	2.5	0.24
×2	ARIADNE	Σ_V	**23.36**	**217.6**	**5.947**	**9.368**	**3.085**	**15.41**	4.574	58.85	13.11	**0.944**
		t_x	107	53	206	50	10	27	35	48	10	15
	CORA	Σ_V	0.675	<u>433.9</u>	0.807	7.862	<u>3.218</u>	4.235	3.911	<u>63.67</u>	14.76	<u>0.952</u>
		t_x	4.0	1.0	127	3.6	2.3	6.2	4.1	4.0	3.3	0.26
	FLOW*	Σ_V	17.49	50.50	N/A	8.828	2.931	8.948	**4.857**	**61.42**	**14.76**	**0.944**
×4	ARIADNE	Σ_V	**11.49**	**60.87**	**1.165**	**4.953**	**1.664**	**8.807**	2.255	29.12	6.570	0.464
		t_x	296	223	5032	185	15	73	71	80	22	23
	CORA	Σ_V	N/A	<u>146.0</u>	N/A	4.517	<u>1.763</u>	1.704	2.450	<u>33.50</u>	7.825	0.465
		t_x	N/A	1.0	N/A	3.6	2.2	6.1	4.0	4.0	3.4	0.75
	FLOW*	Σ_V	N/A	N/A	N/A	4.827	1.577	5.599	**2.670**	**32.23**	**8.322**	**0.465**

Table 5. Comparison with CORA and Flow* for different noise levels, while equalising the execution time t_x with respect to Ariadne. For each approach and each system, the score Σ_V is shown. The highest score between Ariadne and Flow* for each system and each noise level is emphasised in bold. When CORA produces the best result, it is underlined for reference.

Setup		System									
Noise	Tool		HS	CR	LV	JE	PI	J21	LA	RA	J16	DC
$\times\frac{1}{4}$	Ariadne	Σ_V	**109.1**	**1573**	**69.31**	**29.21**	12.82	**36.31**	**33.48**	**385.6**	**58.56**	4.877
		t_x	22	13	12	13	7.1	6.8	9.5	18	3.6	3.9
	CORA	Σ_V	49.42	4656	N/A	27.20	13.00	8.753	12.23	464.8	51.47	7.655
		ρ_h	4.6	3.9	N/A	3.5	3.3	1.1	1.1	4.6	1.0	16.9
	Flow*	Σ_V	64.92	643.3	2.161	26.55	11.10	N/A	14.26	133.5	56.25	**7.725**
		ρ_h	0.8	0.7	0.9	1.7	3.7	N/A	0.8	0.4	1.3	9.5
$\times\frac{1}{2}$	Ariadne	Σ_V	**76.77**	**943.3**	**32.70**	21.85	**8.849**	**30.47**	**17.64**	**221.5**	39.67	3.816
		t_x	27	19	26	19	7.5	9.2	11	20	4.3	5.4
	CORA	Σ_V	43.53	2684	N/A	22.84	9.360	12.96	11.82	270.6	40.70	3.820
		ρ_h	3.0	4.8	N/A	5.3	3.5	1.6	1.4	4.8	1.4	25.0
	Flow*	Σ_V	54.76	384.5	N/A	**22.65**	7.994	N/A	11.56	94.44	**42.42**	**3.860**
		ρ_h	0.9	1.0	N/A	7.4	3.7	N/A	0.9	0.4	1.6	12.1
$\times 1$	Ariadne	Σ_V	**48.91**	**502.4**	**14.54**	15.47	5.492	**23.10**	9.070	**113.8**	23.77	1.906
		t_x	39	26	62	28	8.8	14	18	27	6.1	7.7
	CORA	Σ_V	33.15	1364	N/A	16.50	6.000	16.73	9.900	153.8	27.62	1.902
		ρ_h	3.5	5.7	N/A	8.0	3.8	2.8	2.3	6.6	2.2	35.0
	Flow*	Σ_V	40.50	185.5	N/A	**16.49**	**5.690**	8.974	**9.416**	73.96	**27.90**	**1.924**
		ρ_h	1.3	1.3	N/A	3.5	2.3	0.7	1.5	0.5	2.1	14.6
$\times 2$	Ariadne	Σ_V	**23.36**	**217.6**	**5.947**	9.368	3.085	**15.41**	4.574	**58.85**	13.11	0.944
		t_x	107	53	206	50	10	27	35	48	10	15
	CORA	Σ_V	20.07	612.4	N/A	10.33	3.507	15.24	6.284	79.61	15.85	0.944
		ρ_h	5.8	8.1	N/A	14.0	4.8	5.3	4.5	11.5	3.5	70.0
	Flow*	Σ_V	21.13	69.44	N/A	**10.34**	**3.316**	10.95	**6.045**	53.06	**16.18**	**0.955**
		ρ_h	3.3	2.4	N/A	5.5	2.5	1.4	2.6	0.7	3.0	23.3
$\times 4$	Ariadne	Σ_V	**11.49**	**60.87**	**1.165**	4.953	1.664	8.807	2.255	29.12	6.570	0.464
		t_x	296	223	5032	185	15	73	71	80	22	23
	CORA	Σ_V	1.086	214.1	N/A	5.537	1.909	9.864	3.201	37.97	6.772	0.465
		ρ_h	1.1	17.0	N/A	52.0	7.3	14.6	9.0	18.1	7.5	55.0
	Flow*	Σ_V	1.725	N/A	N/A	**6.421**	**1.836**	**9.133**	**3.286**	**32.23**	**8.452**	**0.471**
		ρ_h	7.3	N/A	N/A	14.5	3.5	3.7	4.4	1.0	5.0	30.3

In Table 4 we evaluate the quality of our approach with respect to Flow* and CORA while varying the noise level and using a fixed step size. The rationale here is that as the level increases, the impact of a more accurate input approximation increases. Systems here are in decreasing order of nonlinearity from left to right. For mostly-linear systems CORA has the best results due to its kernel relying on linearisation of the dynamics; Flow* has similar benefits due to specific optimisations on low-order polynomial representations. On the other hand, it is apparent that Flow* and CORA suffer when the nonlinearity is high, to the point of being unable to complete evolution. An N/A result in FLOW* is due to failing convergence of the flow set over-approximation, while for CORA this is specifically due to a diverging number of split sets required to bound the flow set. Since ARIADNE maintains a larger number of parameters when handling higher noise values, the computation time increases with the noise, whereas FLOW* and CORA feature the same time (shown in Table 4 only for the nominal noise). Summarising, in this setup ARIADNE consistently gives better bounds for systems with medium and high nonlinearity, with comparable computation times with respect to FLOW* for low noise levels, while also avoiding failure for high noise levels.

Table 5 instead compares the three tools by equalising the execution time. This is achieved by using a different step size for FLOW* and CORA in order to obtain roughly the same execution time as ARIADNE's. We express the ratio between the step size and the nominal step size with ρ_h, where $\rho_h > 0$. This approach implicitly abstracts the choice of the step size, which should be treated as a numerical setting rather than part of the system specification. Here we see that the speed advantage of FLOW* on high noise levels can be actually exploited to obtain better results: here we can use $\rho_h > 1$ and obtain the best Σ_V for low/medium nonlinearity in the dynamics. However, even a smaller step size is not sufficient for highly nonlinear systems, which still results in a failure in convergence. For the LV example CORA had significant issues due to splitting if the step size is reduced. Consequently, it was not actually possible to equalise the execution time. On the contrary, for some systems with low noise, a $\rho_h < 1$ is required for equalisation, which further reduces the score in respect to ARIADNE. It should be underlined that a significantly high ρ_h is not without any impact: the resulting larger amount of reachable sets may have a non-negligible cost for operations such as set drawing, (bounded) model checking or convergence for infinite time reachability.

6   Conclusions and Future Work

The work presented in this paper illustrates the importance of higher-order methods (initially presented in [23] and extended here) as more accuracy was achieved with two-parameter approximations on nine out of ten systems considered. Moreover, we found that ARIADNE yields tighter set bounds, as the non-linearity increases, compared with the state-of-the-art tool FLOW* and CORA. Although no analysis of the order of the method is given in [6], we believe that FLOW* has a local error $O(h^2)$, so the global error is intrinsically first-order. Hence a higher quality is to be expected from ARIADNE, since the proposed methodology is able to achieve third-order local errors. On the other hand, our approach introduces extra parameters at each step in the representation of the evolved set, causing a growth in complexity, whereas FLOW* and CORA have a fixed complexity. As a result, the computational cost increases with both the noise level and the total number of steps taken. A comparison with the state-of-the-art using a common time budget indeed suggests that ARIADNE currently provides better bounds for highly nonlinear systems. Consequently, improving ARIADNE's methods for simplifying the description of sets represents a strategic area of ongoing research in order to fully exploit the advantage of the proposed approach.

Currently, we are working towards component-wise derivations of the local error, to better address systems whose variables have scalings of different orders of magnitude. Some extensions on DIs that we plan to implement are outlined in [12]. These include constraint-set representation of uncertainties, including representation via affine and more general convex constraints. Further, we will extend the methodology to nonlinearity in the inputs, in order to maximise the expressiveness in terms of system dynamics.

Acknowledgments. This work was partially supported by MIUR, Project "Italian Outstanding Departments, 2018-2022" and by INDAM, GNCS 2019, "Formal Methods for Mixed Verification Techniques".

The authors would like to thank Xin Chen and Matthias Althoff for the support on setting up their respective softwares and building the examples for the comparison.

References

1. Althoff, M., Grebenyuk, D., Kochdumper, N.: Implementation of Taylor models in CORA 2018. In: Proceedings of the 5th International Workshop on Applied Verification for Continuous and Hybrid Systems, pp. 145–173 (2018)
2. Althoff, M., Guernic, C.L., Krogh, B.H.: Reachable set computation for uncertain time-varying linear systems. In: Hybrid Systems: Computation and Control, pp. 93–102 (2011)
3. Ariadne: an open library for formal verification of cyber-physical systems. http://www.ariadne-cps.org
4. Aubin, J., Cellina, A.: Differential Inclusions. Fundamental Principles of Mathematical Sciences, vol. 264. Springer, Heidelberg (2002)
5. Baier, R., Gerdts, M.: A computational method for non-convex reachable sets using optimal control. In: Proceedings of the European Control Conference 2009, pp. 97–102. IEEE, Budapest (2009). http://ieeexplore.ieee.org/document/7074386/
6. Chen, X.: Reachability analysis of non-linear hybrid systems using Taylor models. Ph.D. thesis, Aachen University (2015)
7. Chen, X., Sankaranarayanan, S.: Decomposed reachability analysis for nonlinear systems. In: 2016 IEEE Real-Time Systems Symposium (RTSS), pp. 13–24, November 2016
8. Collins, P., Bresolin, D., Geretti, L., Villa, T.: Computing the evolution of hybrid systems using rigorous function calculus. In: Proceedings of the 4th IFAC Conference on Analysis and Design of Hybrid Systems (ADHS12), Eindhoven, The Netherlands, pp. 284–290, June 2012
9. Dellnitz, M., Klus, S., Ziessler, A.: A set-oriented numerical approach for dynamical systems with parameter uncertainty. SIAM J. Appl. Dyn. Syst. **16**(1), 120–138 (2017)
10. Filippov, A.F.: Differential Equations with Discontinuous Righthand Sides. Mathematics and its Applications, vol. 18. Kluwer Academic, Dordrecht (1988)

11. Fortuna, L., Nunnari, G., Gallo, A.: Model Order Reduction Techniques with Applications in Electrical Engineering. Springer, London (1992). https://doi.org/10.1007/978-1-4471-3198-4

12. Geretti, L., Bresolin, D., Collins, P., Gonzalez, S.Z., Villa, T.: Ongoing work on automated verification of noisy nonlinear systems with ARIADNE. In: Yevtushenko, N., Cavalli, A.R., Yenigün, H. (eds.) ICTSS 2017. LNCS, vol. 10533, pp. 313–319. Springer, Cham (2017). https://doi.org/10.1007/978-3-319-67549-7_19

13. Han, Z., Cai, X., Huang, J.: Theory of Control Systems Described by Differential Inclusions. Springer Tracts in Mechanical Engineering. Springer, Heidelberg (2016). https://doi.org/10.1007/978-3-662-49245-1

14. Harwood, S.M., Barton, P.I.: Efficient polyhedral enclosures for the reachable set of nonlinear control systems. Math. Control Signals Syst. **28**(8) (2016). https://doi.org/10.1007/s00498-015-0153-2

15. Kurzhanski, A., Valyi, I.: Ellipsoidal Calculus for Estimation and Control. Systems and Control: Foundations and Applications. Birkhäuser, Basel (1997)

16. Lin, Y., Stadtherr, M.A.: Validated solutions of initial value problems for parametric odes. Appl. Numer. Math. **57**(10), 1145–1162 (2007)

17. Ramdani, N., Meslem, N., Candau, Y.: A hybrid bounding method for computing an over-approximation for the reachable set of uncertain nonlinear systems. IEEE Trans. Autom. Control **54**(10), 2352–2364 (2009). https://doi.org/10.1109/TAC.2009.2028974

18. Rungger, M., Reissig, G.: Arbitrarily precise abstractions for optimal controller synthesis. In: 2017 IEEE 56th Annual Conference on Decision and Control (CDC), pp. 1761–1768, December 2017

19. Rungger, M., Zamani, M.: Accurate reachability analysis of uncertain nonlinear systems. In: Proceedings of the 21st International Conference on Hybrid Systems: Computation and Control (Part of CPS Week), HSCC 2018, Porto, Portugal, 11–13 April 2018, pp. 61–70 (2018). https://doi.org/10.1145/3178126.3178127

20. Smirnov, G.V.: Introduction to the Theory of Differential Inclusions. Graduate Studies in Mathematics, vol. 41. American Mathematical Society, Providence (2002)

21. Sprott, J.C.: Some simple chaotic jerk functions. Am. J. Phys. **65**(6), 537–543 (1997)

22. Strogatz, S.H.: Nonlinear Dynamics and Chaos. Studies in Nonlinearity, 2nd edn. CRC Press, Boca Raton (2014)

23. Zivanovic, S., Collins, P.: Numerical solutions to noisy systems. In: IEEE Conference on Decision and Control (CDC), pp. 798–803, December 2010. https://doi.org/10.1109/CDC.2010.5717780

Stochastic Local Search for Solving
Floating-Point Constraints

Shaobo He$^{(\boxtimes)}$, Marek Baranowski, and Zvonimir Rakamarić

School of Computing, University of Utah, Salt Lake City, USA
{shaobo,baranows,zvonimir}@cs.utah.edu

Abstract. We present OL1V3R, a solver for the SMT floating-point theory that is based on stochastic local search (SLS). We adapt for OL1V3R
the key ingredients of related work on leveraging SLS to solve the SMT
fixed-sized bit-vector theory, and confirm its effectiveness by comparing
it with mature solvers. Finally, we discuss the limitations of OL1V3R
and propose solutions to make it more powerful.

1 Introduction

Numeric computations realized by floating-point arithmetic have become ubiquitous. For example, machine learning applications, often implemented in floating-
point arithmetic, are used everywhere. However, unlike its exact real arithmetic
counterpart, floating-point arithmetic exhibits unintuitive properties that com-
plicate developers' reasoning about programs. For example, rounding of floating-
point arithmetic breaks properties that would otherwise hold for exact real arithmetic (e.g., associativity), resulting in unexpected bugs.

Software verifiers based on *satisfiability modulo theories* (SMT) solvers have
been successfully used to help developers (semi-)automatically check correctness
of programs. However, the current successful use cases are limited to integer
programs. The SMT floating-point theory (QF_FP) [2,14] is relatively new compared to the theories used to model integer programs. Moreover, state-of-the-art
decision procedures for QF_FP are based on bit-blasting, which converts SMT
formulas into Boolean circuits solved using highly-efficient SAT solvers. While
bit-blasting can often effectively solve even large formulas in the theory of bit-
vectors (QF_BV), it typically scales poorly in the presence of more complicated
operations such as multiplication. Moreover, Boolean circuits derived from bit-
blasting the QF_FP operations are typically much larger than those produced
for the QF_BV ones, which makes bit-blasting for QF_FP even more brittle.

As a result, search-based incomplete solvers, such as XSat [6], goSAT [9], and
JFS [10,11], emerged as solutions for the scalability issues of bit-blasting. The
basic idea of such solvers is to cast the problem of solving QF_FP constraints
to an optimization problem, which is then solved using off-the-shelf optimizers.

Supported in part by the National Science Foundation (NSF) awards CCF 1552975
and CCF 1704715.

M. Zamani and D. Zufferey (Eds.): NSV 2019, LNCS 11652, pp. 76–84, 2019.
https://doi.org/10.1007/978-3-030-28423-7_5

Such solvers, although demonstrating large speed-ups on certain benchmarks over using bit-blasting, suffer from stability and scalability issues due to relying on external optimization engines not tailored for the particular types of optimization problems they generate. For example, XSat often returns incorrect answers on SMT-LIB [16] benchmarks [11]. Moreover, to the best of our knowledge, none of the existing search-based solvers support arbitrary precision floating-point numbers as allowed by the theory specification.

In this paper, we present our attempt to build a stable search-based QF_FP solver. Our solver, OL1V3R,[1] is based on stochastic local search (SLS) [8], which was previously implemented in the qfbv-sls tactic of Z3 [4] to solve QF_BV constraints [5]. OL1V3R supports common operations specified in the QF_FP theory, including custom-sized floating-points.[2] We evaluate it on a set of SMT-LIB benchmarks and our preliminary results are encouraging: despite using software-emulated arithmetic, OL1V3R achieves performance comparable to mature SMT solvers such as Z3 and MathSAT [3]. Finally, we discuss the lessons we learned and propose directions for improvements.

2 Approach

2.1 Input Grammar

The SMT floating-point theory [2,14] mimics the IEEE standard 754-2008 and also defines conversions between the floating-point and other sorts such as reals. Similar to the qfbv-sls tactic of Z3, we first convert an input formula into its negation normal form with the following grammar:

$$\langle formula \rangle := (\wedge \langle lexpr \rangle^*)$$
$$\langle lexpr \rangle := (\wedge \langle lexpr \rangle^*) \mid (\vee \langle lexpr \rangle^*) \mid \langle atom \rangle \mid \neg \langle atom \rangle$$
$$\langle atom \rangle := \top \mid \bot \mid \langle id \rangle \mid (\langle pred \rangle \langle nlexpr \rangle^*)$$

Here, an atom is either a logical constant, Boolean literal, or predicate over non-logical expressions. Unlike qfbv-sls, we do not reduce predicates into a minimal set, such as by desugaring $x \leq y$ into $x < y \vee x = y$, because reductions like this are not trivial for floating-point predicates due to the existence of NaNs.

2.2 Search Algorithm

We use a simple search algorithm in Fig. 1 to iteratively search for an assignment to variables α that maximizes an objective function which we call the score function. The algorithm takes as input a formula F that follows the grammar we introduced in the previous section. During the initialization (function *initialize*),

---

[1] We made OL1V3R publicly available at https://github.com/soarlab/OL1V3R.
[2] The floating-point formats supported by OL1V3R depend on the capabilities of the underlying "bigfloat" library it employs to evaluate floating-point arithmetic.

```
function SOLVE(F)                          function SELECTMOVE(F, A, α)
    α ← initialize()                           V ← getVars(A)
    i ← 1                                      if uniform(0, 1) ≤ p then
    for i ≤ maxStep do                             return randomWalk(V, α)
        if satisfies(F, α) then return sat     else
        else                                       α' ← getBestMove(F, V, α)
            A ← selectAssertion(F, α)              if score(F, α') ≤ score(F, α) then
            α ← selectMove(F, A, α)                    return random(α)
        end if                                     else
        i ← i + 1                                      return α'
    end for                                        end if
    return unknown                             end if
end function                                end function
```

Fig. 1. Pseudocode of the OL1V3R's algorithm. Function SOLVE performs top-level search, whereas SELECTMOVE invokes the core components (score computation, neighbor selection, randomization). Constants $maxStep$ and p are input parameters of the algorithm.

we assign $+zero$ to each floating-point variable and $true$ to each Boolean variable. When the number of search steps exceeds a preset limit $maxStep$, our algorithm returns $unknown$ and terminates. If the algorithm finds an assignment that satisfies a formula (function $satisfies$), it returns sat. (We describe how we implement $satisfies$ in Sect. 3.) Otherwise, a move (i.e., a mutation to the current assignment) is selected to continue the search. We adopt the heuristic from the qfbv-sls tactic that chooses the candidate variables to mutate from the assertion that is not satisfied and has the highest score (function $selectAssertion$). The selected assertion is passed into function $selectMove$ that generates the next assignment.

In $selectMove$, we first attempt to perform a *random walk* with a probability p (defaults to 0.001), where a neighbor is randomly chosen (function $randomWalk$). Then, the neighbor of the variables reachable from the assertion (function $getVars$) that improves the score of the formula the most (function $getBestMove$) is chosen to continue the search. If there does not exist an improving neighbor, a randomized assignment is used for the next step. This algorithm is akin to the more sophisticated one proposed in Fröhlich et al. [5], and we discuss the potentially useful advanced heuristics in Sect. 4. Our approach is sound (provided the semantics of the SMT floating-point theory are correctly modeled), whereas it is incomplete since it cannot prove that a formula is unsatisfiable. In the rest of this section, we describe the key components of our algorithm.

Score Computation. Score function drives the search, and in Fig. 2 we define it recursively for logical expressions. The score of a satisfying logical expression is 1, which is the maximum score, and otherwise it is in the range $[0, 1)$. Currently, we treat unary predicates, such as $fp.isNaN$, as Boolean variables. Although some of these predicates (e.g., $fp.isInfinite$) describe qualities of floating-point

$$s(\wedge e_1 \ldots e_n, \alpha) = \frac{1}{n} \sum_{i=1}^{n} s(e_i, \alpha)$$

$$s(\vee e_1 \ldots e_n, \alpha) = max(s(e_1, \alpha) \ldots s(e_n, \alpha))$$

$$s(\textit{fp.lt } e_1 \; e_2, \alpha) = \begin{cases} 1 & \textit{fp.lt } e_1|_\alpha \; e_2|_\alpha \\ 0 & e_1|_\alpha = \text{NaN} \vee e_2|_\alpha = \text{NaN} \\ c(1 - \frac{|fpPos(e_1|_\alpha) - fpPos(e_2|_\alpha)|+1}{2^n}) & \text{otherwise} \end{cases}$$

$$s(\neg(\textit{fp.lt } e_1 \; e_2), \alpha) = \begin{cases} 1 & \neg(\textit{fp.lt } e_1|_\alpha \; e_2|_\alpha) \\ c(1 - \frac{|fpPos(e_1|_\alpha) - fpPos(e_2|_\alpha)|}{2^n}) & \text{otherwise} \end{cases}$$

$$s(atom, \alpha) = \begin{cases} 1 & atom|_\alpha \\ 0 & \text{otherwise} \end{cases}$$

$$s(\neg atom, \alpha) = 1 - s(atom, \alpha)$$

Fig. 2. Definition of the score function s. Here, $e|_\alpha$ evaluates an expression e using an assignment α, and $c \in (0,1)$ is a parameter that scales the score of an assignment that is not satisfying (defaults to 0.5). In the last two equations, $atom$ refers only to Boolean variables and unary predicates, and not relational operators such as $fp.eq$, $fp.lt$, and $fp.gt$. For relational operators, we only show the floating-point less-than predicate and its negation; the score for other predicates is computed similarly.

numbers and thus should have designated score function definitions, we leave those for future work.

The qfbv-sls tactic defines the score function of a relational operator $b_1 \bowtie b_2$ using the distance between two integers $bv2nat(b_1)$ and $bv2nat(b_2)$, where $bv2nat$ maps a bit-vector to its unsigned integer value. Similarly, we define our score function of a floating-point relational operator $x_1 \bowtie x_2$ using the distance between two integers $fpPos(x_1)$ and $fpPos(x_2)$, where $fpPos$ is defined as follows:

$$fpPos(x) = \begin{cases} bv2nat(fp2bv(x)) & fp.isPositive(x) \\ 2^{bw-1} - bv2nat(fp2bv(x)) & fp.isNegative(x) \end{cases}$$

Here, function $fp2bv$ converts a non-NaN floating-point number x to its bit representation, and bw is the bit-width of x. For example, $fpPos(+zero) = 0$ and $fpPos(-zero) = 0$. Also, $fpPos$ maps the maximum negative floating-point number to -1. The predicate $x < 0.0$ has higher score when $x = 0.5$ as opposed to $x = 1.0$ since $fpPos(0.5)$ is less than $fpPos(1.0)$. Note that function $fpPos$ is not defined for NaNs, and the score rules in Fig. 2 ensure that a NaN cannot be passed as an argument to it.

Our score definition of equality is different from the qfbv-sls tactic and Niemetz et al. [13], which rely on the Hamming distance between two bit-vectors. In the case of floating-points, using the Hamming distance typically leads to worse performance than using our definition based on floating-point number *positions* as captured by $fpPos$. This is expected because floating-point numbers by definition represent numerical values, whereas bit-vectors are not necessarily interpreted as integers.

Neighborhood Relation. The neighborhood relation, which is used in functions *randomWalk* and *getBestMove* in Fig. 1, maps a candidate assignment into the set of its neighbors. The neighbors of an assignment with respect to a set of variables are the union of all the neighbors of each variable. The core neighbors of a floating-point number x that has a unique bit representation are all floating-point numbers that differ from x by exactly one bit in their bit representations, i.e., they are obtained by flipping a bit in $fp2bv(x)$. For NaN, we assign a randomly generated floating-point number as its neighbor. In addition to the core bit-flipping neighbors, we also include floating-points obtained by adding ± 1 *unit in the last place* into the neighborhood relation.

Randomization. We empirically observed that prioritizing special floating-point numbers, such as $\pm$infinity, during the search exhibits better performance. Hence, the randomization of floating-point values used in OL1V3R (function *random* in Fig. 1) generates special numbers with high probability (default of 0.8), and otherwise it selects a floating-point number uniformly from the set of floating-point numbers.

3   Implementation and Experiments

We implemented OL1V3R in Racket. We use its *math/bigfloat* [17] module to evaluate floating-point expressions (function *satisfies* in Fig. 1), which supports any significant bit-width greater than 2, but only a fixed-size 31-bit exponent. Hence, our implementation checks for overflows and underflows of all floating-point operations with exponent bit-widths less than 31, and handles them as special cases to ensure the soundness of the evaluation. The bigfloat module binds to the GNU MPFR library [12], which emulates arbitrary precision floating-point arithmetic in software. This means that performing arithmetic operations over bigfloats is much slower than over common floating-point types with hardware support. Moreover, we compute the score of a logical expression (once we evaluate its floating-point sub-expressions) using rationals, which gives us precise scores but also causes a slowdown. We discuss potential improvements of these design choices in Sect. 4.

The benchmarks we use for evaluation are a subset of the non-incremental SMT-LIB QF_FP benchmarks [15] obtained as follows. First, we exclude benchmarks in folder *wintersteiger* as they are mostly trivial regressions used to test correctness rather than performance. Then, we run MathSAT and Z3 on the leftover benchmarks using a 15 min time limit, and select only those on which neither tool reports unsat. Finally, all selected benchmarks are preprocessed using the *jfs-opt* tool shipped with JFS because OL1V3R only partially supports the SMT-LIB2 syntax. Our benchmark selection strategy allows us to focus the evaluation on benchmarks that are either satisfiable or possible to be satisfiable since OL1V3R, like other search-based solvers, can only provide sound results for satisfiable formulas. For unsatisfiable formulas, OL1V3R keeps searching for a solution until it hits the time limit, which is also the behavior of JFS.

We evaluate OL1V3R by comparing it with two state-of-the-art SMT solvers, MathSAT [3] (version 5.5.4) and Z3 [4] (version 4.8.4), as well as one search-based solver that uses coverage-guided fuzzing, JFS [10] (commit 2322167). We exclude XSat [6] and goSAT [9] because previous evaluations show that their performance is inferior to JFS [11]. We leverage *benchexec* [1] to obtain repro-ducible and rigorous benchmarking. The time and memory limits are 900 s and 4 GB, respectively; we allocate one CPU core per benchmark. We run the experi-ments on a d820 node of the Utah Emulab [18] cluster with 4 Intel Xeon E5-4620 CPUs and 128 GB DDR3 RAM running Ubuntu 16.04.

Table 1 shows the results of running each tool on the selected benchmarks. We do not observe any inconsistencies between the results returned by the solvers. (MathSAT reports unsat for one benchmark on which it previously timed out because the preprocessing step tends to improve its performance.) In terms of benchmarks solved, MathSAT demonstrates the best performance and Z3 the worst, while JFS and OL1V3R are comparable. In terms of runtimes, OL1V3R is comparable to MathSAT, and also typically better than Z3 and slower than

Table 1. Comparison between OL1V3R and other solvers. Columns **Sat** and **Unsat** show the numbers of benchmarks where a tool returns sat and unsat, respectively. Column **Unknown** shows the number of benchmarks where a tool fails to provide any results due to out-of-memory or crashes. Column **Timeout** shows the number of benchmarks that time out. Column **Other** shows the number of benchmarks where a tool returns sat while OL1V3R times out; column **OL1V3R** shows the opposite.

Tool	Sat	Unsat	Unknown	Timeout	Other	OL1V3R
OL1V3R	113	0	2	82	–	–
MathSAT	125	1	7	64	15	5
Z3	88	0	10	99	3	30
JFS	113	0	0	84	5	7

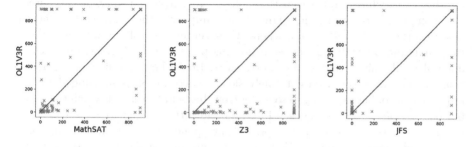

Fig. 3. Comparison of the runtimes of OL1V3R with other solvers.

JFS, as shown by the scatter plots in Fig. 3. However, the runtimes of JFS have an extreme distribution: it either solves a benchmark quickly or times out. Most benchmarks that JFS solves OL1V3R also solves within a reasonable amount of time (around 3 min).

A deeper analysis reveals that both JFS and OL1V3R perform better on benchmarks that contain complex arithmetic such as division and square root. This observation coincides with the JFS' authors' observation that JFS can be complementary to Z3 or MathSAT [11]. Moreover, OL1V3R demonstrates better performance on small benchmarks that permit few models. We believe this can be attributed to the OL1V3R's distance-sensitive score functions. Finally, OL1V3R emulates floating-point arithmetic in software during the evaluation of floating-point expressions in the score computation. On the other hand, JFS evaluates floating-point computations using the underlying hardware. Hence, we expect the performance gap to be easily reduced if we also leverage the floating-point processing hardware (see Sect. 4).

4   Limitations and Proposed Solutions

Evaluation of the score functions can be more efficient. For example, most use cases of floating-point arithmetic are restricted to single/double precision floating-point representations, and those also have fast hardware support on almost all platforms. Hence, we could implement support for these representations as a special case to leverage the underlying hardware. To overcome the potential, albeit unlikely, soundness issues related to the underlying hardware, we can validate the models returned by OL1V3R by either switching back to the software-emulated arithmetic or using sound solvers such as MathSAT and Z3. Moreover, scores can be computed using double-precision floating-point arithmetic as opposed to the expensive rational arithmetic because our experience indicates that double-precision is almost always precise enough for this purpose. Note that this would not compromise the soundness of the algorithm since the computed scores are only used to guide the search. Finally, we can leverage multi-core parallelism to evaluate the scores using a map-reduce paradigm.

Our search strategy suffers from scalability issues on certain benchmarks and could be improved in several ways. The move selection policy is best-improvement, which implies that the score of every neighbor must be computed. The complexity of finding a neighbor that improves the score of the chosen assertion the most is $O(|V|bw)$, where $|V|$ is the number of variables and bw is the maximum bit-width of the used floating-point representations. Our experimental results show that some assertions contain a large number of variables, thus making move selection extremely slow. Hence, we propose using the first-improvement policy, as opposed to the current best-improvement, when the number of variables is above a chosen limit. The intuition is that first-improvement progresses faster whereas best-improvement spends most of its time in computing and comparing scores. However, first-improvement is highly sensitive to the order of neighbors. For example, flipping an exponent bit changes the score much more dramatically than flipping a significand bit. Therefore, we argue that variable neighborhood search [7] could be beneficial not only for the proposed first-improvement policy but also the default best-improvement one.

To be more specific, neighborhood relations are refined to subgroups by sign-bit, exponent bits, and significand bits. This observation is in accordance with the experiments described by Fröhlich et al. [5]. In essence, the chosen search algorithm should capture the fact that the bit representations of floating-point numbers are structured. Furthermore, the scores of assertions being weighted equally leads to frequent violations of assertions that could be easily satisfied, such as intervals of variables, wasting a lot of cycles that should be spent in searching for solutions that satisfy "hard" assertions. This motivates us to adopt in the future the heuristic in qfbv-sls that adds weights to assertions and dynamically adjust them according to the frequency at which an assertion is satisfied.

Like other search-based solvers, OL1V3R has difficulties in handling benchmarks that contain equalities, which are often produced by software verifiers. The reason is obvious: satisfying equalities often requires many more search steps than satisfying other comparison operators, such as $fp.lt$. A straightforward solution that might be effective in many situations is to eliminate equalities whenever possible. For example, if two variables are asserted to be equal, then all the occurrences of one variable can be replaced with the other.

Acknowledgements. We thank Dan Liew for answering our questions related to his work on JFS.

References

1. Beyer, D., Löwe, S., Wendler, P.: Reliable benchmarking: requirements and solutions. Int. J. Softw. Tools Technol. Transfer (STTT) **21**(1), 1–29 (2019). https://doi.org/10.1007/s10009-017-0469-y
2. Brain, M., Tinelli, C., Rümmer, P., Wahl, T.: An automatable formal semantics for IEEE-754 floating-point arithmetic. In: Proceedings of the IEEE International Symposium on Computer Arithmetic (ARITH), pp. 160–167 (2015). https://doi.org/10.1109/ARITH.2015.26
3. Cimatti, A., Griggio, A., Schaafsma, B.J., Sebastiani, R.: The MathSAT5 SMT solver. In: Piterman, N., Smolka, S.A. (eds.) TACAS 2013. LNCS, vol. 7795, pp. 93–107. Springer, Heidelberg (2013). https://doi.org/10.1007/978-3-642-36742-7_7
4. de Moura, L., Bjørner, N.: Z3: an efficient SMT solver. In: Ramakrishnan, C.R., Rehof, J. (eds.) TACAS 2008. LNCS, vol. 4963, pp. 337–340. Springer, Heidelberg (2008). https://doi.org/10.1007/978-3-540-78800-3_24
5. Fröhlich, A., Biere, A., Wintersteiger, C.M., Hamadi, Y.: Stochastic local search for satisfiability modulo theories. In: Proceedings of the AAAI Conference on Artificial Intelligence (AAAI), pp. 1136–1143 (2015)
6. Fu, Z., Su, Z.: XSat: a fast floating-point satisfiability solver. In: Chaudhuri, S., Farzan, A. (eds.) CAV 2016. LNCS, vol. 9780, pp. 187–209. Springer, Cham (2016). https://doi.org/10.1007/978-3-319-41540-6_11
7. Hansen, P., Mladenović, N., Moreno Pérez, J.A.: Variable neighbourhood search: methods and applications. Ann. Oper. Res. **175**(1), 367–407 (2010). https://doi.org/10.1007/s10479-009-0657-6

8. Hoos, H.H., Stützle, T.: Stochastic Local Search: Foundations and Applications. Elsevier, Amsterdam (2004)
9. Khadra, M.A.B., Stoffel, D., Kunz, W.: goSAT: floating-point satisfiability as global optimization. In: Proceedings of the Conference on Formal Methods in Computer Aided Design (FMCAD), pp. 11–14 (2017). https://doi.org/10.23919/FMCAD.2017.8102235
10. Liew, D.S.: Constraint solver based on coverage-guided fuzzing. https://github.com/delcypher/jfs
11. Liew, D.S.: Symbolic execution of verification languages and floating-point code. Ph.D. thesis, Imperial College London (2018)
12. The GNU MPFR library. https://www.mpfr.org
13. Niemetz, A., Preiner, M., Biere, A.: Propagation based local search for bit-precise reasoning. Formal Methods Syst. Des. (FMSD) **51**(3), 608–636 (2017). https://doi.org/10.1007/s10703-017-0295-6
14. Rümmer, P., Wahl, T.: An SMT-LIB theory of binary floating-point arithmetic. In: Informal Proceedings of the International Workshop on Satisfiability Modulo Theories (SMT) (2010)
15. SMT-LIB benchmarks in the QF_FP theory. https://clc-gitlab.cs.uiowa.edu:2443/SMT-LIB-benchmarks/QF_FP
16. SMT-LIB: The satisfiability modulo theories library. http://smtlib.cs.uiowa.edu
17. Toronto, N.: Arbitrary-precision floating-point numbers (Bigfloats). https://docs.racket-lang.org/math/bigfloat.html
18. White, B., et al.: An integrated experimental environment for distributed systems and networks. In: Proceedings of the Symposium on Operating Systems Design and Implementation (OSDI), pp. 255–270 (2002). https://doi.org/10.1145/844128.844152

Evaluating Branching Heuristics in Interval Constraint Propagation for Satisfiability

Calvin Huang[1], Soonho Kong[2], Sicun Gao[3], and Damien Zufferey[4(✉)] (iD)

[1] Scale Labs Inc., San Francisco, USA
[2] Toyota Research Institute, Cambridge, USA
[3] University of California, San Diego, USA
[4] Max Planck Institute for Software Systems, Kaiserslautern, Germany
zufferey@mpi-sws.org

Abstract. Interval Constraint Propagation (ICP) is a powerful method for solving general nonlinear constraints over real numbers. ICP uses interval arithmetic to prune the space of potential solutions and, when the constraint propagation fails, divides the space into smaller regions and continues recursively. The original goal is to find paving boxes of all solutions to a problem. Already when the whole domain needs to be considered, branching methods do matter much. However, recent applications of ICP in decision procedures over the reals need only a single solution. Consequently, variable ordering in branching operations becomes even more important.

In this work, we compare three different branching heuristics for ICP. The first method, most commonly used, splits the problem in the dimension with the largest lower and upper bound. The two other types of branching methods try to exploit an integration of analytical/numerical properties of real functions and search-based methods. The second method, called smearing, uses gradient information of constraints to choose variables that have the highest local impact on pruning. The third method, lookahead branching, designs a measure function to compare the effect of all variables on pruning operations in the next several steps.

We evaluate the performance of our methods on over 11,000 benchmarks from various sources. While the different branching methods exhibit significant differences on larger instance, none is consistently better. This shows the need for further research on branching heuristics when ICP is used to find an unique solution rather than all solutions.

1 Introduction

Interval Constraint Propagation (ICP) is used to find solutions to logic formulas that contain continuous, typically nonlinear, real functions. It is used in a variety of domains such as design and verification of software controller, optimization of parameters of control laws, system biology, etc.

© Springer Nature Switzerland AG 2019
M. Zamani and D. Zufferey (Eds.): NSV 2019, LNCS 11652, pp. 85–100, 2019.
https://doi.org/10.1007/978-3-030-28423-7_6

ICP finds solutions to problems of the form:

$$\exists \boldsymbol{x} \in \mathbb{R}^n. \bigwedge_{i=1}^{n} l_i \leq x_i \leq u_i \ \wedge \ \bigwedge_{i=1}^{m} c_i(\boldsymbol{x})$$

where c_i are arbitrary nonlinear constraints. l_i and u_i are lower and upper bounds that limits the search space. When a solution exists, the algorithm returns *satisfiable* and it returns *unsatisfiable* when the constraints are inconsistent. Along with a satisfiable answer, ICP also returns a solution to the problem.

Typical ICP algorithms uses the branch-and-prune paradigm. Interval extensions of functions are used to prune out sets of points that are not in the solution set and branch on intervals when such pruning cannot be done. This process repeats recursively until a small enough box that may contain a solution is found or inconsistency is observed.

Unfortunately, ICP is exponential in the number of dimension of the solution space and, thus, scales poorly. The original goal of ICP algorithms was to *pave* all solutions and, therefore, covering the entire search space. However, for many applications, finding a single solution is sufficient. In this case, the heuristics that choose the dimension on which to branch are critical for the performance of an ICP solver.

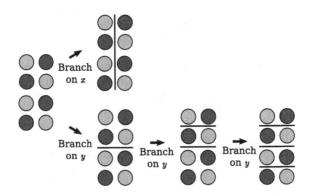

Fig. 1. An example with two variables x and y where branching on x leads to termination in one step, whereas branching on y does need three steps. The example has two constraints represented by (1) the blue circles and (2) the green circles. The pruning steps are shown in Fig. 2. (Color figure online)

Example 1. Figure 1 shows the solution set for the two constraints being the union of four circles each. The two sets of circles do not intersect and, therefore, there is no solution. The order on which the branching is performed changes the number of step performed in the ICP algorithm.

Figure 2 shows how the pruning operations for the different branches. Initially, the pruning cannot do anything as the box containing the blue circles is

After branching on x

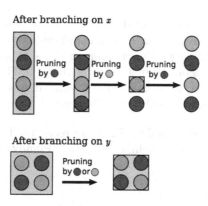

After branching on y

Fig. 2. The pruning step for the example in Fig. 1. The gray square represent the domain D explored by the ICP algorithm. (Color figure online)

the same as the box containing the green ones. After branching on x, the pruning can progressively remove circles from the domain until it is empty. Let us consider the left side of the branch. Pruning with the blue circles removes the top green circle. Pruning with the remaining green circle removes the two blue circles. Finally, pruning again with the blue circles shows a contradiction. The same process repeats on the right side and the problem is shown unsatisfiable.

On the other hand, branching on y result in a situation similar to the initial state but smaller. The pruning does not make progress and two more splits on y are needed before the pruning shows the problem to be unsatisfiable.

In this paper, we compare three branching heuristics for ICP: (1) largest first [5], (2) gradient branching, a method inspired by the maximal smear heuristics [13], (3) lookahead branching [15].

Largest first selects the variable with the largest domain The gradient branching uses the Jacobian of the constraints and branches on the variable maximizing the magnitude of the gradient. The lookahead branching performs exhaustive splitting over each of the variables, and keeps the branch which results in the largest amount of progress during the subsequent pruning. Both methods introduce parameters that can be fine-tuned based on characteristics of different benchmark sets.

More complex variations of the heuristics have been proposed, e.g., doing random lookahead at the beginning, scoring each variables, and combining the score with another heuristic like maximal smear [16]. However, to better isolate the effect of each heuristics we use simple version of each heuristic and do not combine them.

Contributions. In this paper, we study branching heuristics for ICP. More specifically:

– We show the importance of branching heuristics for constraints solving over a *continuous* domain for satisfiability. Branching heuristics have been

intensively studied in solving constraints over discrete domains and over continuous domain for paving. Our experimental evaluations show that different heuristics can lead to very different running times on some instances.
- An implementation of our heuristics in the dReal SMT solver and an experimental evaluation on more than 11,000 benchmarks from varied sources. Surprisingly, all the methods have similar overall performances.

The paper is organized as follow. First, we recall the basics of the ICP algorithm. Then we explain the branching heuristics. Finally, we present an experimental evaluation.

2   Preliminaries

We consider first-order formulas interpreted over the real numbers. Our special focus is formulas that can contain arbitrary nonlinear functions that are *Type 2 computable* [20]. Intuitively, Type 2 computability corresponds to *numerical computability*.

We look at δ-decision procedures [9] that are based on Interval Constraint Propagation (ICP). The framework of δ-decision procedures formulates a relaxed notion of logical decisions, by allowing one-sided δ-bounded errors [7]. Instead of asking whether a formula has a satisfiable assignment or not, we ask if it is "δ-satisfiable" or "unsatisfiable". Here, a formula is δ-satisfiable if it would be satisfiable under some δ-perturbation on the original formula. On the other hand, when the algorithm determines that the formula is "unsatisfiable", it is a definite answer and no numerical error can be involved.

ICP [3] finds solutions to a system of real constraints using the branch-and-prune method, combining interval arithmetic and constraint propagation. The idea is to use interval extensions of functions to prune out sets of points that are not in the solution set, and recursively branch on intervals when such pruning can not be done, until a small enough box that may contain a solution is found or inconsistency is observed. A high-level description of the decision version of ICP is given in Algorithm 1. The boxes, or interval domains, are written as $\boldsymbol{D}$ and c_i denotes the ith constraint.

The core ICP algorithm uses a branch-and-prune loop that aims to either find a small enough box that witnesses δ-satisfiability, or detect that no solution exists. The loop consists of two main steps: pruning and branching.

Prune($\boldsymbol{D}, c_i$) (line 4–6) The pruning operator removes from the current box $\boldsymbol{D}$ parts of the state space that does not contain solutions to the constrain c_i. It uses interval arithmetic to maintain an overapproximation of the solution sets.

Branch($\boldsymbol{D}, i$) (line 9) When the pruning operation ceases to make progress, one performs a depth-first search by branching on variables and restarts pruning operations on a subset of the domain. Typically, branching selects the variable with the largest domain, e.g., D_i, and partition it into two equally large subintervals. More concretely, line 9 selects $i = \arg\max_{\{i. \ |D_i| > \epsilon\}} |D_i|$.

Algorithm 1. ICP$(c_1, ..., c_m, \boldsymbol{D} = D_1 \times \cdots \times D_n, \delta)$

1: S.push($\boldsymbol{D}$)
2: **while** $S \neq \emptyset$ **do**
3:     $\boldsymbol{D} \leftarrow S$.pop()
4:     **while** $\exists 1 \leq i \leq m, \boldsymbol{D} \neq_\delta$ Prune$(\boldsymbol{D}, c_i)$ **do**
5:         $\boldsymbol{D} \leftarrow$ Prune$(\boldsymbol{D}, c_i)$
6:     **end while**
7:     **if** $\boldsymbol{D} \neq \emptyset$ **then**
8:         **if** $\exists 1 \leq i \leq n, |D_i| \geq \varepsilon$ **then** $\triangleright \varepsilon$ is some computable factor of δ
9:             $\{\boldsymbol{D}_1, \boldsymbol{D}_2\} \leftarrow$ Branch$(\boldsymbol{D}, i)$
10:             S.push($\boldsymbol{D}_1$)
11:             S.push($\boldsymbol{D}_2$)
12:         **else**
13:             **return** sat
14:         **end if**
15:     **end if**
16: **end while**
17: **return** unsat

Notation 1. *To simplify the presentation, throughout this paper we assume that* $0/0 = 0$.

Notation 2. *In the rest of this paper, we denote the pruning fixed-point, i.e., the line 4–6 of Algorithm 1, by* Prune$(\boldsymbol{D})$.

3   Gradient Branching

Branching on the size of the interval does not exploit information specific about the constraints in the problems. Instead, we can use a branching heuristic based on the gradient that exploits analytical/numerical properties of the constraints. One method uses gradient information of constraints to choose variables that have the highest local impact on pruning. The method we present is a variation of the maximal smearing method [13]. On top of this method, we add weight to different elements (gradient, size of the intervals). Also, we directly work in the log-space and sum rather than multiply the coefficients.

The algorithm is shown in Algorithm 2. The final score is a combination of two factors: (1) the size of the interval and (2) the gradient. The size of the interval (line 2) is a term similar to the standard heuristic that picks the larger interval for branching. The importance of that factor is controlled by the parameter p_3, usually a small value. The main factor is the gradient at the center of the current box (line 7). The midpoint method returns the point at the center of the box $\boldsymbol{D}$. The gradient is obtained using the Jacobian of the constraints. $Jacobian(c_j)(p)$ computes the Jacobian of c_j at the point p and return a vector g of size n where g_i is the derivative value of the ith variable.

Algorithm 2 integrates in Algorithm 1 at line 4. The algorithm depends on three parameters p_1, p_2, and p_3. We set the parameters to 1000, 1000, and 0.01

respectively. We found these values empirically by exploring a range of values and keeping the ones performing the best on a small set of examples.

Remark 1. Since the ranges of the variables can be vastly different from one another, we do not want to give disproportionate weight to the variables where the range is much larger, so we use the `asinh` function to score the range of a variable. We choose `asinh` rather than `log` because it has better behavior for small values.

Algorithm 2. Gradient($c_1, ..., c_m, \boldsymbol{D} = D_1 \times \cdots \times D_n$)

1: $p \leftarrow$ midpoint($\boldsymbol{D}$)
2: **for all** $i \in [1; n]$ **do** $scores[i] \leftarrow$ asinh($|D_i|p_1)p_3$
3: **end for**
4: **for all** $j \in [1; m]$ **do**
5:     $g \leftarrow Jacobian(c_j)(p)$
6:     **for all** $i \in [1; n]$ **do**
7:         $scores[i] \leftarrow scores[i] +$ asinh(abs($g_i)|D_i|p_2)$
8:     **end for**
9: **end for**
10: **return** arg max$_i$ $scores[i]$

---

4   Lookahead Branching

Due to the nonlinearity of the constraints, it is difficult to predict a priori the effect of branching on the subsequent pruning steps. An alternative is to use a posteriori information, i.e. try to branch on multiple variables, prune, and keep the branching which results in the most progress. This is the lookahead strategy [15].

The lookahead strategy makes locally optimal branching choices, but it is computationally expensive as the results of many pruning steps are discarded. However, a *bad* choice in branching, i.e. a branching leading to little or no pruning also has a cost on the total running time.

Example 2. Making a bad choice can double the amount of subsequent computations. Let us consider an unsatisfiable set of constraints $\mathcal{C}(X)$ over the set of variables X. Furthermore, assume that the ICP algorithm takes T seconds to return unsat.

Now let us add a fresh variable $y \in [-\delta; \delta]$ and let $\mathcal{C}'(X \cup \{y\})$ be $C(X) \wedge y = y$. In the best case, the ICP algorithm running on $\mathcal{C}'$ does not branch on y and runs on $\mathcal{C}'$ like it ran on $\mathcal{C}$. In the worst case, it first branch on y. After branching on y, $\mathcal{C}'$ is the same as $\mathcal{C}$. However, the ICP needs to show that *both* sides of the branch do not contain any solution. In the first case solving $\mathcal{C}'$ takes T seconds and in the second case it takes $2T$ seconds. The more the ICP branches on y, the more the running time increases.

We present a modified ICP algorithm which uses lookahead. The main components are (1) a way of measuring the progress made during pruning, (2) a lookahead algorithm which preserves some of the progress made during the pruning, and (3) a modified ICP loop which can mix lookahead and normal branching decisions.

Using only lookahead is prohibitively expensive on problems with a large number of variables. Therefore, our algorithm has two important features. First, the lookahead procedure preserves some information about the results of the discarded pruning steps. Second, the modified ICP loop can mix lookahead with another cheaper branching policy.

Measuring Progress. To evaluate the progress of pruning steps we need a way of quantifying the progress made by pruning steps, i.e., measure the D. The most natural measure of a box is its volume. However, the volume is not resistant to degenerate intervals, e.g., $[0; 0]$. The volume of any box containing a degenerate interval is 0. Instead we use the *linear dimension* of the box to measure progress. The linear dimension is defined as the sum of the interval sizes:

$$\mathrm{ld}(D) = \sum_i |D_i|$$

Computing the Scores of Variables. To decide on which variable to branch, we give a score to each variable and pick the variable with the maximal score. A variable's score is computed by branching on that variable, pruning the two resulting boxes, and measuring the progress made during the pruning. Furthermore, the variables scores can be amortized in a decaying sum. Since we do not perform the lookahead at every step, this helps identifying the variables which are globally more important from the local variations. The decaying sum is inspired by the variable state independent decaying sum [14] which is a very successful heuristic for SAT solvers. Algorithm 3 shows the details of the computation.

A crucial optimization of the lookahead procedure is the hull on line 9. Instead of repeatedly branching only on the initial D, we take the hull, i.e., smallest box containing D_1 and D_2. This preserves some of the work done during the pruning.

The algorithm depends on the coefficient p_1 that amortises the scoring over the entire run of the ICP algorithm. In our experiment, we set p_1 to 0.5.

Modified ICP Algorithm. Algorithm 4 is a modified version of Algorithm 1 to track additional information about the search. The stack S does not only contains boxes but also keeps track of the depth of the box in the search tree built by the algorithm. Two additional variables l and dl keep track of how long ago the last lookahead performed was, and at what depth. This extra information is used to decide when to use lookahead. Between lookahead steps, the same variable is split repeatedly or if its interval is too small, the algorithm can revert to another policy (line 15).

Algorithm 4 depends on three parameters: p_1, p_2, and p_3. These parameters control how often the lookahead step is performed on line 10 of Algorithm 4.

Algorithm 3. Lookahead$(c_1, ..., c_m, \boldsymbol{D} = D_1 \times \cdots \times D_n)$

```
1: scores ← 0                                                  ▷ only the first time
2: i ← 1
3: while i ≤ n ∧ D ≠ ∅ do
4:     if |Dᵢ| > ε then
5:         {D₁, D₂} ← Branch(D, i)
6:         D'₁ ← Prune(D₁)
7:         D'₂ ← Prune(D₂)
8:         score[i] ← score[i] p₁ + (1 − p₁)(ld(D₁)/ld(D'₁) + ld(D₂)/ld(D'₂))
9:         D ← hull(D'₁, D'₂)
10:    end if
11:    i ← i + 1
12: end while
13: return (D, arg maxᵢ scores[i])
```

Algorithm 4. ICP2$(c_1, \ldots, c_m, \boldsymbol{D} = D_1 \times \cdots \times D_n, \delta)$

```
1: l ← −p₁                                    ▷ how long since the last lookahead
2: dl ← 0                                       ▷ depth from the last lookahead
3: i ← 0                                                      ▷ branching index
4: S.push(0, D)
5: while S ≠ ∅ do
6:     (d, D) ← S.pop()
7:     D ← Prune(D)
8:     l ← l + 1
9:     if D ≠ ∅ then
10:        if l < 0 ∨ l > p₂ ∨ d ≤ dl − p₃ then
11:            (D, i) ← Lookahead(c₁, ..., cₘ, D)
12:            l ← min(l, 0)
13:            dl ← d
14:        end if
15:        if |Dᵢ| ≥ ε ∨ ∃1 ≤ i ≤ n, |Dᵢ| ≥ ε then
16:            {D₁, D₂} ← Branch(D, i)
17:            S.push(d + 1, D₁)
18:            S.push(d + 1, D₂)
19:        else
20:            return sat
21:        end if
22:    end if
23: end while
24: return unsat
```

The lookahead is performed at a fixed frequency, except at the start where is it performed more often, and after backtracking.

- $l < 0$ and $l \leftarrow -p_1$ (line 1) forces the lookahead for the first p_1 iteration of the algorithm. Due to the DFS nature of the ICP algorithm, making good choices at the early stage of the search is very important. Therefore, we perform more lookahead steps at the beginning.

- $l > p_2$ controls the maximal interval between two lookahead steps.
- $d \leq dl - p_3$ forces lookahead if the depth d is p_3 less than the depth dl at which that the lookahead was last computed, i.e. if the search backtracks more than p_3 steps in the search tree. After backtracking, the search may continue in a very different region of the solution space. Therefore, we need to update the score of the variables to make sure it is still relevant to the region currently being explored.

In our experiments we set p_1, p_2, and p_3 to 10.

5 Evaluation

We implemented the heuristics presented above in the dReal SMT solver [8] and evaluated their efficiency. dReal already implements the baseline heuristic to bisect the largest dimension by default. Our benchmarks come from:

- the dReal test suite;
- information theory: search for probabilistic encoding minimizing power consumption [19];
- control theory: certifying Lyapunov functions;
- automated theorem proving: proof obligations extracted from the Flyspeck project [9,11];
- Geometric problems: intersection of objects in high-dimensional spaces, and computing the inverse kinematics for robotic planning;
- The QF_NRA examples from SMT-LIB [1].

The benchmarks are available at https://github.com/dreal/benchmarks.

In this work we focus on branching and our examples do not contain any ordinary differential equations. Examples with ODEs are less interesting as solving the differential part dominates the running time.

We run two experiments. In the first experiment, we run dReal on the whole set of 11789 benchmarks with a 300 s timeout. For the second experiment, we keep only the benchmarks with more than 7 variables to filter out the smaller, easier examples. Furthermore, we exclude the hycomp benchmarks from the SMT-LIB set because, even though they have many variables, they are solved using pruning only. The second set has 896 benchmarks and we run dReal with a 1800 s timeout. We run our experiments in parallel on a server with AMD Opteron 6174 CPUs at 2.2 GHz and 500 GB of RAM. dReal is single threaded and memory consumption is not an issue. Additionally, we run dReal with --polytope and --stat to use the polytope contractor and to collect statistics of the runs.

Table 1. Summary of the experiments. We show the number of instances solved by each method. The virtual best/worst solver represent the best/worst results of any heuristic on each benchmarks. We also show how many benchmarks could only be solved using a single method.

Instances	Small (Δ)	Large (Δ)
#Benchmarks	11789	896
Solved Baseline	10654	**292**
Solved Gradient	10654 (+0)	266 (−26)
Solved Lookahead	**10667** (+13)	283 (−9)
Virtual Best	10827 (+173)	337 (+45)
Virtual Worst	10439 (−206)	222 (−70)
Unique Baseline	34	19
Unique Gradient	**65**	5
Unique Lookahead	19	**31**

The results are shown in Table 1 and Figs. 3, 4, 5, 6 and 7. The table includes the number of instances solved by each method. We also include the virtual best and virtual worst solver for the three methods. In the total number of instances solved, the three branching heuristics give roughly similar results. The lookahead is better overall and, surprisingly, the baseline performs better on the large instances. However, there is a large variation from benchmark to benchmark. This can be seen with the virtual best/worst solver, the unique instances, i.e, the instances solved by only one method, and this is also visible on the Figures.

Figures 4 and 5 compare the gradient and lookahead against the baseline heuristic. There is a large cluster of easy instances in the bottom left corner. However, the most interesting feature of these graphs are the number of points which are on the timeout lines. Also, we can observe that the gradient is faster than the baseline on the easy instances and the lookahead is slower on average but times out less often.

Figures 6 and 7 show more information about the internals of the search. Each solved problem is shown by a (x, y) dot where y is the number of dimensions in the problem and x is the number of pruning or branching steps performed by the solver. The gradient and baseline are roughly comparable with an average of around 9,000 branches and 1,400,000 pruning steps. However, the lookahead search is quite different with around 5,300 branches and 3,072,000 pruning steps, trading off branching for pruning. It is easy to see that the lookahead search performs much more pruning. On the other hand, it branches less often. The branching difference is less visible, but the cost of additional branches is more important, see Example 2.

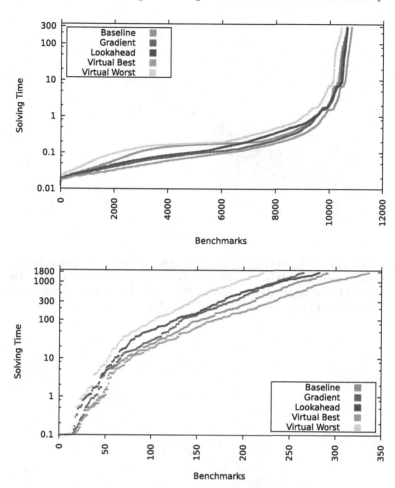

Fig. 3. Cactus plot of the running times of the baseline, gradient, and lookahead heuristics. A (x, y) point means x instances are solved with a y-second timeout. The higher graph shows all the benchmarks with a 300 s. timeout. The lower graph shows the large instances with a 1800 s. timeout.

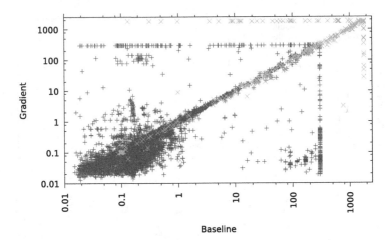

Fig. 4. Scatter plot of the running times of the gradient heuristic against the baseline. The + are the tests with a 300 s. timeout and the × are the tests with a 1800 s. timeout. The gradient is faster for smaller instances. Notice the large number of instance that can be solved easily by one method but not the other.

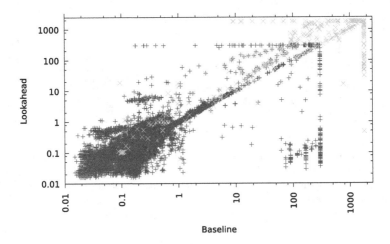

Fig. 5. Scatter plot of the running times of the lookahead heuristic against the baseline. The + are the tests with a 300 s. timeout and the × are the tests with a 1800 s. timeout. The lookahead solves more instances, but is slower overall.

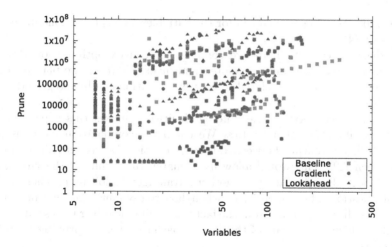

Fig. 6. The number of pruning steps against the number of variables. The lookahead performs more pruning and the gradient and baseline are comparable.

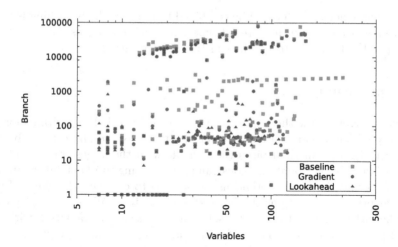

Fig. 7. The number of branching steps against the number of variables. The lookahead branches less often that the other two heuristics.

6   Related Work and Discussion

Branching is extensively studied in the discrete CSP community [17] and many techniques developed in this setting are applicable to an ICP algorithm for continuous domain. For instance, iSAT [6] implements an integrated ICP+SAT algorithm and uses the SAT solver heuristics for branching. In this work, we try to exploit some information specific to the real numbers, such as the gradient, to improve the variable selection for branching. In the future, we plan to evaluate more complex scoring mechanism for the variables as has been done in the SAT community [4].

Gradient descent methods are common for convex optimisation [18]. Our problems are nonlinear and, therefore, nonconvex. However, we plan to further investigate how technique related to convex relaxation can be integrated in ICP algorithms.

The difference between the different heuristics makes this a prime candidate for combination of heuristics. We could try combination methods using weights [16], alternating between different selection heuristics [10], or portfolio approach [12]. This would allow us to match the results of the virtual best solver. A portfolio approach has another advantage: exploiting parallelism. This also ask questions about identifying when/how to exchange information between solvers. The difficulty stems from the fact that while the solver works with convex objects, i.e. boxes. The part of the search space removed by pruning operations is not convex.

A new direction, we have not yet optimized which branch of the search is explored first after a bisection. Paving always need to explore both sides. However, a satisfiability check may stop after finding a solution on the first side explored.

Another avenue which could be combined to improve the branching is to ask the pruning step to return more information which can be used for decide at which point within an interval the splitting must occur [2].

7   Conclusion

In this paper, we show the importance of branching in ICP algorithms for satisfiability of non-linear constraints over the reals. We compare three branching heuristics. One method picks the variable with the largest range and does not use information about the constraints. One using gradient information of constraints and the other method use lookahead to estimate the effect of variables on pruning operations in the next several steps. We have implemented these heuristics in the dReal SMT solver and present an evaluation with over 11,000 problem instances. The different branching methods exhibit significant differences on larger instance. However, no heuristics is consistently better. This shows the need for further research on branching heuristics when using ICP for satisfiability.

Acknowledgements. We thank the reviewers for their feedback and comments which helped us improve the paper. Calvin Huang was studying at MIT when that work was done. Damien Zufferey was funded in part by the DFG under Grant Agreement 389792660-TRR 248 and by the ERC under the Grant Agreement 610150.

References

1. Barrett, C., Fontaine, P., Tinelli, C.: The Satisfiability Modulo Theories Library (SMT-LIB) (2019). www.smtlib.org/
2. Batnini, H., Michel, C., Rueher, M.: Mind the gaps: a new splitting strategy for consistency techniques. In: van Beek, P. (ed.) CP 2005. LNCS, vol. 3709, pp. 77–91. Springer, Heidelberg (2005). https://doi.org/10.1007/11564751_9
3. Benhamou, F., Granvilliers, L.: Continuous and interval constraints. In: Rossi, F., van Beek, P., Walsh, T. (eds.) Handbook of Constraint Programming, Chap. 16. Elsevier (2006)
4. Biere, A., Fröhlich, A.: Evaluating CDCL variable scoring schemes. In: Heule, M., Weaver, S. (eds.) SAT 2015. LNCS, vol. 9340, pp. 405–422. Springer, Cham (2015). https://doi.org/10.1007/978-3-319-24318-4_29
5. Csendes, T., Ratz, D.: Subdivision direction selection in interval methods for global optimization. SIAM J. Numer. Anal. **34**(3), 922–938 (1997). https://doi.org/10.1137/S0036142995281528
6. Fränzle, M., Herde, C., Teige, T., Ratschan, S., Schubert, T.: Efficient solving of large non-linear arithmetic constraint systems with complex Boolean structure. JSAT **1**(3–4), 209–236 (2007)
7. Gao, S., Avigad, J., Clarke, E.M.: δ-complete decision procedures for satisfiability over the reals. In: Gramlich, B., Miller, D., Sattler, U. (eds.) IJCAR 2012. LNCS (LNAI), vol. 7364, pp. 286–300. Springer, Heidelberg (2012). https://doi.org/10.1007/978-3-642-31365-3_23
8. Gao, S., Kong, S., Clarke, E.M.: dReal: an SMT solver for nonlinear theories over the reals. In: Bonacina, M.P. (ed.) CADE 2013. LNCS (LNAI), vol. 7898, pp. 208–214. Springer, Heidelberg (2013). https://doi.org/10.1007/978-3-642-38574-2_14
9. Gao, S., Kong, S., Clarke, E.M.: Proof generation from detla-decisions. In: Winkler, F., et al. (eds.) 16th International Symposium on Symbolic and Numeric Algorithms for Scientific Computing, SYNASC 2014, Timisoara, Romania, 22–25 September 2014, pp. 156–163. IEEE Computer Society (2014). https://doi.org/10.1109/SYNASC.2014.29
10. Granvilliers, L.: Adaptive bisection of numerical CSPs. In: Milano, M. (ed.) CP 2012. LNCS, pp. 290–298. Springer, Heidelberg (2012). https://doi.org/10.1007/978-3-642-33558-7_23
11. Hales, T.C., et al.: A formal proof of the Kepler conjecture. Forum Math. Pi **5**, e2 (2017). https://doi.org/10.1017/fmp.2017.1
12. Hamadi, Y., Ringwelski, G.: Boosting distributed constraint satisfaction. J. Heuristics **17**(3), 251–279 (2011). https://doi.org/10.1007/s10732-010-9134-2
13. Kearfott, R.B., Novoa, M.: Algorithm 681: INTBIS, a portable interval Newton/bisection package. ACM Trans. Math. Softw. **16**(2), 152–157 (1990). https://doi.org/10.1145/78928.78931
14. Moskewicz, M.W., Madigan, C.F., Zhao, Y., Zhang, L., Malik, S.: Chaff: engineering an efficient SAT solver. In: Design Automation Conference, pp. 530–535 (2001). https://doi.org/10.1145/378239.379017
15. Purdom, P.W., Brown, C.A., Robertson, E.L.: Backtracking with multi-level dynamic search rearrangement. Acta Inf. **15**(2), 99–113 (1981). https://doi.org/10.1007/BF00288958
16. Reyes, V., Araya, I.: Probing-based variable selection heuristics for NCSPs. In: 2014 IEEE 26th International Conference on Tools with Artificial Intelligence, pp. 16–23, November 2014. https://doi.org/10.1109/ICTAI.2014.14

17. Rossi, F., van Beek, P., Walsh, T. (eds.): Handbook of Constraint Programming. Elsevier, New York (2006)
18. Snyman, J.: Practical Mathematical Optimization: An Introduction to Basic Optimization Theory and Classical and New Gradient-Based Algorithms. Springer, New York (2005). https://doi.org/10.1007/b105200
19. Stanley-Marbell, P., Francese, P.A., Rinard, M.: Encoder logic for reducing serial I/O power in sensors and sensor hubs. In: 2016 IEEE Hot Chips 28 Symposium (HCS), Cupertino, CA, USA, 21–23 August 2016, pp. 1–2. IEEE (2016). https://doi.org/10.1109/HOTCHIPS.2016.7936231
20. Weihrauch, K.: Computable Analysis: An Introduction. Texts in Theoretical Computer Science. Springer, Heidelberg (2000). https://doi.org/10.1007/978-3-642-56999-9

Approximate Probabilistic Relations for Compositional Abstractions of Stochastic Systems

Abolfazl Lavaei[1]([✉]), Sadegh Soudjani[2], and Majid Zamani[3,4]

[1] Department of Electrical Engineering,
Technical University of Munich, Munich, Germany
lavaei@tum.de
[2] School of Computing, Newcastle University,
Newcastle upon Tyne, UK
Sadegh.Soudjani@newcastle.ac.uk
[3] Department of Computer Science,
University of Colorado Boulder, Boulder, USA
majid.zamani@colorado.edu
[4] Department of Computer Science,
Ludwig Maximilian University of Munich, Munich, Germany

Abstract. In this paper, we propose a compositional approach for constructing abstractions of general Markov decision processes (gMDPs) using approximate probabilistic relations. The abstraction framework is based on the notion of δ-lifted relations, using which one can quantify the distance in probability between the interconnected gMDPs and that of their abstractions. This new approximate relation unifies compositionality results in the literature by allowing abstract models to have either finite or infinite state spaces. To this end, we first propose our compositionality results using the new approximate probabilistic relation which is based on lifting. We then focus on a class of stochastic nonlinear dynamical systems and construct their abstractions using both model order reduction and space discretization in a unified framework. Finally, we demonstrate the effectiveness of the proposed results by considering a network of four nonlinear dynamical subsystems (together 12 dimensions) and constructing finite abstractions from their reduced-order versions (together 4 dimensions) in a unified compositional framework.

Keywords: Approximate probabilistic relations ·
Compositional abstractions · General Markov decision processes ·
Policy refinement

This work was supported in part by the H2020 ERC Starting Grant AutoCPS (grant agreement No. 804639).

M. Zamani and D. Zufferey (Eds.): NSV 2019, LNCS 11652, pp. 101–109, 2019.
https://doi.org/10.1007/978-3-030-28423-7_7

1   Introduction

Control systems with stochastic uncertainty can be modeled as Markov decision processes (MDPs) over general state spaces. Synthesizing policies for satisfying complex temporal logic properties [4] over MDPs evolving on uncountable state spaces is inherently a challenging task due to the computational complexity. Since closed-form characterization of such policies is not available in general, a suitable approach is to approximate these models by simpler ones possibly with finite or lower dimensional state spaces. A crucial step is to provide formal guarantees during this approximation phase, such that the analysis or synthesis on the simpler model can be refined back over the original one.

Similarity relations over finite-state stochastic systems have been studied, either via exact notions of probabilistic (bi)simulation relations [12,18] or approximate versions [6,7]. Similarity relations for models with general, uncountable state spaces have been also proposed in the literature. These relations either depend on stability requirements on model outputs via martingale theory or contractivity analysis [10,24] or enforce structural abstractions of a model [5] by exploiting continuity conditions on its probability laws [1,3].

There have been also several results on the construction of (in)finite abstractions for stochastic systems. Construction of finite abstractions for formal verification and synthesis is presented in [2]. An adaptive gridding approach is proposed in [19] with the dedicated tool FAUST^2 [21]. Extension of such techniques to automata-based controller synthesis and infinite horizon properties is studied in [11] and [23], respectively. Compositional construction of finite abstractions using dynamic Bayesian networks is discussed in [20]. Compositional construction of infinite abstractions (reduced-order models) is respectively proposed in [13,16] using small-gain type conditions and dissipativity-type properties of subsystems and their abstractions. Compositional construction of finite abstractions is studied in [14,15]. Recently, compositional synthesis of large-scale stochastic systems using a relaxed dissipativity approach is proposed in [17].

In this paper, we provide conditions under which the proposed similarity relations between individual gMDPs can be extended to relations between their respective interconnections. These conditions enable compositional quantification of the distance in probability between the interconnected gMDPs and that of their abstractions. Our compositional scheme allows constructing both infinite and finite abstractions in a unified framework.

Similarities between two gMDPs have been recently studied in [8] using a notion of δ-lifted relation. This notion is used in [9] for temporal logic control of gMDPs. These two works are focused on single gMDPs. One of the main contributions of this paper is to extend this notion such that it can be applied to networks of gMDPs. Furthermore, we provide an approach for the construction of finite MDPs in a unified framework for a class of stochastic nonlinear dynamical systems, considered as gMDPs, whereas the construction scheme in [8,9] only handles the class of linear systems.

2   General Markov Decision Processes

In our framework, we consider the class of general Markov decision processes (gMDPs), as in the next definition, that evolves over continuous or uncountable state spaces. This class of models generalizes the usual notion of MDP [4] by including internal inputs that are employed for composition [15], and by adding an output space over which properties of interest are defined [8].

Definition 1. *A general Markov decision process (gMDP) is a tuple*

$$\Sigma = (X, W, U, \pi, T, Y, h), \tag{1}$$

where

- $X \subseteq \mathbb{R}^n$ *is a Borel space as the state space of the system. We denote by* $(X, \mathcal{B}(X))$ *the measurable space with* $\mathcal{B}(X)$ *being the Borel sigma-algebra on the state space;*
- $W \subseteq \mathbb{R}^p$ *is a Borel space as the* internal *input space of the system;*
- $U \subseteq \mathbb{R}^m$ *is a Borel space as the* external *input space of the system;*
- $\pi = \mathcal{B}(X) \rightarrow [0,1]$ *is the initial probability distribution;*
- $T : \mathcal{B}(X) \times X \times W \times U \rightarrow [0,1]$ *is a conditional stochastic kernel that assigns to any* $x \in X$, $w \in W$, *and* $\nu \in U$, *a probability measure* $T(\cdot|x, w, \nu)$ *on the measurable space* $(X, \mathcal{B}(X))$. *This stochastic kernel specifies probabilities over executions* $\{x(k), k \in \mathbb{N}\}$ *of the gMDP such that for any set* $\mathcal{A} \in \mathcal{B}(X)$ *and any* $k \in \mathbb{N}$,

$$\mathbb{P}(x(k+1) \in \mathcal{A} \,\big|\, x(k), w(k), \nu(k)) = \int_{\mathcal{A}} T(dx(k+1)|x(k), w(k), \nu(k)).$$

- $Y \subseteq \mathbb{R}^q$ *is a Borel space as the output space of the system;*
- $h : X \rightarrow Y$ *is a measurable function that maps a state* $x \in X$ *to its output* $y = h(x)$.

Evolution of the state of a gMDP Σ, can be alternatively described by

$$\Sigma : \begin{cases} x(k+1) = f(x(k), w(k), \nu(k), \varsigma(k)), \\ y(k) = h(x(k)), \end{cases} \quad k \in \mathbb{N}, \; x(0) \sim \pi, \tag{2}$$

for input sequences $w(\cdot) : \mathbb{N} \rightarrow W$ and $\nu(\cdot) : \mathbb{N} \rightarrow U$, where $\varsigma := \{\varsigma(k) : \Omega \rightarrow V_\varsigma, \; k \in \mathbb{N}\}$ is a sequence of independent and identically distributed (i.i.d.) random variables on a set V_ς with sample space Ω. Vector field f together with the distribution of ς give the stochastic kernel T. If X, W, U are finite sets, system Σ is called finite, and infinite otherwise.

Next section presents approximate probabilistic relations that can be used for relating two gMDPs while capturing probabilistic dependency between their executions.

3   Approximate Probabilistic Relations Based on Lifting

Definition 2. *Let $X, \hat{X}$ be two sets with associated measurable spaces $(X, \mathcal{B}(X))$ and $(\hat{X}, \mathcal{B}(\hat{X}))$. Consider a relation $\mathscr{R}_x \in \mathcal{B}(X \times \hat{X})$. We denote by $\bar{\mathscr{R}}_\delta \subseteq \mathcal{P}(X, \mathcal{B}(X)) \times \mathcal{P}(\hat{X}, \mathcal{B}(\hat{X}))$, the corresponding δ-lifted relation such that $\Phi \bar{\mathscr{R}}_\delta \Theta$ if there exists a probability space $(X \times \hat{X}, \mathcal{B}(X \times \hat{X}), \mathscr{L})$ (equivalently, a lifting $\mathscr{L}$) satisfying*

- *$\forall \mathcal{A} \in \mathcal{B}(X)$, $\mathscr{L}(\mathcal{A} \times \hat{X}) = \Phi(\mathcal{A})$,*
- *$\forall \hat{\mathcal{A}} \in \mathcal{B}(\hat{X})$, $\mathscr{L}(X \times \hat{\mathcal{A}}) = \Theta(\hat{\mathcal{A}})$,*
- *for the probability space $(X \times \hat{X}, \mathcal{B}(X \times \hat{X}), \mathscr{L})$, it holds that $x\mathscr{R}_x\hat{x}$ with probability at least $1 - \delta$, equivalently, $\mathscr{L}(\mathscr{R}_x) \geq 1 - \delta$.*

For a given relation $\mathscr{R}_x \subseteq X \times \hat{X}$, the above definition specifies required properties for lifting relation $\mathscr{R}_x$ to a relation $\bar{\mathscr{R}}_\delta$ that relates probability measures over X and $\hat{X}$.

We are interested in using δ-*lifted* relation for specifying similarities between a gMDP and its abstraction. Therefore, internal inputs of the two gMDPs should be in a relation denoted by $\mathscr{R}_w$. Next definition gives conditions for having a stochastic simulation relation between two gMDPs.

Definition 3. *Consider gMDPs $\Sigma = (X, W, U, \pi, T, Y, h)$ and $\hat{\Sigma} = (\hat{X}, \hat{W}, \hat{U}, \hat{\pi}, \hat{T}, Y, \hat{h})$ with the same output space. System $\hat{\Sigma}$ is (ϵ, δ)-stochastically simulated by Σ, i.e. $\hat{\Sigma} \preceq_\epsilon^\delta \Sigma$, if there exist relations $\mathscr{R}_x \subseteq X \times \hat{X}$ and $\mathscr{R}_w \subseteq W \times \hat{W}$ for which there exists a Borel measurable stochastic kernel $\mathscr{L}_T(\cdot \mid x, \hat{x}, w, \hat{w}, \hat{\nu})$ on $X \times \hat{X}$ such that*

- *$\forall (x, \hat{x}) \in \mathscr{R}_x$, $\|h(x) - \hat{h}(\hat{x})\| \leq \epsilon$,*
- *$\forall (x, \hat{x}) \in \mathscr{R}_x$, $\forall \hat{w} \in \hat{W}$, $\forall \hat{\nu} \in \hat{U}$, there exists $\nu \in U$ such that $\forall w \in W$ with $(w, \hat{w}) \in \mathscr{R}_w$,*

$$T(\cdot \mid x, w, \nu) \; \bar{\mathscr{R}}_\delta \; \hat{T}(\cdot \mid \hat{x}, \hat{w}, \hat{\nu}), \text{ with lifting } \mathscr{L}_T(\cdot \mid x, \hat{x}, w, \hat{w}, \hat{\nu}),$$

- *$\pi \; \bar{\mathscr{R}}_\delta \; \hat{\pi}$.*

Definition 3 can be applied to gMDPs without internal inputs that may arise from composing gMDPs via their internal inputs. For such gMDPs, we eliminate $\mathscr{R}_w$, thus the definition reduces to that of [8].

Definition 3 enables us to quantify the error in probability between a concrete system Σ and its abstraction $\hat{\Sigma}$. In any (ϵ, δ)-approximate probabilistic relation, δ is used to quantify the distance in probability between gMDPs and ϵ for the closeness of output trajectories as stated in the next theorem. This theorem is adapted from [8] and provides the probabilistic closeness guarantee between interconnected gMDPs and that of their compositional abstractions which are discussed in Sect. 4.

Theorem 1. *If $\widehat{\Sigma} \preceq_{\epsilon}^{\delta} \Sigma$ and $(w(k), \hat{w}(k)) \in \mathscr{R}_w$ for all $k \in \{0, 1, \dots, T_d\}$, then for all policies on $\widehat{\Sigma}$ there exists a policy for Σ such that, for all measurable events $\mathsf{A} \subset Y^{T_d+1}$,*

$$\mathbb{P}\{\{\hat{y}(k)\}_{0:T_d} \in \mathsf{A}^{-\epsilon}\} - \gamma \leq \mathbb{P}\{\{y(k)\}_{0:T_d} \in \mathsf{A}\} \leq \mathbb{P}\{\{\hat{y}(k)\}_{0:T_d} \in \mathsf{A}^{\epsilon}\} + \gamma, \quad (3)$$

with constant $1 - \gamma := (1 - \delta)^{T_d+1}$, and with the ϵ-expansion and ϵ-contraction of A defined as

$$\mathsf{A}^{\epsilon} := \{y(\cdot) \in Y^{T_d+1} | \exists \bar{y}(\cdot) \in \mathsf{A} \text{ with } max_{k \leq T_d} \|\bar{y}(k) - y(k)\| \leq \epsilon\},$$
$$\mathsf{A}^{-\epsilon} := \{y(\cdot) \in \mathsf{A} \mid \bar{y}(\cdot) \in \mathsf{A} \text{ for all } \bar{y}(\cdot) \text{ with } max_{k \leq T_d} \|\bar{y}(k) - y(k)\| \leq \epsilon\}.$$

In the next section, we define composition of gMDPs via their internal inputs and discuss how to relate them to a network of interconnected abstractions based on their individual relations.

4   Compositional Abstractions of Interconnected gMDPs

4.1   Interconnected gMDPs

Let Σ be a network of $N \in \mathbb{N}_{\geq 1}$ gMDPs

$$\Sigma_i = (X_i, W_i, U_i, \pi_i, T_i, Y_i, h_i), \quad i \in \{1, \dots, N\}. \quad (4)$$

We partition internal input and output of Σ_i as

$$w_i = [w_{i1}; \dots; w_{i(i-1)}; w_{i(i+1)}; \dots; w_{iN}], \quad y_i = [y_{i1}; \dots; y_{iN}], \quad (5)$$

and also output space and function as

$$h_i(x_i) = [h_{i1}(x_i); \dots; h_{iN}(x_i)], \quad Y_i = \prod_{j=1}^{N} Y_{ij}. \quad (6)$$

The outputs y_{ii} are denoted as *external* ones, whereas the outputs y_{ij} with $i \neq j$ as *internal* ones which are employed for interconnection by requiring $w_{ji} = y_{ij}$. This can be explicitly written as

$$w_i = g_i(x_1, \dots, x_N) = [h_{1i}(x_1); \dots; h_{(i-1)i}(x_{i-1}); h_{(i+1)i}(x_{i+1}); \dots; h_{Ni}(x_N)]. \quad (7)$$

Now, we formally define the *interconnected gMDP Σ* as follows.

Definition 4. *Consider $N \in \mathbb{N}_{\geq 1}$ gMDPs $\Sigma_i = (X_i, W_i, U_i, \pi_i, T_i, Y_i, h_i), i \in \{1, \dots, N\}$, with the input-output configuration as in (5) and (6). The interconnection of Σ_i, $i \in \{1, \dots, N\}$, is a gMDP $\Sigma = (X, U, \pi, T, Y, h)$, denoted by $\mathcal{I}(\Sigma_1, \dots, \Sigma_N)$, such that $X := \prod_{i=1}^{N} X_i$, $U := \prod_{i=1}^{N} U_i$, $Y := \prod_{i=1}^{N} Y_{ii}$, and $h = \prod_{i=1}^{N} h_{ii}$, with the following constraints:*

$$\forall i, j \in \{1, \dots, N\}, \ i \neq j : \quad w_{ji} = y_{ij}, \quad Y_{ij} \subseteq W_{ji}. \quad (8)$$

Moreover, one has conditional stochastic kernel $T := \prod_{i=1}^{N} T_i$ and initial probability distribution $\pi := \prod_{i=1}^{N} \pi_i$.

4.2 Compositional Abstractions of Interconnected gMDPs

We assume that we are given N gMDPs as in Definition 1 together with their corresponding abstractions $\widehat{\Sigma}_i = (\hat{X}_i, \hat{W}_i, \hat{U}_i, \hat{\pi}_i, \hat{T}_i, Y_i, \hat{h}_i)$ such that $\widehat{\Sigma}_i \preceq_{\epsilon_i}^{\delta_i} \Sigma_i$ for some relation $\mathscr{R}_{x_i}$ and constants ϵ_i, δ_i. Next theorem shows the main compositionality result of the paper.

Theorem 2. *Consider the interconnected gMDP $\Sigma = \mathcal{I}(\Sigma_1, \ldots, \Sigma_N)$ induced by $N \in \mathbb{N}_{\geq 1}$ gMDPs Σ_i. Suppose $\widehat{\Sigma}_i$ is (ϵ_i, δ_i)-stochastically simulated by Σ_i with the corresponding relations $\mathscr{R}_{x_i}$ and $\mathscr{R}_{w_i}$ and lifting $\mathscr{L}_i$. If*

$$g_i(x)\mathscr{R}_{w_i}\hat{g}_i(\hat{x}), \quad \forall (x, \hat{x}) \in \mathscr{R}_{x_i}, \tag{9}$$

with interconnection constraint maps $g_i, \hat{g}_i$ defined as in (7), then $\widehat{\Sigma} = \mathcal{I}(\widehat{\Sigma}_1, \ldots, \widehat{\Sigma}_N)$ is (ϵ, δ)-stochastically simulated by $\Sigma = \mathcal{I}(\Sigma_1, \ldots, \Sigma_N)$ with relation $\mathscr{R}_x$ defined as

$$\begin{bmatrix} x_1 \\ \vdots \\ x_N \end{bmatrix} \mathscr{R}_x \begin{bmatrix} \hat{x}_1 \\ \vdots \\ \hat{x}_N \end{bmatrix} \Leftrightarrow \begin{cases} x_1 \mathscr{R}_{x_1} \hat{x}_1, \\ \vdots \\ x_N \mathscr{R}_{x_N} \hat{x}_N, \end{cases}$$

and constants $\epsilon = \sum_{i=1}^{N} \epsilon_i$, and $\delta = 1 - \prod_{i=1}^{N}(1 - \delta_i)$. Lifting $\mathscr{L}$ and interface ν are obtained by taking products $\mathscr{L} = \prod_{i=1}^{N} \mathscr{L}_i$ and $\nu = \prod_{i=1}^{N} \nu_i$, and then substituting interconnection constraints (8).

5 Construction of Abstractions for Nonlinear Systems

Here, we focus on a specific class of stochastic nonlinear dynamical systems Σ as

$$\Sigma : \begin{cases} x(k+1) = Ax(k) + E\varphi(Fx(k)) + Dw(k) + B\nu(k) + R\varsigma(k), \\ y(k) = Cx(k), \end{cases} \tag{10}$$

where $\varsigma(\cdot) \sim \mathcal{N}(0, \mathbb{I}_n)$, and $\varphi : \mathbb{R} \to \mathbb{R}$ satisfies

$$0 \leq \frac{\varphi(c) - \varphi(d)}{c - d} \leq b, \quad \forall c, d \in \mathbb{R}, c \neq d, \tag{11}$$

for some $b \in \mathbb{R}_{>0} \cup \{\infty\}$. We use the tuple $\Sigma = (A, B, C, D, E, F, R, \varphi)$ to refer to the class of nonlinear systems of the form (10).

Existing compositional abstraction results for this class of models are based on either model order reduction [13, 16] or finite MDPs [14, 15]. Our proposed results here combine these two approaches in one unified framework. In other words, our abstract model is obtained by discretizing the state space of a reduced-order version of the concrete model.

5.1 Construction of Finite Abstractions

Consider a nonlinear system $\Sigma = (A, B, C, D, E, F, R, \varphi)$ and its reduced-order version $\widehat{\Sigma}_r = (\hat{A}_r, \hat{B}_r, \hat{C}_r, \hat{D}_r, \hat{E}_r, \hat{F}_r, \hat{R}_r, \varphi)$. Note that index r in the whole paper signifies the reduced-order version of the original model. Construction of a finite gMDP from $\widehat{\Sigma}_r$ follows the approach of [19,22]. Denote the state and input spaces of $\widehat{\Sigma}_r$ respectively by $\hat{X}_r, \hat{W}_r, \hat{U}_r$. We construct a finite gMDP by selecting partitions $\hat{X}_r = \cup_i X_i$, $\hat{W}_r = \cup_i W_i$, and $\hat{U}_r = \cup_i U_i$, and choosing representative points $\bar{x}_i \in X_i$, $\bar{w}_i \in W_i$, and $\bar{\nu}_i \in U_i$, as abstract states and inputs. The finite abstraction of Σ is a gMDP $\widehat{\Sigma} = (\hat{X}, \hat{W}, \hat{U}, \hat{\pi}, \hat{T}, Y, \hat{h})$, where

$$\hat{X} = \{\bar{x}_i, i = 1, \ldots, n_x\}, \ \hat{U} = \{\bar{u}_i, i = 1, \ldots, n_u\}, \ \hat{W} = \{\bar{w}_i, i = 1, \ldots, n_w\}.$$

Transition probability matrix $\hat{T}$ is constructed according to the dynamics $\hat{x}(k + 1) = \hat{f}(\hat{x}(k), \hat{w}(k), \hat{\nu}(k), \varsigma(k))$ with

$$\hat{f}(\hat{x}, \hat{\nu}, \hat{w}, \varsigma) := \Pi_x(\hat{A}_r\hat{x} + \hat{E}_r\varphi(\hat{F}_r\hat{x}) + \hat{D}_r\hat{w} + \hat{B}_r\hat{\nu} + \hat{R}_r\varsigma), \tag{12}$$

where $\Pi_x : \hat{X}_r \to \hat{X}$ is the map that assigns to any $\hat{x}_r \in \hat{X}_r$, the representative point $\bar{x} \in \hat{X}$ of the corresponding partition set containing $\hat{x}_r$. The output map $\hat{h}(\hat{x}) = \hat{C}\hat{x}$. The initial state of $\widehat{\Sigma}$ is also selected according to $\hat{x}_0 := \Pi_x(\hat{x}_r(0))$ with $\hat{x}_r(0)$ being the initial state of $\widehat{\Sigma}_r$.

Abstraction map Π_x satisfies the inequality $\|\Pi_x(\hat{x}_r) - \hat{x}_r\| \le \beta$ for all $\hat{x}_r \in \hat{X}_r$, where β is the state discretization parameter defined as $\beta := \sup\{\|\hat{x}_r - \hat{x}_r'\|, \ \hat{x}_r, \hat{x}_r' \in X_i, \ i = 1, 2, \ldots, n_x\}$.

5.2 Establishing Probabilistic Relations

Here, we candidate relations

$$\mathscr{R}_x = \left\{(x, \hat{x}) | (x - P\hat{x})^T M (x - P\hat{x}) \le \epsilon^2\right\}, \tag{13}$$

$$\mathscr{R}_w = \left\{(w, \hat{w}) | (w - P_w\hat{w})^T M_w (w - P_w\hat{w}) \le \epsilon_w^2\right\}, \tag{14}$$

where $P \in \mathbb{R}^{n \times \hat{n}}$ and $P_w \in \mathbb{R}^{m \times \hat{m}}$ are matrices of appropriate dimensions (potentially with the lowest $\hat{n}$ and $\hat{m}$), and M, M_w are some positive-definite matrices.

Next theorem gives conditions for having $\widehat{\Sigma} \preceq_\epsilon^\delta \Sigma$ with relations (13) and (14).

Theorem 3. Let $\Sigma = (A, B, C, D, E, F, R, \varphi)$ and $\widehat{\Sigma}_r = (\hat{A}_r, \hat{B}_r, \hat{C}_r, \hat{D}_r, \hat{E}_r, \hat{F}_r, \hat{R}_r, \varphi)$ be two nonlinear systems with the same additive noise. Suppose $\widehat{\Sigma}$ is a finite gMDP constructed from $\widehat{\Sigma}_r$ (cf. Subsection 5.1). Then $\widehat{\Sigma}$ is (ϵ, δ)-stochastically simulated by Σ with relations (13)–(14) if there exist matrices K, Q, S, L_1, L_2 and $\tilde{R}$ such that

$$M \succeq C^T C, \tag{15}$$

$$\hat{C}_r = CP, \tag{16}$$

$$\hat{F}_r = FP, \tag{17}$$

$$E = P\hat{E}_r - B(L_1 - L_2), \tag{18}$$

$$AP = P\hat{A}_r - BQ, \tag{19}$$

$$DP_w = P\hat{D}_r - BS, \tag{20}$$

$$\mathbb{P}\{(H + PG)^T M (H + PG) \leq \epsilon^2\} \succeq 1 - \delta, \tag{21}$$

where

$$H = ((A + BK) + \bar{\delta}(BL_1 + E)F)(x - P\hat{x}) + D(w - P_w\hat{w}) + (B\tilde{R} - P\hat{B}_r)\hat{\nu} + (R - P\hat{R}_r)\varsigma,$$
$$G = \hat{A}_r\hat{x} + \hat{E}_r\varphi(\hat{F}_r\hat{x}) + \hat{D}_r\hat{w} + \hat{B}_r\hat{\nu} + \hat{R}_r\varsigma - \Pi_x(\hat{A}_r\hat{x} + \hat{E}_r\varphi(\hat{F}_r\hat{x}) + \hat{D}_r\hat{w} + \hat{B}_r\hat{\nu} + \hat{R}_r\varsigma).$$

6   Case Study

We applied our results to a network of four stochastic nonlinear systems (totally 12 dimensions). We constructed finite gMDPs from their reduced-order versions (together 4 dimensions). We guaranteed that the distance between outputs of Σ and of $\hat{\Sigma}$ would not exceed $\epsilon = 6$ during the time horizon $T_d = 10$ with probability at least 97% ($\gamma = 0.03$).

References

1. Abate, A.: Approximation metrics based on probabilistic bisimulations for general state-space Markov processes: a survey. Electron. Notes Theor. Comput. Sci. **297**, 3–25 (2013)
2. Abate, A., Prandini, M., Lygeros, J., Sastry, S.: Probabilistic reachability and safety for controlled discrete-time stochastic hybrid systems. Automatica **44**(11), 2724–2734 (2008)
3. Abate, A., Kwiatkowska, M., Norman, G., Parker, D.: Probabilistic model checking of labelled Markov processes via finite approximate bisimulations. In: van Breugel, F., Kashefi, E., Palamidessi, C., Rutten, J. (eds.) Horizons of the Mind. A Tribute to Prakash Panangaden. LNCS, vol. 8464, pp. 40–58. Springer, Cham (2014). https://doi.org/10.1007/978-3-319-06880-0_2
4. Baier, C., Katoen, J.P.: Principles of Model Checking. MIT Press, Cambridge (2008)
5. Desharnais, J., Gupta, V., Jagadeesan, R., Panangaden, P.: Metrics for labelled Markov processes. Theor. Comput. Sci. **318**(3), 323–354 (2004)
6. Desharnais, J., Laviolette, F., Tracol, M.: Approximate analysis of probabilistic processes: logic, simulation and games. In: Proceedings of the 5th International Conference on Quantitative Evaluation of System, pp. 264–273 (2008)
7. D'Innocenzo, A., Abate, A., Katoen, J.: Robust PCTL model checking. In: Proceedings of the 15th ACM international conference on Hybrid Systems: Computation and Control, pp. 275–286 (2012)

8. Haesaert, S., Soudjani, S., Abate, A.: Verification of general Markov decision processes by approximate similarity relations and policy refinement. SIAM J. Control Optim. **55**(4), 2333–2367 (2017)
9. Haesaert, S., Soudjani, S., Abate, A.: Temporal logic control of general Markov decision processes by approximate policy refinement. In: Proceedings of the 6th IFAC Conference on Analysis and Design of Hybrid Systems, vol. 51, pp. 73–78 (2018)
10. Julius, A.A., Pappas, G.J.: Approximations of stochastic hybrid systems. IEEE Trans. Autom. Control **54**(6), 1193–1203 (2009)
11. Kamgarpour, M., Summers, S., Lygeros, J.: Control design for specifications on stochastic hybrid systems. In: Proceedings of the 16th ACM International Conference on Hybrid Systems: Computation and Control, pp. 303–312 (2013)
12. Larsen, K.G., Skou, A.: Bisimulation through probabilistic testing. Inf. Comput. **94**(1), 1–28 (1991)
13. Lavaei, A., Soudjani, S., Majumdar, R., Zamani, M.: Compositional abstractions of interconnected discrete-time stochastic control systems. In: Proceedings of the 56th IEEE Conference on Decision and Control, pp. 3551–3556 (2017)
14. Lavaei, A., Soudjani, S., Zamani, M.: Compositional synthesis of finite abstractions for continuous-space stochastic control systems: a small-gain approach. In: Proceedings of the 6th IFAC Conference on Analysis and Design of Hybrid Systems, vol. 51, pp. 265–270 (2018)
15. Lavaei, A., Soudjani, S., Zamani, M.: From dissipativity theory to compositional construction of finite Markov decision processes. In: Proceedings of the 21st ACM International Conference on Hybrid Systems: Computation and Control, pp. 21–30 (2018)
16. Lavaei, A., Soudjani, S., Zamani, M.: Compositional construction of infinite abstractions for networks of stochastic control systems. Automatica **107**, 125–137 (2019)
17. Lavaei, A., Soudjani, S., Zamani, M.: Compositional synthesis of large-scale stochastic systems: a relaxed dissipativity approach. Nonlinear Analysis: Hybrid Systems (2019, accepted)
18. Segala, R., Lynch, N.: Probabilistic simulations for probabilistic processes. Nordic J. Comput. **2**(2), 250–273 (1995)
19. Soudjani, S., Abate, A.: Adaptive and sequential gridding procedures for the abstraction and verification of stochastic processes. SIAM J. Appl. Dyn. Syst. **12**(2), 921–956 (2013)
20. Soudjani, S., Abate, A., Majumdar, R.: Dynamic Bayesian networks as formal abstractions of structured stochastic processes. In: Proceedings of the 26th International Conference on Concurrency Theory, pp. 1–14 (2015)
21. Soudjani, S.E.Z., Gevaerts, C., Abate, A.: FAUST^2: formal abstractions of uncountable-state stochastic processes. In: Baier, C., Tinelli, C. (eds.) TACAS 2015. LNCS, vol. 9035, pp. 272–286. Springer, Heidelberg (2015). https://doi.org/10.1007/978-3-662-46681-0_23
22. Soudjani, S.: Formal abstractions for automated verification and synthesis of stochastic systems. Ph.D. thesis, Technische Universiteit Delft, The Netherlands (2014)
23. Tkachev, I., Abate, A.: On infinite-horizon probabilistic properties and stochastic bisimulation functions. In: Proceedings of the 50th IEEE Conference on Decision and Control and European Control Conference (CDC-ECC), pp. 526–531 (2011)
24. Zamani, M., Mohajerin Esfahani, P., Majumdar, R., Abate, A., Lygeros, J.: Symbolic control of stochastic systems via approximately bisimilar finite abstractions. IEEE Trans. Autom. Control **59**(12), 3135–3150 (2014)

Polytopic Trees for Verification
of Learning-Based Controllers

Sadra Sadraddini[1(✉)], Shen Shen[1], and Osbert Bastani[2]

[1] Massachusetts Institute of Technology, Cambridge, USA
{sadra,shenshen}@mit.edu
[2] University of Pennsylvania, Philadelphia, USA
obastani@seas.upenn.edu

Abstract. Reinforcement learning is increasingly used to synthesize controllers for a broad range of applications. However, formal guarantees on the behavior of learning-based controllers are elusive due to the black-box nature of machine learning models such as neural networks. In this paper, we propose an algorithm for verifying learning-based controllers—in particular, deep neural networks with ReLU activations, and decision trees with linear decisions and leaf values—for deterministic, piecewise affine (PWA) dynamical systems. In this setting, our algorithm computes the safe (resp., unsafe) region of the state space—i.e., the region of the state space on which the learned controller is guaranteed to satisfy (resp., fail to satisfy) a given reach-avoid specification. Knowing the safe and unsafe regions is substantially more informative than the boolean characterization of safety (i.e., safe or unsafe) provided by standard verification algorithms—for example, this knowledge can be used to compose controllers that are safe on different portions of the state space. At a high level, our algorithm uses convex programming to iteratively compute new regions (in the form of polytopes) that are guaranteed to be entirely safe or entirely unsafe. Then, it connects these polytopic regions together in a tree-like fashion. We conclude with an illustrative example on controlling a hybrid model of a contact-based robotics problem.

1 Introduction

Recently, there has been a great deal of success using reinforcement learning to synthesize controllers for challenging control tasks, including grasping [20], autonomous driving [24], and walking [9]. Reinforcement learning provides a number of advantages compared to traditional approaches to control—for example, it can be used to compress computationally expensive online controllers into computationally efficient control policies [21], it can be used to solve challenging nonconvex optimization problems such as grasping [4], and it can be used to adapt controllers to handle unmodeled real-world dynamics [1,9].

Despite these successes, reinforcement learning has had limited applicability in real-world control tasks. An important obstacle is the inability to provide

This research was partially supported by ONR award N00014-17-1-2699.

M. Zamani and D. Zufferey (Eds.): NSV 2019, LNCS 11652, pp. 110–127, 2019.
https://doi.org/10.1007/978-3-030-28423-7_8

formal guarantees on the behavior of learned controllers. For instance, real-world control tasks are usually safety-critical in nature. Furthermore, the more general problem of computing safe regions (i.e., sets of states from which the controller is guaranteed to be safe) is also an important tool for composing controllers [32].

The challenge is that learned controllers are typically deep neural networks (DNNs), which are hard to formally analyze due to their large number of parameters and lack of internal structure [5,16]. The lack of guarantees is particularly concerning since even in the supervised learning setting, DNNs are not robust [5,11,14,16,25,29,31,34,36]—i.e., even if an input is correctly classified, a small, adversarially chosen perturbation can typically cause the input to become misclassified. For closed-loop control, the lack of robustness would imply that even if a DNN controller produces a safe trajectory from a given initial state, a small perturbation to the initial state can cause the trajectory to become unsafe. This setting is particularly challenging for formal analysis, since we must reason about repeated application of the DNN controller.

In this paper, we propose an algorithm for computing safe regions (as well as unsafe regions—i.e., for which the system is guaranteed to be unsafe) for learning-based controllers. We are interested in *reach-avoid* specifications, which are safety properties expressed as (i) a goal region that is considered to be safe, (ii) a safety constraint specifying states that are known to be unsafe. Then, our goal is to classify each state as either safe (i.e., reaches the goal region without entering the unsafe region), or unsafe (i.e., it reaches the unsafe region). For example, consider the task of stabilizing an inverted pendulum. Then, the goal region may be a small region $|\theta| \leq \theta_{safe}$ around the upright position $\theta = 0$, where the closed-loop system is known to be safe (e.g., verified using stability analysis [32]), and the safety constraint may say that the pendulum should not fall over—i.e., $|\theta| > \theta_{unsafe}$, where $\theta_{unsafe} \in \mathbb{R}$. Our goal is to compute the set of states from which the learning-based controller successfully reaches the goal region without entering the unsafe region.

We build on recent work that verify DNNs with rectified-linear units (ReLUs), which are piecewise affine [5,16]. As a consequence, for the supervised learning setting, safety properties can then be encoded as a mixed-integer linear program [33], which can be checked using standard solvers. For our setting of closed-loop control, we consider dynamical systems with piecewise affine (PWA) dynamics, where each piece is a *polytopic region* (i.e., defined by the intersection of linear half-spaces). These systems are commonly encountered in control tasks; even systems that are not PWA can typically be (locally) closely approximated by one that is PWA. For PWA systems, safety properties for the closed-loop dynamics can be formulated as a mixed-integer linear program [15]. However, this approach can only be used to verify whether a given set of initial states is a safe region, and cannot be used to compute safe and unsafe regions.

At a high level, our algorithm iteratively constructs the safe and unsafe regions as follows. On each iteration, it first samples an unclassified state x from the state space, and determines whether x is safe or unsafe using a simple forward simulation. In particular, x is safe if the feedforward simulation reaches the current safe region, and unsafe if it reaches the current unsafe region. Finally, our algorithm expands x into a polytopic region around x with the same correctness property as x (i.e., safe or unsafe). Thus, our algorithm is essentially growing two tree-like data structures (which we call *polytopic trees*) - one representing safe states and the other for unsafe states. Then, our algorithm continues iteratively growing these polytopic trees until the entire state space has been classified.

The key challenge is expanding x into a polytopic region. We leverage the fact that the closed-loop dynamics is PWA—in particular, it computes a polytopic region around x such that the closed-loop dynamics is linear on that region. Then, it uses convex programming to restrict this region to a polytopic sub-region that has the same correctness property (i.e., safe or unsafe) as x. In summary, our contributions are:

- We formulate the problem of computing safe and unsafe regions for learning-based controllers (Sect. 2).
- We propose an algorithm for computing safe and unsafe regions (Sect. 5). A subroutine computes safe and unsafe polytopic regions around a given initial state for the closed-loop dynamical system (Sects. 4 and 3).
- We perform an extensive case study to evaluate our approach (Sect. 6).

Related Work. The closest work is [30], which studies the problem of finding the safe states of a linear systems controlled with ReLU-based DNNs. Their solution is based on partitioning the work-space and computing reachable sets to obtain a finite-state abstraction. The end result is an under-approximation of the safe region. This approach suffers from the resolution quality of the workspace partitioning, which is known to scale badly in high dimensions. Our approach does not require partitioning, which helps the algorithm scale better. Moreover, in high dimensions, it is common to only verify a desirable part of the state space, where sampling-based strategies are naturally powerful. On the other hand, fine partitioning of the whole state-space is still necessary to obtain a finite abstraction that represents the original system by the needed accuracy.

Another line of work in formal verification of learning-based controllers is searching for counterexamples within a given region. For example, [6] takes this approach to verify controllers obtained using reinforcement learning. If no counterexample is found, then the whole given region is verified as safe. The counterexample search can be formulated as an SMT problem [10]. While this approach allows for one shot verification of the specification over a given region, it does not allow for direct computation of the safe region. In many applications in robot control, counterexamples are abundant, and safe regions are complex subsets of the state space. Therefore, this approach to verification has limited applicability. Similarly, [15] provides a boolean answer to the verification problem by checking a property over a given region. The method is based on formulating the verification problem as the reachability problem of a hybrid system, which is verified using state-of-the art solvers such as dReach [17] and Flow* [8]. They also do not provide a direct way to compute safe and unsafe regions.

The authors in [37] and [38] explicitly compute the forward reachable sets of DNN-based controllers. The exact computations are formidable, so they use over-approximations. Our work also computes reachable sets, albeit in a backward manner. We efficiently grow the backward reachable set using trees, thus eliminating the need for roll-out of reachable sets for a large horizon. Moreover, we are able to provide probabilistic completeness properties, whereas methods based on over-approximations are inherently conservative.

2   Problem Statement and Approach

Notation. We denote the sets of real and non-negative real numbers by $\mathbb{R}$ and $\mathbb{R}_+$, respectively. Given a set $\mathbb{S} \subseteq \mathbb{R}^n$, we use $\text{int}(\mathbb{S})$ to denote the interior of $\mathbb{S}$. Given $\mathbb{S} \subset \mathbb{R}^n$ and $A \in \mathbb{R}^{n_A \times n}$, we use $A\mathbb{S}$ to denote the set $\{As \mid s \in \mathbb{S}\}$. For a vector $x \in \mathbb{R}^n$, we use $|x|$ to denote the cardinality of the vector, i.e., $|x| = n$. All matrix inequality relations are interpreted element-wise. A *polyhedron* $\mathbb{H} \subset \mathbb{R}^n$ is the intersection of a finite number of closed half-spaces in the form $\mathbb{H} = \{x \in \mathbb{R}^n \mid Hx \leq h\}$, where $H \in \mathbb{R}^{n_H \times n}, h \in \mathbb{R}^{n_H}$ define the hyperplanes. A bounded polyhedron is called a *polytope*. A *piecewise affine (PWA) function* f is a function $f : \mathbb{H} \to \mathbb{R}^{n_f}$, where the domain $\mathbb{H} \subseteq \mathbb{R}^n$ is a union $\mathbb{H} = \bigcup_{i=1}^k \mathbb{H}_i$ of disjoint polyhedra $\mathbb{H}_1, \ldots, \mathbb{H}_k$, and where for each i, $f(x) = A_i x + b_i$ for all $x \in \mathbb{H}_i$ for some $A_i \in \mathbb{R}^{n \times n_f}$ and $b_i \in \mathbb{R}^{n_f}$.

Problem Formulation. Consider a deterministic control system

$$x_{t+1} = F(x_t, u_t)$$
$$u_t = g(x_t),$$

where $x_t \in \mathbb{X} \subseteq \mathbb{R}^n$ is the state, $u_t \in \mathbb{U} \subseteq \mathbb{R}^m$ is the control input at time $t \in \mathbb{N}$, and $F : \mathbb{X} \times \mathbb{U} \to \mathbb{R}^n$ is the system dynamics, and $g : \mathbb{R}^n \to \mathbb{U}$ is the controller. We assume that F and g are both PWA functions. Note that it is possible that there exists $x \in \mathbb{X}, u \in \mathbb{U}$ such that $F(x, u) \notin \mathbb{X}$. One of the primary tasks of the controller is to keep the state within the constraint set $\mathbb{X}$. Also, we assume that $\mathbb{X}$ is bounded. Note that one or both of F and g may be machine learning components with PWA structure. Examples include feedforward neural networks with ReLU activation functions, and decision trees with linear predicates. The closed-loop system is given as:

$$x_{t+1} = F(x_t, g(x_t)) = F_{cl}(x_t), \tag{1}$$

where F_{cl} itself is a PWA system:

$$F_{cl}(x) = A_i x + b_i, \quad \forall x \in \mathbb{C}_i, \tag{2}$$

where $\mathbb{C}_i, i = 1, \cdots, N$, are interior-disjoint polytopes, $\bigcup_{i=1}^N \mathbb{C}_i = \mathbb{X}$. The number of pieces N is dependent on the structure of F and g, but upper-bounded by the number pieces in F times the number pieces in g.

Problem 1. Given closed-loop system of the form (1), and a goal region $X_G \subseteq \mathbb{X}$, compute the two followings sets:

- $X_s \subseteq \mathbb{X}$, where all trajectories originating from it reach X_G in finite time (the *safe region*).
- $X_f \subseteq \mathbb{X}$, where all trajectories originating from it leave $\mathbb{X}$ in finite time (the *unsafe region*).

We assume that X and X_G are both given as a union of finite number of polytopes. This assumption is common in most control problems as any bounded set can be reasonably approximated using a finite number of polytopes.

Approach. The complete solution to Problem 1 partitions $X \setminus X_G$ into 3 regions: $X_s^{\max}$, the largest possible set of X_s, $X_f^{\max}$, the largest possible set of X_f, and $X_a^{\min} := X \setminus (X_s^{\max} \cup X_f^{\max})$, where $X_a^{\min}$ is the set of states from which originating trajectories neither reach the goal or violate the constraints in finite time. Therefore, $X_a^{\min}$ is a forward-invariant set. Although in most control tasks the forward-invariant sets around an equilibrium point or a limit cycle are desirable and the user typically designs X_G within it, it is possible that learning-based controllers inadvertently create invariant sets outside of X_G, where trajectories are trapped and thus is an undesirable behavior—examples of this behavior in DNN-based controllers is shown in Sect. 6.

Our solution to Problem 1 is an anytime sampling-based algorithm that gradually grows X_s and X_f, and shrinks X_a. Initially, $X_s = X_G, X_f = \emptyset$, and $X_a = X \setminus X_G$. As shown in the paper, our algorithm has probabilistic completeness: if $x \in X_s^{\max}$ or $x \in X_f^{\max}$, the probability that our solution verifies it as the algorithm runs approaches one.

Example. As an example of the safe and unsafe regions computed using our algorithm, consider the following figures:

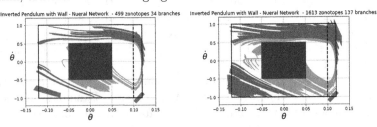

These figures plot the safe region X_s (green), unsafe region X_f (red), and unclassified region X_a (white) for a neural network controller trained to stabilize a torque-limited inverted pendulum, after 34 iterations (left) and 137 iterations (right) of our algorithm. This task is complicated by the presence of a wall, which the controller can use to "bounce" off of to aid stabilization. The presence of the contact dynamics makes the problem challenging for traditional control synthesis algorithms. On the other hand, reinforcement learning can be directly applied to solve this problem. The blue region is the goal region X_G, where the linear controller synthesized using LQR on the linearized dynamics can provably stabilize the inverted pendulum. Reinforcement learning is used to train a neural network or decision tree controller with the goal of driving the system into the blue region X_G. The region inside the black square is the constraint set $\mathbb{X}$.

At each iteration, our algorithm grows either the safe region or the unsafe region from a randomly chosen state $x \in X_a$. Some of the regions added on each iteration can be distinguished in the figure above—they tend to be elongated subsets of the state space, since they are computed by expanding a trajectory (which has measure zero) into a small region around that trajectory (which has positive measure). Comparing the two figures, we can also see how safe and unsafe regions are added over time. As can be seen, X_s tends to grow outward from X_G as the number of iterations increases. Similarly, X_f tends to grow inward from the region $\mathbb{R}^2 \setminus \mathbb{X}$. These patterns reflect the tree-like way in which the safe and unsafe regions are grown.

3   Local Constrained Affine Dynamics

We provide a framework to characterize the local affine dynamics of (1) around a given point. Recall that (1) is PWA with affine dynamics in polytopic cells.

Definition 1. *An affine cell is defined as a tuple* $\mathcal{A} = (A, b, H, h)$, *where* $F_{cl}(x) = Ax + b, \forall x \in \{x \in \mathbb{R}^n | Hx \leq h\}$.

Let the set of all affine cells be defined as $\mathbb{A}$. In this section, we explain how to derive a function $\mathcal{L} : \mathbb{X} \rightarrow \mathbb{A}$, which takes a point $x \in X$, and provides the affine cell which it belongs to. The basic idea is to fix (i) the mode of the dynamical system (if it is PWA) and (ii) the activations of the machine learning structure used in the controller. In decision trees, this means the path to the leaf is fixed. In DNNs, it means all the ReLU activations remain the same. Note that there exists a finite number of affine cells in (1). However, computing all of them in advance may not be possible. For decision trees, the number of affine cells is equivalent to the number of leaves, which is often a manageable number. For neural networks, on the other hand, the number of affine cells can be as much as $2^{|\# \text{ neurons}|}$, which can be extremely large to save on a memory. Therefore, it is better that $\mathcal{L}(x)$ is computed on-the-fly, i.e. while the algorithm is running.

Decision Trees. A depth d decision tree τ is a binary tree with $2^d - 1$ internal nodes and 2^d leaf nodes (we ignore leaf nodes when measuring depth). Each internal node of the tree is labeled with tuple (i, t), where $i \in \{1, \ldots, n\}$ (where n is the dimension of the state space) and $t \in \mathbb{R}$; we interpret this tuple as a predicate $x_i \leq t$. Each leaf node is labeled with a control input $u \in \mathbb{U}$.

We let $\mathsf{root}(\tau)$ denote the root of τ, and $\mathsf{leaves}(\tau)$ denote the leaf nodes of τ. For each leaf node ν in τ, we let $\mathsf{path}(\nu; \tau) = ((\nu_1, s_1), \ldots, (\nu_d, s_d))$ denote the sequence of internal nodes on the path from $\mathsf{root}(\tau)$ to ν (so $\nu_1 = \mathsf{root}(\tau)$ and ν_d is the parent of ν in τ). The variable $s_i \in \{\pm 1\}$ is $+1$ if ν_{i+1} is the left child of ν_i, and -1 if it is the right child (where we let $\nu_{d+1} = \nu$). Then, we associate each leaf node ν with the affine cell $\mathcal{A}_\nu = (A_\nu, b_\nu, H_\nu, h_\nu)$, where A_ν is the zero matrix, $b_\nu = u$ (where u is the label on ν), and (H_ν, h_ν) define the polyhedron $\mathbb{H}_\nu$ that is the intersection of the half-spaces

$$\{s \cdot x_i \leq t \mid (\nu', s) \in \mathsf{path}(\nu; \tau) \text{ has label } (i, t)\}. \tag{3}$$

It is clear that the polyhedra $\mathbb{H}_\nu$ associated with the leaf nodes $\nu \in \mathsf{leaves}(\tau)$ are disjoint and cover $\mathbb{R}^n$. Thus, we can interpret τ as a function $\tau : \mathbb{X} \to \mathbb{U}$, where

$$\tau(x) = \sum_{\nu \in \mathsf{leaves}(\tau)} (A_\nu x + b_\nu) \cdot \mathbb{I}[x \in \mathbb{H}_\nu],$$

where $\mathbb{I}$ is the indicator function. Thus, given $x \in \mathbb{X}$, we define $\mathcal{L}(x) = A_\nu$, where ν is the (unique) leaf node such that $x \in \mathbb{H}_\nu$.

Neural Networks. Consider a k-layer ReLU-based network. For a single layer i, let its input be x_i and output be x_{i+1}. Also, let the layer weights be $A_i \in \mathbb{R}^{|x_{i+1}| \times |x_i|}$ and the bias be $b_i \in \mathbb{R}^{|x_{i+1}|}$. The layer i input-output relationship is $x_{i+1} = \max(A_i x_i + b_i, 0)$ where $\max(\cdot)$ is taken element-wise.

To derive the polytopic cell expression, we first introduce binary vector $s_i \in \{0, 1\}^{|x_{i+1}|} = S(A_i x_i + b_i)$ where the scalar function $S(\alpha) := \mathbb{I}[\alpha \geq 0]$ is applied element-wise. Therefore, we equivalently have $x_{i+1} = \hat{A}_i x_i + \hat{b}_i$ where $\hat{A}_i = s_i \odot A_i$, $\hat{b}_i = s_i \odot b_i$ and $\odot$ is the element-wise multiplication. By recursive expansion, the network final output x_{k+1} in terms of the first layer input x_1 is

$$x_{k+1} = \underbrace{\prod_{i=1}^{k} \hat{A}_i \, x_1}_{A} + \underbrace{\sum_{i=1}^{k-1} \prod_{j=i+1}^{k} \hat{A}_j \hat{b}_i + \hat{b}_k}_{b}, \tag{4}$$

which is PWA with the pieces (defined by polytopes to be derived) dependent on the s_i. Also, since matrix multiplication is not commutative, it is worth pointing out that the enumeration is left-multiplied: $\prod_{i=1}^{k} \hat{A}_i = \hat{A}_k \hat{A}_{k-1} \ldots \hat{A}_1$.

To get the H-representation for the polytopes, we use one single layer with one single ReLU for illustration. In this case, x_2 can take on two possible values depending on if $s_1 = 1$, i.e., $A_1 x_1 + b_1 \geq 0$, or if $s_1 = 0$, i.e. $A_1 x_1 + b_1 < 0$. These two case conditions can be equivalently described as checking if $H_1 x_1 \leq h_1$, with $H_1 := (2s_1 - 1) \odot A_1$, and $h_1 := -(2s_1 - 1) \odot b_1$.

It is then straightforward, albeit tedious, to generalize that for any particular layer i, the hyperplanes defining a particular polytope is

$$H_i = (2s_i - e) A_i \prod_{j=1}^{i-1} \hat{A}_j, h_i = (2s_i - e) b_i + H_i \left(\sum_{l=1}^{i-1} \prod_{j=l+1}^{i-2} \hat{A}_j \hat{b}_l + \hat{b}_i \right) \tag{5}$$

where e is the all-one vector, such that $(2s_1 - e) \in \{-1, 1\}^{|x_{i+1}|}$ and easier for sign-flipping. For the entire network, the affine cell of a particular input x_1 is then $\mathcal{A}(x_1) = (A, b, H, h)$ with A, b as defined in (4), and H and h as simply the column concatenation of the individual H_i and h_i in (5).

Affine Cells of the Closed-Loop System. Once given a state query $x_q \in X$ and obtained affine cell for the controller $g(x) = A_u x + b_u, \forall x \in \mathbb{C}_u, x_q \in \mathbb{C}_u$, we combine it with $F(x, u) = A_F x + b_F u + c_F, \forall x \in \mathbb{C}_F, x_q \in \mathbb{C}_F$ to derive the affine cell of the closed-loop dynamics:

$$F_{cl}(x) = (A_F + b_F A_u) x + (b_F b_u + c_F), \forall x \in \mathbb{C}_u \cap \mathbb{C}_F. \tag{6}$$

4 Polytopic Trajectories

In this section we introduce *polytopic trajectories*, which is central to our verification approach. Recall that by simulating the system forward we obtain a trajectory that is a region with zero measure. A key property of this trajectory is that the points in the trajectory are either all safe or all unsafe (since the dynamics and controller are deterministic). Our algorithm expands this trajectory into a region with positive measure, such that the points in the region are either all safe or all unsafe. Doing so enables our algorithm to verify a nonzero fraction of the state space at each iteration. To obtain such a region, our algorithm expands each point in this trajectory into a polytopic region, resulting in a trajectory of polytopic regions, which we refer to as a polytopic trajectory.

Parametrization. First, we define the space of all polytopic trajectories. A polytopic trajectory is a sequence of polytopes $\mathbb{P}_t, t = 0, 1, \cdots, T$, with the constraint that $\mathbb{P}_t \subseteq \mathbb{X}$ is mapped to $\mathbb{P}_{t+1} \subseteq \mathbb{X}$ by the closed-loop dynamics. As standard, the polytopes are individually parameterized as follows:

$$\mathbb{P}_t = \bar{x}_t + G_t \mathbb{P}_b, \tag{7}$$

where $\mathbb{P}_b \subseteq \mathbb{R}^q$ is a user-defined base polytope, and $\bar{x}_t \in \mathbb{R}^n, G_t \in \mathbb{R}^{n \times q}$ are parameters characterizing $\mathbb{P}_t$ as an affine transformation of $\mathbb{P}_b$. The matrix G_t is called the *generator*. When $\mathbb{P}_b$ is chosen to be the unit hypercube in $\mathbb{R}^q$, the polytopes are referred to as *zonotopes*. Due to their balance between expressiveness and computational efficiency, zonotopes are a popular way to parameterize polytopes when verifying dynamical systems [2,12]. The remaining parameter q is chosen by the user. A typical choice is $q = n$ to obtain zonotopes of order one.

Next, we describe how our algorithm enforces the constraint on $\mathbb{P}_t$ and $\mathbb{P}_{t+1}$—i.e., that the closed-loop dynamics maps $\mathbb{P}_t$ to $\mathbb{P}_{t+1}$. If we restrict $\mathbb{P}_t$ to entirely lie in an affine cell of (1), then $\mathbb{P}_t$ will be subject to an affine transformation. In this case, $\mathbb{P}_{t+1}$ will also be a polytope. However, if $\mathbb{P}_t$ has points in multiple cells of (1), then its image under the closed-loop dynamics would be a union of polytopes (but may not itself be a polytope); the number of polytopes in this union may grow exponentially in the number of time steps. Therefore, we enforce a constraint that each polytope is contained within a single affine cell. In particular, letting the affine dynamics be $x_{t+1} = A_t x_t + b_t$, we have

$$\mathbb{P}_{t+1} = A_t \bar{x}_t + b_t + A_t G_t \mathbb{P}_b. \tag{8}$$

Therefore, we obtain linear relations for the parameters of the polytopes:

$$\bar{x}_{t+1} = A_t \bar{x}_t + b_t, G_{t+1} = A_t G_t. \tag{9}$$

Finally, we remark that in many control problems, the underlying system evolves in continuous-time. Therefore, it is preferable to include the states between $\mathbb{P}_t$ and $\mathbb{P}_{t+1}$ in the polytopic region, since those states are traversed between two polytopes. One reasonable approximation is computing the convex hull of $\mathbb{P}_t$ and $\mathbb{P}_{t+1}$, but this approximation is computationally demanding. An alternative is adding $x_{t+1} - x_t$ as an additional column to G_t, which elongates the zonotope alongside the trajectory path. Due to its simplicity, we use the latter method.

Optimization. Next, we describe how our algorithm computes the parameters $\{(\bar{x}_t, G_t)\}_{t=0,\cdots,T-1}$ of a polytopic trajectory that satisfies the property that the states in the polytopic trajectory are either all safe or all unsafe. Our algorithm uses a convex program to do so. Let the sampled trajectory be $x_0, x_1, \cdots, x_T$, where x_T is already known to be safe or unsafe. Suppose that $x_T \in \mathbb{P}_{\text{target}}$, where the *target polytope* $\mathbb{P}_{\text{target}}$ is a polytope around x_T that is known to be safe or unsafe. The existence of such a polytope is guaranteed since our algorithm keeps track of safe and unsafe regions as a union of polytopes—in particular, the target polytope may be one of the following regions: X_G, $\mathbb{R}^n \setminus X_G$, or a polytope in X_s or X_f. Details are in Sect. 5; for now, we suppose that $\mathbb{P}_{\text{target}}$ is given.

We compute a polytopic trajectory using the following optimization problem:

$$\{(\bar{x}_t, G_t)\}_{t=0,\cdots,T-1} = \arg\min \ \alpha\left(\{(\bar{x}_t, G_t)\}_{t=0,\cdots,T-1}\right)$$
$$\text{subj. to } \ G_{t+1} = A_t G_t, \bar{x}_{t+1} = A_t \bar{x}_t + b_t, \bar{x}_0 = x_0,$$
$$\bar{x}_t + G_t \mathbb{P}_b \subseteq \mathbb{C}_t, \bar{x}_T + G_T \mathbb{P}_b \subseteq \mathbb{P}_{\text{target}}, \quad (10)$$
$$(A_t, b_t, \mathbb{C}_t) = \mathcal{L}(x_t), t \in \{0, \cdots, T-1\}.$$

where $\alpha : \prod_{i=0}^{T-1} \mathbb{R}^n \times \mathbb{R}^{n \times q} \to \mathbb{R}$ is a cost function that is user-defined. The first line of constraints in (10) encode the closed-loop dynamics $\mathbb{P}_t$ to $\mathbb{P}_{t+1}$ and the initial state. The second line is polytope containment constraints that ensure that the whole $\mathbb{P}_t$ is subject to a single affine dynamics and the final polytope is contained in the target polytope $\mathbb{P}_{\text{target}}$. The details on how to encode polytope containment problems into a set of linear constraints using auxiliary variables and constraints is available in [27]. Thus, all the constraints in (10) are linear.

We wish to design α to promote larger volumes for the polytopes. The volume of zonotopes is generally a non-convex objective [18]. Thus we use heuristics for designing α. A useful, simple, form of α is

$$\alpha = \text{Tr}\begin{pmatrix} G_0 & 0 \\ 0 & G_0^T \end{pmatrix}. \quad (11)$$

Note that if $\mathbb{P}_b$ is the unit hypercube, it follows from symmetry that restricting the diagonal terms in the matrix in (11) to be non-negative does not have any effect on $\mathbb{P}_0$ as zonotopes are invariant with respect to multiplication of the columns of their generator by -1. A notable difference between (10) and computing the region of attraction of LQR controllers in [32] is that in the latter, the verified regions are centered around the nominal trajectory. In contrast, there is no such restriction in (10), so the polytopic trajectory can shift around the nominal trajectory. This fact is important since constructing polytopes centered at the points of the trajectory can lead to very small polytopes if only one time point of the trajectory lies close to the boundary of its affine cell.

Computational Complexity. Using (11), the optimization problem in (10) becomes a linear program which its size scales quadratically with n, the dimension of the state, and linearly in length of the trajectory. The polytope containment constraints introduce auxiliary variables whose size grows linearly with n

---

Algorithm 1. Construction of Polytopic Verification Trees

Require: System (1) and X_G ▷ The closed loop system and the goal
Require: $i^{\max}, T^{\max}, \mathcal{L} : X \to \mathbb{L}$ ▷ The number of iterations, the maximum time of forward simulation, and local constrained affine system generator
  $i = 0, X_s = X_G, X_f = \emptyset$ ▷ Initialization
  while $i \leq i^{\max}$ **do**
    $x_0 \leftarrow$ sample from $X \setminus (X_s \cup X_f), t = 0$
    while $t \leq T^{\max}$ **do**
      if $x_t \in \mathbb{P}, \mathbb{P} \subseteq X_s$ **then** ▷ $\mathbb{P}$ is a polytope
        flag $\leftarrow$ safe
        Compute polytopic trajectory $\mathbb{P}_0, \mathbb{P}_1, \cdots, \mathbb{P}_{t-1}$ using (10) with $\mathbb{P}_{\text{target}} = \mathbb{P}$
        Add branch to the tree and add $\mathbb{P}_0, \mathbb{P}_1, \cdots, \mathbb{P}_{t-1}$ to X_s
        Break
      if $x_t \in \mathbb{P}, \mathbb{P} \subseteq X_f$ or $x_t \notin \mathbb{X}$ **then** ▷ $\mathbb{P}$ is a polytope
        flag $\leftarrow$ unsafe
        Compute polytopic trajectory $\mathbb{P}_0, \mathbb{P}_1, \cdots, \mathbb{P}_{t-1}$ using (10) with $\mathbb{P}_{\text{target}} = \mathbb{P}$
        Add branch to the tree and add $\mathbb{P}_0, \mathbb{P}_1, \cdots, \mathbb{P}_{t-1}$ to X_f
        Break
      $x_{t+1} = F_{cl}(x_t)$ ▷ Simulate system forward
      $\mathbb{C}_{t+1} = \mathcal{L}(x_{t+1})$ ▷ Compute the polytopic linear system
  return X_s, X_f

---

and with the number of rows of the hyperplane, where the latter grows linearly with (i) the depth of the decision tree, (ii) the number of nodes in the DNN. Therefore, obtaining polytopic trajectories is a very efficient procedure.

5 Polytopic Trees

We describe our polytopic tree algorithm (outlined in Algorithm 1).

5.1 Sampling Unclassified States and Checking Membership

At each iteration, we first sample a point from the *unclassified states* $\mathbb{X} \setminus (X_s \cup X_f)$. A straightforward approach is to use rejection sampling—i.e., sample x from X, and reject it if it belongs to $(X_s \cup X_f)$. However, the subroutine of checking whether $x \in (X_s \cup X_f)$ can be computationally challenging as $(X_s \cup X_f)$ grows with the number of iterations. Recall that both X_s and X_f consist of a finite number of polytopes. There are several approaches to checking if $x \in (X_s \cup X_f)$.

The first approach is to check the feasibility of $x = \bar{x}_i + G_i p$, for $p \in \mathbb{P}_b$ and $i \in \{1, \cdots, N\}$, where $\bar{x}_i, G_i$ are the parameters of the ith polytope in $(X_s \cup X_f)$, and N is the total number of polytopes. This approach requires at most N linear programs, which the size of each is linear in n and q, and very small. The second approach is to precompute the hyperplanes of all polytopes; then, instead of checking feasibility of linear programs, we can evaluate the partial order relation required to check if a point is within the intersection of multiple hyperplanes.

However, finding the hyperplanes may also be computationally challenging. Both methods can be greatly accelerated using binary search methods for manipulating a large number of polytopes [35].

5.2 Growing the Polytopic Tree

A *polytopic tree* is a tree-like data structure where each node is labeled with a polytope; in general, these "trees" may have multiple roots. Our algorithm represents the regions X_s and X_f as polytopic trees, where we require that the parent $\mathbb{P}'$ of a polytope $\mathbb{P}$ contains the image of $\mathbb{P}$ under the closed-loop dynamics. The regions X_s and X_f are simply the union of all polytopes in the tree. Initially, we represent $X_s = X_G$ as the "tree" where each polytope in X_G is its own root, and represent $X_f = \emptyset$ as the empty tree.

We iteratively grow the polytopic trees representing X_s and X_f by sampling an unclassified state x_0 from $\mathbb{X} \setminus (X_s \cup X_f)$, forward simulating the system from x_0 to obtain a trajectory, and then expanding the resulting trajectory into a polytopic trajectory. More precisely, during forward simulation, once we have state x_t of the trajectory, we compute $\mathbb{C}_t = \mathcal{L}(x_t)$, and check whether to stop at x_t. There are 4 cases: (i) $x_t \in X_G$ (i.e., the goal is reached), (ii) $x_t \notin \mathbb{X}$ (i.e., the state bounds are violated), (iii) $x_t \in (X_s \cup X_f)$ (i.e., the state is already known to be safe or unsafe), or (iv) $t > T^{\max}$, where $T^{\max}$ is a bound on the trajectory length specified by the user. In cases (i), (ii), and (iii), we terminate the trajectory (so $T = t$), and compute a polytopic trajectory by solving (10) with initial state x_0, sequence of affine cells $\mathbb{C}_0, \cdots, \mathbb{C}_{T-1}$, and target polytope $\mathbb{P}_T$ chosen to be the polytope encountered in X_G (case (i)), $\mathbb{R} \setminus \mathbb{X}$ (case (ii)), or $X_s \cup X_f$ (case (iii)). In case (iii), we can determine $\mathbb{P}_T$ since our algorithm represents X_s and X_f each as a finite union of polytopes. In case (iv), we assume that the trajectory belongs to the set $X_a^{\min}$, and ignore the trajectory.

Once we have computed the polytopic trajectory, we insert the polytopes $\mathbb{P}_0, \ldots, \mathbb{P}_{T-1}$ into the appropriate polytopic tree—i.e., the tree representing X_s if $\mathbb{P}_T$ is safe, and the tree representing X_f if $\mathbb{P}_T$ is unsafe. To do so, we simply set the parent of $\mathbb{P}_t$ to be $\mathbb{P}_{t+1}$ for each $t \in \{0, 1, \ldots, T-1\}$. Except in case (ii), $\mathbb{P}_T$ is already in the tree; in case (ii), if $\mathbb{P}_T$ is not yet in the polytopic tree representing X_f, then we add it as a new root node. The following result is straightforward:

Theorem 1 (Correctness). *Algorithm 1 returns X_s and X_f, from which all originating trajectories reach X_G and $\mathbb{R}^n \setminus \mathbb{X}$, respectively, in finite time.*

5.3 Probabilistic Completeness

We state the completeness result of our algorithm. We require two mild assumptions, which are similar to the assumptions made in [32].

Assumption 1. *For any measurable $\mathbb{Y} \subseteq \mathbb{X}$, the sampler chooses a point from $\mathbb{Y}$ with non-zero probability.*

Assumption 2. *Given* $x_0 \in int(X_s^{\max} \cup X_f^{\max})$, *there is a non-zero probability that the polytopic trajectory optimization* (10) *provides* $\mathbb{P}_0$ *with non-zero volume* $vol(\mathbb{P}_0) \geq \lambda > 0$ *for some uniform constant* λ.

Assumption 1 is not restrictive as we are often able to sample uniformly from $\mathbb{X}$. Assumption 2 relies on the heuristics used in (10). We empirically have observed that the polytopes always have non-zero volume. If a polytope with zero volume is obtained (even after elongating it across the trajectory, as explained in Sect. 4), we can discard it and use another heuristic. Moreover, the assumption that a uniform constant exists is not restrictive as there exists a finite number of affine cells with non-zero volume. Therefore, the assumption boils down to (10) being able to find a polytopic inner-approximation to an affine cell that covers a certain fraction of its volume if provided an appropriate cost function.

Theorem 2 (Probabilistic Completeness). *Let* X_s^i *and* X_f^i *be the* X_s *and* X_f *computed Algorithm 1 by the* i'th *iteration. Then if Assumption 1 and Assumption 2 both hold, the following holds:*

$$Pr\left(\lim_{i \to \infty} int(X_s^{\max} \setminus X_s^i) \cup int(X_f^{\max} \setminus X_f^i) = \emptyset\right) = 1. \tag{12}$$

Proof. In Appendix A.

6   Example

We adopt example 1 from [23] and [28]. The model represents an inverted pendulum with a spring-loaded wall on one side, as illustrated in Fig. 1 [Left]. The control input is the torque. The system is constrained to $|\theta| \leq 0.12$, $|\dot{\theta}| \leq 1$, $|u| \leq 4$, and the wall is located at $\theta = 0.1$. The problem is to steer the state toward the origin. We set $X_G = [-0.05, 0.05] \times [-0.5, 0.5]$. We know from [23] that X_G is within the region of attraction of the linear quadratic regulator (LQR) controller of the contact-free dynamics (which is Ω in Fig. 1 [Left]). Therefore, once the trajectories end in X_G, they are guaranteed to asymptotically reach the origin. The dynamics is a hybrid model with two modes associated with "contact-free" and "contact". The piecewise affine dynamics is:

$$A_1 = \begin{pmatrix} 1 & 0.01 \\ 0.1 & 1 \end{pmatrix}, A_2 = \begin{pmatrix} 1 & 0.01 \\ -9.9 & 1 \end{pmatrix}, B_1 = B_2 = \begin{pmatrix} 0 \\ 0.01 \end{pmatrix}, c_1 = \begin{pmatrix} 0 \\ 0 \end{pmatrix}, c_2 = \begin{pmatrix} 0 \\ 1 \end{pmatrix},$$

where mode 1 and 2 correspond to contact-free ($\theta \leq 0.1$) and contact dynamics ($\theta > 0.1$), respectively.

6.1   Controller Based on Formal Synthesis

It is non-trivial to control this hybrid system. Both [23] and [28] use approximate explicit hybrid model predictive control (MPC) to compute an inner-approximation of the safe region. The method in [28] is sampling-based and it achieves probabilistic feedback coverage. As shown in Fig. 1 (right), the safe region is **not** the whole state-space and it takes a very non-trivial shape.

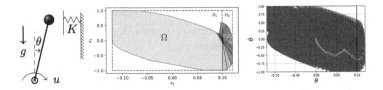

Fig. 1. Example: The inverted pendulum with wall (left). The model-based safe regions as obtained from figures in [23] (middle), and [28] (right).

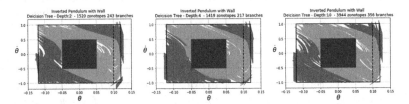

Fig. 2. Example: Verified regions for system controlled with a decision tree. X_G, X_s, X_f are shared in blue, green, and red, respectively. (Color figure online)

6.2   Decision Tree Controllers

Training. We use the VIPER algorithm to learn decision trees [6]. Learning decision tree controllers is challenging due to their discrete structure—in particular, the gradient of the loss function for a decision tree is zero almost everywhere. To address this challenge, VIPER first learns a neural network controller using standard reinforcement learning algorithms. Then, it uses *imitation learning* to train a decision tree controller that "mimics" the neural network controller [26]. In particular, given an "oracle controller" (i.e., the neural network), imitation learning reduces the reinforcement learning problem for the decision tree controller to a supervised learning problem. Thus, we can use standard CART algorithm for learning decision trees [7]. See [6] for details.

Verification. The results are shown in Fig. 2. Since all decision trees are extracted from the same neural network, their performance looks quite similar, albeit the smallest decision tree with depth 2 performs slightly weaker than the others, which is interpreted by the larger unsafe region and smaller safe region. All the decision trees perform superb handling the contact, which is due to the fact that constant controller in this area of the state space is sufficient. On the other hand, the decision tree behaves very poorly with negative angle and small velocities as piecewise constant decisions are not sufficient to conduct a maneuver that brings the state to get into the goal.

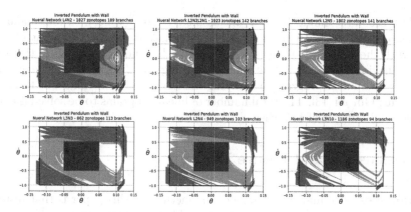

Fig. 3. Example: Verified regions for system controlled with a neural network. X_G, X_s, X_f are shared in blue, green, and red, respectively. (Color figure online)

6.3 Neural Network Controllers

Training. The neural network used to guide the training of the decision tree is too large for our algorithm to verify. It is known that neural networks must be vastly overparameterized to obtain good performance (otherwise, they are susceptible to local optima) [22], which explains why we can approximate a large neural network with small decision trees. Indeed, we found that training a small neural network using reinforcement learning was intractable. Instead, we used supervised learning—we run the model-based PWA controller described in [23] to generate state-control pairs, and construct ReLU-based DNN of various depth and size to minimize the mean-square-error between the network prediction and those labels. Using this approach, the neural networks still performed poorly, even though they were comparable in size to the smallest decision tree. Nevertheless, this experiment complements the decision tree experiment—the emphasis for decision trees is on the verifying "good" behaviors, whereas the emphasis here is on identifying "bad" behaviors.

Verification. Figure 3 shows the verified regions of various neural network controllers. We name the network by its size and depth, e.g. L4N2 means the network has four layers with two ReLUs each, and L2N2L2N1 means the first two layers have two ReLUs each and the last two layers have just one each; in addition to these ReLU-based layers, all networks also have a final affine layer.

We observe that on average, the algorithm covers a larger falsified region, which is to be expected since the network is not an ideal stabilizing controller. The plots in each column exhibit a variety of different traits. For example, the figures in the first column exhibit lack of robustness of the neural network—around the vertical strip of between $[0.05, 0.10]$, there is a slim unsafe region encompassed by a large safe region. In particular, in this portion of the state space, even a very small deviation from the state space can lead to unsafety.

The second column has an unclassified region (white). Upon manually inspecting the control behavior, we observe chattering near the point of contact with the wall—i.e., the system repeatedly hit and bounced off of the wall. This behavior showcases a limitation of learning-based controllers. The average time for each linear program in verifying the largest NN controller was less than 0.1 s using Gurobi [13]. The total number of linear programs to be solved is equal to the total number of branches.

7   Discussion and Future Work

Advantages. The main advantage of the method in this paper is that instead of verifying a property over a region, it is able to compute regions of safe and unsafe states, which is more relevant in problems where the set of safe states is a complex subset of the state space. Our approach is easy to deploy as it based on anytime algorithm that only requires sampling, forward simulation, and linear programming, and unlike most related verification techniques, it has the potential to be applied to large-scale problems.

Limitations. The last advantage point above is conditioned on the number of samples and polytopic branches required to provide a reasonable volume of verified regions. A major drawback of our approach stems from the fact that it relies on each polytope to be contained within a single affine cell. For many machine learning components, especially DNNs, these affine cells can be very small, thus making polytopes small hence requiring denser trees for proper coverage. This issue was alleviated for decision tree controllers, where the number of affine cells scales linearly with the number of leaves. A promising direction to resolve this issue is focusing on interpretable neural networks [3,19], which are trained in a way that they are less fragile and typically have fewer and larger affine cells. This limitation is less severe in many applications that we are only interested in verifying regions around a nominal point or trajectory.

Another limitation of our approach is the restriction to PWA dynamical systems and controllers. While the linearity assumption around a nominal trajectory is reasonable, this restriction limits us from constructing larger verified regions that are able to incorporate nonlinearities.

Future Directions. An immediate future direction is characterizing $X_a^{\max}$. A potential approach is searching for equilibria or limit cycles and applying the methods in this paper to characterize states leading to limit cycles. Moreover, we are planning to leverage the results in this paper to develop compositional methods for controller synthesis and verification. For instance, by learning a controller that steers trajectories from the unsafe region of another controller to its safe regions, we can compose controllers in a hierarchical manner. This approach has the potential to provide a framework for learning-based control synthesis in a more scalable, interpretable, and formally correct way.

A   Appendix

A.1   Proof of Theorem 2

Proof. Let $X_r^i = X_s^{\max} \setminus X_s^i$. We need to show that $\lim_{i \to \infty} \text{int}(X_r^i) = \emptyset$ with probability one. The same argument holds for $X_f^{\max} \setminus X_f^i$. We prove by contradiction. Let $\lim_{i \to \infty} X_r^i$ be a measurable set. It follows from Assumption 1 that we obtain a sample from X_r^∞ with non-zero probability. Then we simulate the system forward from the sampled state x_0. Once the trajectory is obtained, the polytopic trajectory is computed, and by Assumption 2, we obtain a measurable $\mathbb{P}_0$, centered at $x_0 \in \text{int}(X_r^\infty)$ that has non-empty intersection with X_r^∞. Therefore, by non-zero probability, the volume of X_r^i shrinks in one iteration by at least λ. Thus we reach a contradiction.

References

1. Abbeel, P., Coates, A., Quigley, M., Ng, A.Y.: An application of reinforcement learning to aerobatic helicopter flight. In: Advances in Neural Information Processing Systems, pp. 1–8 (2007)
2. Althoff, M., Stursberg, O., Buss, M.: Computing reachable sets of hybrid systems using a combination of zonotopes and polytopes. Nonlinear Anal.: Hybrid Syst. 4(2), 233–249 (2010)
3. Alvarez-Melis, D., Jaakkola, T.S.: Towards robust interpretability with self-explaining neural networks. arXiv preprint arXiv:1806.07538 (2018)
4. Andrychowicz, M., et al.: Learning dexterous in-hand manipulation. arXiv preprint arXiv:1808.00177 (2018)
5. Bastani, O., Ioannou, Y., Lampropoulos, L., Vytiniotis, D., Nori, A., Criminisi, A.: Measuring neural net robustness with constraints. In: Advances in Neural Information Processing Systems, pp. 2613–2621 (2016)
6. Bastani, O., Pu, Y., Solar-Lezama, A.: Verifiable reinforcement learning via policy extraction. arXiv preprint arXiv:1805.08328 (2018)
7. Breiman, L.: Classification and Regression Trees. Routledge, Abingdon (2017)
8. Chen, X., Abraham, E., Sankaranarayanan, S.: Taylor model flowpipe construction for non-linear hybrid systems. In: 2012 IEEE 33rd Real-Time Systems Symposium (RTSS), pp. 183–192. IEEE (2012)
9. Collins, S., Ruina, A., Tedrake, R., Wisse, M.: Efficient bipedal robots based on passive-dynamic walkers. Science 307(5712), 1082–1085 (2005)
10. Gao, S., Kong, S., Clarke, E.M.: dReal: an SMT solver for nonlinear theories over the reals. In: Bonacina, M.P. (ed.) CADE 2013. LNCS, vol. 7898, pp. 208–214. Springer, Heidelberg (2013). https://doi.org/10.1007/978-3-642-38574-2_14
11. Gehr, T., Mirman, M., Drachsler-Cohen, D., Tsankov, P., Chaudhuri, S., Vechev, M.: AI2: safety and robustness certification of neural networks with abstract interpretation
12. Girard, A.: Reachability of uncertain linear systems using zonotopes. In: Morari, M., Thiele, L. (eds.) HSCC 2005. LNCS, vol. 3414, pp. 291–305. Springer, Heidelberg (2005). https://doi.org/10.1007/978-3-540-31954-2_19
13. Gurobi Optimization, Inc.: Gurobi optimizer reference manual (2016). http://www.gurobi.com

14. Huang, X., Kwiatkowska, M., Wang, S., Wu, M.: Safety verification of deep neural networks. In: Majumdar, R., Kunčak, V. (eds.) CAV 2017. LNCS, vol. 10426, pp. 3–29. Springer, Cham (2017). https://doi.org/10.1007/978-3-319-63387-9_1

15. Ivanov, R., Weimer, J., Alur, R., Pappas, G.J., Lee, I.: Verisig: verifying safety properties of hybrid systems with neural network controllers. arXiv preprint arXiv:1811.01828 (2018)

16. Katz, G., Barrett, C., Dill, D.L., Julian, K., Kochenderfer, M.J.: Reluplex: an efficient SMT solver for verifying deep neural networks. In: Majumdar, R., Kunčak, V. (eds.) CAV 2017. LNCS, vol. 10426, pp. 97–117. Springer, Cham (2017). https://doi.org/10.1007/978-3-319-63387-9_5

17. Kong, S., Gao, S., Chen, W., Clarke, E.: dReach: δ-reachability analysis for hybrid systems. In: Baier, C., Tinelli, C. (eds.) TACAS 2015. LNCS, vol. 9035, pp. 200–205. Springer, Heidelberg (2015). https://doi.org/10.1007/978-3-662-46681-0_15

18. Kopetzki, A.K., Schürmann, B., Althoff, M.: Efficient methods for order reduction of zonotopes. In: Proceedings of the 56th IEEE Conference on Decision and Control (2017)

19. Lei, T., Barzilay, R., Jaakkola, T.: Rationalizing neural predictions. arXiv preprint arXiv:1606.04155 (2016)

20. Levine, S., Finn, C., Darrell, T., Abbeel, P.: End-to-end training of deep visuomotor policies. J. Mach. Learn. Res. 17(1), 1334–1373 (2016)

21. Levine, S., Koltun, V.: Guided policy search. In: International Conference on Machine Learning, pp. 1–9 (2013)

22. Li, Y., Liang, Y.: Learning overparameterized neural networks via stochastic gradient descent on structured data. In: Advances in Neural Information Processing Systems, pp. 8168–8177 (2018)

23. Marcucci, T., Deits, R., Gabiccini, M., Biechi, A., Tedrake, R.: Approximate hybrid model predictive control for multi-contact push recovery in complex environments. In: 2017 IEEE-RAS 17th International Conference on Humanoid Robotics (Humanoids), pp. 31–38. IEEE (2017)

24. Pan, Y., et al.: Learning deep neural network control policies for agile off-road autonomous driving. In: The NIPS Deep Reinforcement Learning Symposium (2017)

25. Raghunathan, A., Steinhardt, J., Liang, P.S.: Semidefinite relaxations for certifying robustness to adversarial examples. In: Advances in Neural Information Processing Systems, pp. 10900–10910 (2018)

26. Ross, S., Gordon, G., Bagnell, D.: A reduction of imitation learning and structured prediction to no-regret online learning. In: Proceedings of the Fourteenth International Conference on Artificial Intelligence and Statistics, pp. 627–635 (2011)

27. Sadraddini, S., Tedrake, R.: Linear encodings for polytope containment problems. arXiv preprint arXiv:1903.05214 (2019)

28. Sadraddini, S., Tedrake, R.: Sampling-based polytopic trees for approximate optimal control of piecewise affine systems. In: International Conference on Robotics and Automation (ICRA) (2019)

29. Su, J., Vargas, D.V., Sakurai, K.: One pixel attack for fooling deep neural networks. IEEE Trans. Evol. Comput. (2019)

30. Sun, X., Khedr, H., Shoukry, Y.: Formal verification of neural network controlled autonomous systems. arXiv preprint arXiv:1810.13072 (2018)

31. Szegedy, C., et al.: Intriguing properties of neural networks. In: ICLR (2014)

32. Tedrake, R., Manchester, I.R., Tobenkin, M., Roberts, J.W.: LQR-trees: feedback motion planning via sums-of-squares verification. Int. J. Robot. Res. 29(8), 1038–1052 (2010)

33. Tjeng, V., Tedrake, R.: Verifying neural networks with mixed integer programming. arXiv preprint arXiv:1711.07356 (2017)
34. Tjeng, V., Xiao, K.Y., Tedrake, R.: Evaluating robustness of neural networks with mixed integer programming (2018)
35. Tøndel, P., Johansen, T.A., Bemporad, A.: Evaluation of piecewise affine control via binary search tree. Automatica **39**(5), 945–950 (2003)
36. Wong, E., Kolter, Z.: Provable defenses against adversarial examples via the convex outer adversarial polytope. In: International Conference on Machine Learning, pp. 5283–5292 (2018)
37. Xiang, W., Lopez, D.M., Musau, P., Johnson, T.T.: Reachable set estimation and verification for neural network models of nonlinear dynamic systems. In: Yu, H., Li, X., Murray, R.M., Ramesh, S., Tomlin, C.J. (eds.) Safe, Autonomous and Intelligent Vehicles. UST, pp. 123–144. Springer, Cham (2019). https://doi.org/10.1007/978-3-319-97301-2_7
38. Xiang, W., Tran, H.D., Johnson, T.T.: Specification-guided safety verification for feedforward neural networks. arXiv preprint arXiv:1812.06161 (2018)

Mutant Accuracy Testing for Assessing the Implementation of Numerical Algorithms

Ruining (Ray) Wu[1,2] and Ian M. Mitchell[1(✉)] (iD)

[1] Department of Computer Science,
The University of British Columbia, Vancouver, Canada
`ian.mitchell@ubc.ca`
[2] Department of Computer Science, University of Toronto, Toronto, Canada
`rwu@cs.toronto.edu`
`http://www.cs.ubc.ca/~mitchell`

Abstract. Despite their widespread use, implementations of numerical computing algorithms are generally tested manually with fuzzily defined thresholds determining success or failure. Modern software testing methods, such as automated regression testing, are difficult to apply because both test oracles and algorithm output are approximate. Based on the observation that high accuracy numerical algorithms appear to be fragile by design to errors in their parameters, we propose to compare the error of target implementations to mutated versions of themselves with the expectation that the mutants will suffer degraded accuracy. We test the idea on MATLAB implementations of some basic numerical algorithms, and find that most mutants are worse while the few which are better show a distinctive pattern of mutation.

Keywords: Mutation testing · Numerical algorithms ·
Oracle problem · Hypothesis testing

1 Introduction

Testing is a well-refined art in most areas of computing; for example, automated regression and mutation testing are used to ensure that intended code changes do not introduce bugs and that test suites provide sufficient coverage to detect artificially introduced bugs respectively. But much of this infrastructure depends on knowing the correct output for each test; in other words, the test oracle is exact. Although accurate numerical calculation has been a known challenge since before modern computers [3] and has been the subject of serious academic research for

This work was supported by National Science and Engineering Research Council of Canada (NSERC) Discovery Grant RGPIN-2017-04543 and an Undergraduate Student Research Award (USRA).

M. Zamani and D. Zufferey (Eds.): NSV 2019, LNCS 11652, pp. 128–144, 2019.
https://doi.org/10.1007/978-3-030-28423-7_9

more than seventy years (for example, [14]), the state of the art for testing implementations of numerical algorithms is much more manual [12]. A key reason is that approximation is everywhere in numerical computing. Not only are test oracles approximate, but implementations will generate output containing error when coded correctly, and different implementations may generate different but still correct output. Even the most rigorous categories of testing, such as convergence rate studies, often involve heuristically enforced thresholds; for example, is a fourth order accurate Runge-Kutta scheme for numerically solving initial value ordinary differential equation problems correctly implemented if the measured convergence rate is 3.95? What about 3.89?

Our goal with the technique described in this paper was to develop a testing approach for numerical implementations which:

- Eliminated the need for threshold checks to determine correctness, or at least made the outcome less sensitive to the precise value of that threshold.
- Could be automated to encourage more widespread use of regression testing.

To test a target implementation, we propose to generate a collection of mutant implementations and compare their accuracy against the target, with the hypothesis that the accuracy of mutants of correct targets will degrade significantly, while those of incorrect targets will degrade much less.

We test this idea on MATLAB implementations—both correct and with artificially introduced bugs—of three basic numerical algorithms. Most mutants show degraded accuracy, most buggy implementations show less fragility, and results for a given algorithm do not depend strongly on our choice of threshold. Unfortunately, some mutants have better accuracy, some buggy implementations are more fragile, and different algorithms show quantitatively different responses. Because of this variability, it is unclear how the technique might be automated; however, manual inspection of the mutants which demonstrated better accuracy was enlightening and may prove useful for evaluating the quality of an implementation.

It should be noted that we focus on software designed to produce numerical approximations to mathematical problems. Software for symbolic mathematics (such as the SageMath system, Mathematica, or Maple) is also in widespread use; however, we believe that such implementations are more amenable to traditional software testing approaches because approximation plays a smaller role in typical symbolic mathematics tasks.

2   Background

Numerically approximating the solution of a scientific or other real-world problem is subject to many types of error, so we first categorize these errors and identify which we consider in this paper. We then discuss the limitations of oracles available for numerical computing problems and the types of testing often performed on numerical implementations. We conclude the section with a brief discussion of mutation testing, which is typically used for enterprise software but which has at least once been repurposed for numerical implementations, albeit in a manner different than what we propose.

2.1 Sources of Error in Numerical Computations

Because computer hardware implements only arithmetic and perhaps a few elementary functions, most mathematical tasks on computers involve approximations of various kinds. Demonstrating the correctness of a numerical approximation can be divided into two tasks [12]:

- Validation: Determining whether the mathematical models are sufficiently accurate; in other words, "did you solve the right equations?"
- Verification: Determining whether the implementation produces an accurate approximation of the solution; in other words, "did you solve the equations right?"

Here we will explore only verification, but it is worth keeping in mind that because most real problems involve modeling error, driving implementation error all the way to zero would be wasted effort.

The field of numerical analysis has for decades focused on the construction of algorithms for approximating various mathematical models which are accurate, in the sense that the difference (or error) between the true solution of the equations and the computed approximation are small. Accuracy can be broken into two components [5]. Problem conditioning measures the effect on the solution of perturbing the problem's parameters. Computational error measures the effect on the solution of errors made during computation. We again narrow our focus in this paper to questions of the latter, but we will assume that our target problems are well-conditioned and the primary sources of error are computational.

Finally, we will distinguish two different categories of computational error. Roundoff error arises because we use floating point rather than real numbers to represent values, and at regular intervals during computation results must be rounded to some finite precision. Truncation (or discretization) error arises when we terminate what is mathematically an infinite object or process; for example, represent a continuous function by its value at finitely many points, truncate a Taylor series after finitely many terms, or stop an infinite recurrence after finitely many iterations. While finite precision arithmetic could be considered a form of truncation, we distinguish these two cases because in typical computing environments the user has very limited ability to choose the precision of the arithmetic (for example, choosing either single or double precision floating point numbers), while truncation error can often be tuned more finely with a user controlled parameter (for example, step size in ODE solvers).

2.2 Oracles

An oracle [7] is a mechanism by which we can determine the correctness of a test case. When an exact oracle exists, testing computer programs is relatively straightforward: Run the test case through the program and compare the computed result to the oracle's answer. While it is impractical in most cases to test every possible input, with each correct test case our confidence in the program increases.

Two key challenges arise in testing numerical algorithms. First, an exact oracle may not be available. The class of test cases for which analytic solutions are known can be quite restricted, so testing only within this class may not properly exercise the implementation. In some cases, including the ones considered in Sect. 4, we can work around this constraint using the method of manufactured solutions (MMS) (for example, see [10, 12, 13]). In MMS, we start from an analytic solution and work backwards to define a problem with that solution; for example, to test a one dimensional quadrature (numerical integration) routine, we start with an arbitrary differentiable function $f(x)$ and suitable endpoints $a, b \in \mathbb{R}$. The test problem is defined as $\int_a^b f'(x)\, dx$, where $f'(x)$ is easily found by analytic differentiation, and the analytic solution is given by $f(b) - f(a)$. However, even if an analytic solution is known, its constituent elements may not be finitely computable and/or representable on the computer; for example, if $f(x)$ in the example above includes a term involving $\sin(x)$. Consequently, we should expect that only approximate oracles are available in practice.

Second, not only do we expect an approximate answer from our implementation, but we typically do not have a precise a priori bound at the time algorithms are designed, implemented and tested for either the expected error in the approximation or the desired accuracy.[1] The former arises because rigorous quantitative analysis of even the computational sources of error is complicated enough that it is rarely done, and the latter because non-computational sources of error (such as modeling and propagated data error) are often poorly quantified, leading to decreased certainty about the level of tolerable computational error.

In summary, for much of the numerical computing domain we cannot use the common approach to testing software implementations which asserts the presence of a bug if the program's output on a test case does not exactly match that of the oracle. Consequently, the practice of testing numerical algorithms has diverged from the rest of the testing community.

2.3 Testing Numerical Algorithms

A number of approaches have been designed to manage or analyze computational error. The first is simply to ensure that the algorithm chosen is stable; in other words, that errors made in early steps of the computation (including in the representation of the input data) do not grow dramatically in later steps [1, 5]. More quantitatively, interval arithmetic can be used to bound computational sources of error; for example, VNODE-LP is a software package for

---

[1] These quantities may be known when it comes time to solve a particular problem, but outside of introductory numerical analysis courses most problems are solved by calling a library routine or legacy implementation; consequently, those who design, implement and test such routines should not assume knowledge of these values.

computing solutions to ordinary differential equations which produces intervals within which the true solution is known to lie [11]. An alternative quantitative approach focused on estimating the effect of roundoff error is the Contrôle et Estimation STochastic des Arrondis de Calculs (CESTAC) method implemented in the CADNA library [9], which essentially repeats the calculation several times under different rounding regimes and thereby provides a probabilistic estimate of both the approximate solution and the magnitude of the roundoff error. However, approaches like these are intended to quantify the computational error incurred during a calculation, not to demonstrate correct implementation: Even if the error between the approximation and oracle for all test cases lies within the computed bounds, there may still be bugs.

In contrast, there has been work in the domain of automatic theorem proving to formally demonstrate implementation correctness; for example, Gappa is a tool which makes it easier to construct formal proof obligations which would demonstrate that for a C implementation of a floating point algorithm the error would lie within a specified interval; these proof obligations can then be passed to an automated proof checker for validation [2]. This level of rigour is wonderful when it can be accomplished, but even Gappa currently requires a careful manual rewriting of the underlying C code and heuristically chosen hints to guide proof procedure, while direct use of theorem provers is beyond the capabilities of most programmers.

While techniques such as those described above bring a pleasing level of quantitative rigour to implementation analysis, in this paper we will focus on testing a much more common pattern encountered in numerical software: The algorithm is designed so that truncation error converges asymptotically toward zero as some tuning parameter is varied, and then implemented in a floating point precision sufficiently high that roundoff error will (hopefully) be negligible compared to other sources of error. For concreteness, we will call the tuning parameter which controls truncation error "h" and assume that the truncation error decreases as h does. In many cases the truncation error can be theoretically bounded as an explicit function of the form $\mathcal{O}(h^p)$ for some $p > 0$, in which case we call p the "order of accuracy" of the approximation algorithm. Four levels of testing for such numerical algorithms have been defined [13]; in order of increasing rigor they are:

1. Expert judgment: The algorithm's output approximation is given to an expert who is asked to determine whether it is sufficiently correct.
2. Error quantification: The error between the approximation and the oracle is computed, and then an expert is asked to determine whether it is sufficiently small.
3. Convergence: The algorithm is run with a sequence of decreasing values of h, and it is checked that the error is decreasing. This level of testing requires the program to converge, but not at a particular order of accuracy.
4. Order of accuracy: As with convergence, but the rate of convergence is checked against the theoretically derived order of accuracy for the algorithm.

While the strongest in this hierarchy, the order of accuracy approach is still surprisingly dependent on expert judgment in practice: The implementation on a test case is run for a series of decreasing values of h, the approximate oracle is used to compute an approximate error for each h, and then the logarithm of the ratio of the errors for two (typically consecutive) values of h is used to estimate the experimental order of accuracy. Assuming that more than two values of h are used, multiple estimates are produced; some can be discarded as being outside the regime in which the asymptotic truncation error analysis applies, but the remainder are to be compared to the theoretical order of accuracy. How closely must they match? Consider these two prescriptions:

- From [10, p. 30]: "In general, one should not expect the trend in the observed order-of-accuracy to match the theoretical order-of-accuracy to more than two or three significant figures..."
- From [12, p. 195]: "Note that only for the simplest scientific computing cases (e.g., linear elliptic problems) will the observed order of accuracy match the formal order to more than approximately two significant figures during a successful order verification test."

Beyond the fuzziness of such a procedure (which order of accuracy estimates are compared, how should "significant figures" be mapped into a quantitative threshold), this process is not easily automated; consequently, regression testing of even minor code modifications becomes labour intensive and is often skipped.

In this paper we are not advocating that this approach to testing be abandoned; in fact, we have long found it highly efficient for identifying and correcting bugs during initial design and implementation. Instead, we are seeking to add a subsequent layer of testing once an implementation has satisfied order of accuracy convergence tests such as those described above. We will assume a collection of test cases with approximate oracles such as would be used in these convergence tests, and our goal is not necessarily more rigorous testing, but rather automating the testing so that regression approaches can be easily applied to subsequent code modifications.

2.4   Mutation Testing

Mutation Testing (MT) [8] is a testing technique designed to verify the strength of a test set for some "target" source code once that target passes all of the tests (in the sense that its outputs match the test oracles' output). Hundreds or thousands of "mutant" versions of the target are produced by a source code generator which systematically introduces source code modifications designed to simulate bugs that a programmer might accidentally introduce. The mutants are then run against the same test set, and those whose outputs fail to match the oracles' are "killed." Any mutants which survive represent potential bugs that would not be detected by the test set. A test set could then be strengthened by examining any surviving mutants and designing test cases that would kill them.

MT cannot be directly applied to numerical algorithms: We do not have exact oracles against which to compare for equality, and the standard techniques for testing numerical algorithms described in Sect. 2.3 are not automated; hence it is infeasible to scale them to test hundreds or thousands of mutants. A necessary step in the application of MT to numerical algorithms is therefore a method of automatically evaluating the correctness of a mutant on a test case.

At first glance, it might appear that Mutation Sensitivity Testing (MST) [6] would satisfy this objective. Instead of using exact comparisons, the error of the mutants' output relative to the oracle is compared against a specified tolerance, and the contribution of the paper is an exploration of how the choice of this tolerance and the type of test cases (random or designed) affected the fraction of mutants which were killed, with the conclusions that:

- A small number of tests with low tolerance is more effective than a large number of tests with high tolerance in killing mutants. Unfortunately, higher accuracy oracles are needed for lower tolerance tests.
- Random and designed tests should be used together for maximum effectiveness.

However, the authors of [6] did not intend for their approach to be used directly to verify numerical code; in fact, they considered the target code itself to be the oracle, and the goal of their study (like traditional MT) was guidance on how to design effective test suites.

In contrast, our goal is a test criterion which does not rely (or at least is only weakly dependent on) the choice of parameters. We note that in pursuit of this goal, we will make a stronger assumption than [6] that we have access to an approximate but reasonably accurate oracle separate from the target code.

3 Mutant Accuracy Testing

While MT is traditionally used to evaluate the strength of a test suite, here we propose to use it to evaluate the correctness of a numerical implementation. We believe that code mutation might yield a useful measure of correctness for numerical algorithms with high orders of accuracy (anything with order of accuracy $p > 1$) because such algorithms appear to be fragile to perturbation by design: They achieve their high order of accuracy by the use of carefully chosen parameters which combine to cancel the lower order terms in the truncation error. If the code mutation process introduces changes to these parameters, then the lower order terms should reappear and cause the error in the output approximation to grow significantly.

3.1 Mutant Generation

MATmute [6] is a freely available mutant generator for MATLAB code. Given a target MATLAB function or file, MATmute generates a collection of mutants by systematically applying *mutation operations* on source code. The operations that MATmute performs are the following:

- Statement deletion: A statement is commented out.
- Branch negation: A branch condition is negated, forcing the opposite decision.
- Constant replacement: A hard-coded constant is replaced with another.
- Operator replacement: A mathematical operator is replaced by another.
- Assignment perturbation: The right hand side of an assignment statement is multiplied by a constant before the assignment is completed.

For each mutant MATmute generates both a mutant source code file and a summary of what mutation operation was applied.

For a given test run, any mutants which do not compile or otherwise fail to generate an intelligible result are removed from consideration. The error for the remaining "viable" mutants is compared to that of the target, and any which are bitwise identical are also removed. These "equivalent" mutants are fairly common because the difference between the target and a given mutant may be in code that is not executed for a given test case; consequently, they are not diagnostically useful for that test case. The remaining viable but nonequivalent mutants and their results are then used to evaluate the target code.

3.2 Mutant Evaluation

We treat the computed error of the approximation produced by a code (either target or mutant) on a test case as an observation of a random process. For a given mutant, we define the hypotheses:

- Null hypothesis: The mutant does not produce approximations with larger error than the target.
- Alternative hypothesis: The mutant produces approximations with larger error than the target.

For a given mutant, we collect all of the test cases for which it was viable and non-equivalent to the target code. We can pair the observation of the mutant's error for each of these test cases with the observation of the target's error for the same test case. We apply a one-sided sign test [15] to the collection of observation pairs to determine the probability of seeing the observations given that the null hypothesis holds; in other words, the p-value. We choose the sign test rather than alternatives like the Wilcoxon signed-rank or paired t-test because it makes the fewest assumptions about the underlying distributions.

Based on our belief that the accuracy of numerical algorithms is fragile, we expect that most mutants will produce approximations with larger error. Therefore, we expect to collect observations that are highly unlikely under the null hypothesis, and the p-value will be low. We can choose a threshold p-value p_k and declare any mutant i with a lower p-value $p_i < p_k$ to be killed.

4 Experiments

We describe the conditions under which we tested our approach.

Table 1. Sample Implementation Statistics. All algorithms were implemented as MAT-LAB m-files.

Algorithm name	Number of		
	Lines	Test cases	Buggy versions
Composite Simpson's	4	3	9
Cubic spline	32	3	9
RK4	25	3	22

4.1   Reference Numerical Implementations

We chose some frequently used higher order accurate algorithms for common basic numerical analysis tasks:

- Quadrature (numerical integration) in one dimension: Composite Simpson's rule. Panels of equal size are chosen to cover the interval of integration and h controls the size of these panels.
- Interpolation in one dimension: Complete cubic spline. Abscissae are chosen equally spaced between the end points of the interpolation, and h controls the space between abscissae.
- Initial value problem for ordinary differential equation: Runge-Kutta fourth order (RK4). Constant stepsize is used and h is the step size.

Additional details of the algorithms are included in Appendix A. Coincidentally, the chosen algorithms all have order of accuracy $p = 4$ (so their error should be bounded by $\mathcal{O}(h^4)$), but our proposed approach does not require knowledge of the order of accuracy and hence it should apply to any convergent scheme.

Reference implementations of each algorithm were coded by the first author in MATLAB based on descriptions in [1], and then reviewed for correctness by the second author. Table 1 provides some quantitative measures of the code.

Although versions of all of these algorithms are available in the standard MATLAB libraries, the MATLAB versions are much more general and hence include an enormous amount of code to handle different input and output cases. This kind of data manipulation code is much more amenable to traditional testing strategies and we wanted to focus on testing the core numerical calculation; however, due to limitations with MATmute we could not easily generate mutations only in a subset of lines in a routine. Therefore, we chose to code our own versions which contained only the core numerical calculation.

4.2   Test Cases

MMS was used to design a collection of test cases for each algorithm. For each test case and value of the tuning parameter h, a scalar measure of error can be evaluated:

- Composite Simpson's: Absolute error of the integral.

Table 2. Sample Algorithm Mutation Statistics (reference implementations)

Algorithm name	Number of mutants		
	Total	Viable	Nonequivalent
Composite Simpson's	184	122	172
Cubic spline	677	213	287
RK4	531	127	218

- Cubic spline: Maximum absolute error of the approximation at the test points.
- RK4: Absolute error at the end of the time interval.

More details can be found in Appendix A.

To further build confidence in the implementations, the convergence rate of each algorithm on each test case was qualitatively confirmed experimentally as described in Sect. 2.3.

4.3 Buggy Versions

When proposing a test criterion for code, we must demonstrate both that it passes correct code and that it fails incorrect or buggy code. For this preliminary exploration, we created buggy versions of our reference implementations by hand based on our experience with incorrect code generated by students in introductory numerical analysis classes, examination of mutants of our reference implementations which did and did not pass the hypothesis test, and careful design to elicit certain error behaviours. We considered only buggy versions which would still be convergent, although not necessarily with the designed order of accuracy, on the basis that non-convergent implementations are easily diagnosed as buggy.

5 Results

Table 2 provides some statistics about the number and type of mutants produced by MATmute for each of the reference implementations. The number of nonequivalent (and in a few cases even viable) mutants does vary slightly depending on the test case. The statistics when using the buggy versions of the algorithms as target code are similar.

Figure 1 shows the distribution of p-values for mutants of the reference composite Simpson's target. Other targets produced similar distributions. The red curve in Fig. 2 provides similar information in a different form: Threshold p-values p_k against the fraction of mutants which will survive ($p_i \geq p_k$). We observe that the survival rate is dropping slightly between $p_k = 0.2$ and $p_k = 0.4$, but is fairly flat across a wide range of thresholds. The remaining black curves in Fig. 2 show the corresponding survival rates for mutants of the buggy Simpson's targets. We observe that three of the buggy targets are roughly as fragile as the

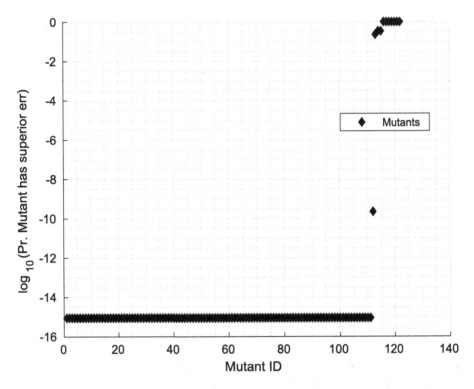

Fig. 1. Distribution of p-values for viable, non-equivalent mutants of the reference implementation of Composite Simpson's. Mutants are ordered by their p-value from smallest on the left to largest on the right. Most mutants have p-values very near zero, and of the rest most are near one. Similar distributions were seen for other target codes (reference and buggy).

reference implementation, in the sense that their mutants are unlikely to survive, and two of the buggy targets are even more fragile.

Figures 3 and 4 show the corresponding survival rates for the cubic spline and RK4 implementations.

6 Discussion

While the statistical test proposed in Sect. 3.2 still requires choosing a threshold parameter p_k, the results in Figs. 2, 3 and 4 provide some evidence that the survival rate is relatively insensitive to the precise value of this parameter. Unfortunately, this insensitivity does not extend between algorithms, as the survival rate for the reference code in Fig. 2 is 5–9% while that in Fig. 3 is well below 1%. And even once p_k is chosen, the result is a collection of surviving mutants. Consequently, this procedure will not achieve our goal of fully automating the testing process for numerical algorithms.

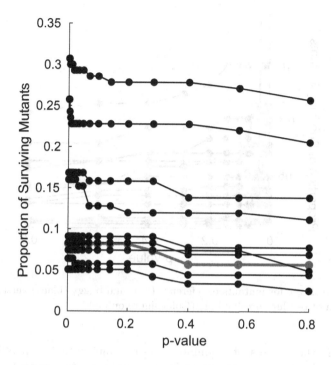

Fig. 2. Survival rate for mutants of reference (red) and buggy (black) versions of composite Simpson's as a function of p-value threshold p_k. (Color figure online)

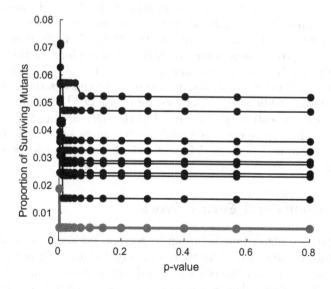

Fig. 3. Survival rate for mutants of reference (red) and buggy (black) versions of cubic spline as a function of p-value threshold p_k. (Color figure online)

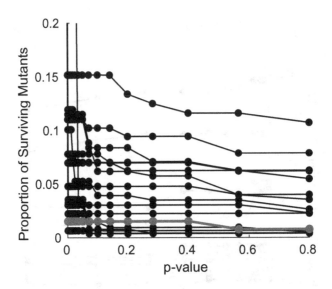

Fig. 4. Survival rate for mutants of reference (red) and buggy (black) versions of RK4 as a function of p-value threshold p_k. (Color figure online)

However, the process of examining the mutants with low p-value proved enlightening. In every case, the mutation operation had inadvertently improved the accuracy of the algorithm, typically by reducing the effective h parameter; for example, replacing h with $0.9h$, $h/2$ or h^2. This increased accuracy is the numerical equivalent of turning your amplifier up to eleven [4], since the user could already adjust the input h parameter to achieve the same outcome.

A similar effect is responsible for the two "buggy" versions of composite Simpson's which proved more fragile than the reference implementation, in the sense that the survival rate of mutants was below that of the reference implementation for all p-value thresholds. In one of these versions the "bug" was to explicitly reduce h, while in the other an error of size $\mathcal{O}(h^4)$ was introduced (the same size as the truncation error expected in the reference implementation). It is clear that such implementations would not be caught by a standard order of accuracy criterion, and perhaps debatable whether they should be considered buggy at all.

7   Conclusions and Future Work

Despite numerical algorithms being an important workload from the earliest days of computing and over sixty years of study, testing their accuracy is still often a manual and qualitative process. Based on the observation that numerical algorithms with higher orders of accuracy are constructed with carefully chosen parameters to cancel out the lower order truncation errors, we hypothesized that their accuracy might be fragile to small changes in the source code. At the same time, tools for automatically generating such small changes in source code have been developed in the domain of mutation testing. Therefore, we proposed to measure the error of mutants and a target implementation over a range of test cases, and use a standard statistical test to estimate the probability of seeing those errors under the null hypothesis that the mutant is as accurate as the target.

For a set of representative but small numerical algorithms implemented in MATLAB and mutated with the MATmute tool, the p-values of most mutants were very small and few mutants had intermediate p-values, at least partially supporting the fragility hypothesis. Moreover, this evaluation process could be fully automated. Although we considered only higher order accurate convergent algorithms, nothing in the evaluation process depends on the order of accuracy, or even that the algorithm is convergent, providing that a sufficient number of test cases could be constructed.

Unfortunately, the distinction in this p-value metric between correct reference implementations and artificially produced buggy versions was algorithm dependent and in some cases lacking; consequently, it does not appear to be directly usable as an automated test of implementation correctness. However, the process may still prove useful if mutants with high p-values can be manually inspected. For our simple reference implementations, it was easy to determine that the mutations in these cases would not reduce (and in many cases would increase) the accuracy of the output. We hypothesize that if a mutant with low p-value were found whose apparent accuracy relative to the target implementation could not be easily explained by code inspection, then there would be strong evidence that the reference implementation was not achieving its design accuracy (or that the mutation engine had stumbled onto an interesting alternative algorithm).

It has become clear that our set of toy implementations and artificially generated bugs is insufficient to properly assess the usefulness of any proposed testing criterion; consequently, we are currently collecting a sample of numerical routines from open source software projects and cataloging wild bugs that have been detected and corrected in them. We plan to make this collection publicly available in the hope that other researchers will take on the challenge of how to better automate the testing of numerical algorithms.

Acknowledgements. The authors would like to thank Kevin Jayamanna for doing related preliminary work in his undergrad thesis, and Daniel Hook for providing MATmute to the community.

A   Numerical Algorithms

Our implementations are based on the descriptions in [1]. In this section we briefly describe each of the algorithms, the error measurement for that algorithm, and the test case generation procedure.

A.1   Simpson's Method

The definite integral problem is to evaluate

$$I = \int_a^b f(x)\, dx$$

for a specified $a, b \in \mathbb{R}$ and scalar function $f(x)$.

Simpson's method is a fourth order accurate method that is used to approximate definite integrals. It is given by:

$$I_{Simp} = \frac{b-a}{6} \left[f(a) + 4f\left(\frac{b+a}{2}\right) + f(b) \right]$$

Composite Simpson's method involves dividing the domain of integration into subintervals called "panels," applying Simpson's method to each panel, and summing the result. Let r, the number of panels, be even. The formula is

$$S_{comp} = \frac{h}{3} \left[f(a) + 2 \sum_{k=1}^{r/2-1} f(t_{2k}) + 4 \sum_{k=1}^{r/2} f(t_{2k-1}) + f(b) \right]$$

where $t_i = a + ih$, $i = \{1, 2, ..., r\}$.

For analysis purposes, we define the error as the absolute value of the difference between the algorithm's output and the (floating point approximation of the) analytic answer. It can be shown that composite Simpson's method has an error bound of

$$\frac{\|f^{(4)}\|_\infty}{180} (b-a) h^4.$$

A typical 3-line implementation of composite Simpson's method in MAT-LAB generates 180–190 mutants using MATmute, of which roughly 120–130 are viable.

Test cases are generated either using pen-and-paper integration, or by MMS.

A.2   Complete Cubic Spline

A cubic spline is a continuously differentiable, piecewise cubic scalar function $v(x)$ that interpolates points $\{(x_1, f(x_1)), ..., (x_n, f(x_n))\}$, meaning that $v(x_i) = f(x_i)$. We call the spline "complete" because the derivatives at the endpoints $f'(x_1)$ and $f'(x_n)$ are also provided, and we choose $v(x)$ such that $v'(x_1) = f'(x_1)$ and $v'(x_n) = f'(x_n)$.

For analysis purposes, we generate a set of test points between the interpolation points, compute the difference between the value of the interpolant and the value of the original function at these test points, and report the greatest absolute difference across all test points as the error.

MATmute generates roughly 680–700 mutants from our 30-line implementation of a complete cubic spline.

For this problem analytic solutions are trivial to construct: We pick a function f and a set of points $\{x_i\}$. Then, we use $\{x_i\}$ and $\{f(x_i)\}$ as the input to our cubic spline algorithm. The exact answers can be obtained directly from the function f.

A.3 Runge-Kutta Schemes

Runge-Kutta methods are used to solve initial value problems for ordinary differential equations. This class of problems is defined by:

$$\frac{dx(t)}{dt} = f(x, t) \text{ such that } x(t_0) = x_0,$$

where $f(x)$ and x_0 are specified. While $x(t)$ may be a vector in general, for our purposes we considered only scalar cases.

We used the classic fourth order accurate Runge-Kutta method. It is given by the following set of update formulae:

$$y_{n+1} = y_n + \frac{1}{6}(k_1 + k_2 + k_3 + k_4),$$
$$k_1 = hf(t_n, y_n),$$
$$k_2 = hf(t_n + h/2, y_n + k_1/2),$$
$$k_3 = hf(t_n + h/2, y_n + k_2/2),$$
$$k_4 = hf(t_n + h, y_n + k_3),$$

where y_n is the approximation at time t_n and a fixed stepsize h has been assumed.

For analysis purposes, we define the error in our Runge-Kutta implementation as the absolute value of the difference between the algorithm's output and the analytic answer at a final time.

MATmute generates roughly 480–500 mutants from a typical 4th order Runge-Kutta implementation.

Test cases are generated by MMS: Starting with a function for $x(t)$, supply

$$f(x, t) = \frac{dx(t)}{dt} \text{ and } x_0 = x(t_0)$$

as the inputs.

References

1. Ascher, U.M., Greif, C.: A First Course on Numerical Methods. SIAM (2011)
2. de Dinechin, F., Lauter, C.Q., Melquiond, G.: Assisted verification of elementary functions using Gappa. In: ACM Symposium on Applied Computing, pp. 1318–1322 (2006). https://doi.org/10.1145/1141277.1141584
3. Grcar, J.: John von Neumann's analysis of Gaussian elimination and the origins of modern numerical analysis. SIAM Rev. **53**(4), 607–682 (2011). https://doi.org/10.1137/080734716

4. Guest, C., McKean, M., Shearer, H., Reiner, R.: This is spinal tap. film (1984). Director: Rob Reiner, producer: Karen Murphy
5. Heath, M.T.: Scientific Computing: An Introductory Survey. SIAM (2018)
6. Hook, D., Kelly, D.: Mutation sensitivity testing. Comput. Sci. Eng. **11**(6), 40–47 (2009)
7. Howden, W.E.: Theoretical and empirical studies of program testing. In: Proceedings of the 3rd International Conference on Software Engineering, pp. 305–311 (1978)
8. Howden, W.E.: Weak mutation testing and completeness of test sets. IEEE Trans. Softw. Eng. **4**, 371–379 (1982)
9. Jézéquel, F., Chesneaux, J.M.: CADNA: a library for estimating round-off error propagation. Comput. Phys. Commun. **178**(12), 933–955 (2008). https://doi.org/10.1016/j.cpc.2008.02.003
10. Knupp, P., Salari, K.: Verification of Computer Codes in Computational Science and Engineering. Chapman & Hall/CRC, Boca Raton (2002)
11. Nedialkov, N.S.: VNODE-LP: a validated solver for initial value problems in ordinary differential equations. Technical report CAS-06-06-NN, Department of Computing and Software, McMaster University (2006)
12. Oberkampf, W.L., Roy, C.J.: Verification and Validation in Scientific Computing. Cambridge University Press, Cambridge (2010)
13. Roy, C.J.: Review of code and solution verification procedures for computational simulation. J. Comput. Phys. **205**(1), 131–156 (2005)
14. Von Neumann, J., Goldstine, H.H.: Numerical inverting of matrices of high order. Bull. Am. Math. Soc. **53**(11), 1021–1099 (1947)
15. Wikipedia contributors: Sign test—Wikipedia, the free encyclopedia (2019). https://en.wikipedia.org/wiki/Sign_test. Accessed 30 Apr 2019

Author Index

Printed in the United States
By Bookmasters